# DIDIER DROGBA

# DIDIER DROGBA

## PORTRAIT OF A HERO

### JOHN McSHANE

JOHN BLAKE

Published by John Blake Publishing Ltd,
3 Bramber Court, 2 Bramber Road,
London W14 9PB, England

www.blake.co.uk

First published in paperback in 2008

ISBN: 978-1-84454-590-2

British Library Cataloguing-in-Publication Data:

A catalogue record for this book is available from the British Library.

Design by www.envydesign.co.uk

Printed in Great Britain by CPI Bookmarque, Croydon, CRO 4TD

1 3 5 7 9 10 8 6 4 2

© Text copyright John McShane

Photographs reproduced courtesy of Getty Images, Clevamedia, Rex Features, Empics
and Action Images

Papers used by John Blake Publishing are natural, recyclable products made from
wood grown in sustainable forests. The manufacturing processes conform to the
environmental regulations of the country of origin.

Every attempt has been made to contact the relevant copyright-holders, but some
were unobtainable. We would be grateful if the appropriate people could contact us.

# Contents

# Prologue

The 98,000 spectators who were crammed in the Nou Camp stadium, Barcelona, had seen one of the most pulsating and melodramatic games that even that famous football cathedral had been privileged to witness for years.

Harassed Italian referee Stefano Farina took an anxious look at his watch and saw he had already played three minutes of injury time in a Champions League game that had seen the best, and worst, that the finest players in the world could produce. Ten men had already been booked, three breathtaking goals had been scored, there were running vendettas all over the pitch and a heady cocktail of pain-inducing fouls, mixed with theatrical play-acting more suited to Hollywood, had kept countless millions around the world as transfixed to the televised events on the field as those privileged to be at the ground that humid October night in 2006.

But now the battle between the feuding giants of Barcelona and Chelsea seemed all but over, with the spoils of war going to the Catalan club 2–1. The tired legs of all the men on field longed for an end to their ordeal and the epic encounter was virtually over –

until Didier Drogba, six foot two inches and over thirteen stone of ferocious talent, decided to take control.

A high centre into the Barcelona area was headed down by Chelsea's powerhouse captain John Terry and Drogba burst into the area like a newly released stallion tasting freedom for the first time. He shrugged aside a challenge from the man who had been following him like an assassin all night, ponytailed Mexican defender Rafael Márquez, and powered on towards goal. And then, with the delicacy of a gentle breeze on a summer night, somehow he kept his strength and momentum under control and calmly slid the ball under the giant Barcelona goalkeeper Victor Valdez as he rushed out to meet him.

On the touchline Chelsea coach José Mourinho slid along on his knees in joy and on the field a disgusted home fan threw a peach at Drogba, who paused only to pick it up and take a bite. Moments later the whistle blew and Barcelona boss Frank Rijkaard was on the pitch angrily protesting to the referee. The Chelsea players, in their unfamiliar Real Madrid-style white strip, huddled together in the centre circle and in their middle was Drogba, a man born surrounded by poverty in Africa almost three decades earlier, and who had arrived at this night of glory through years of rejection by teams and fans – often including his own club's supporters – that would have destroyed a lesser character.

As the disappointed Spanish crowd left the stadium in their thousands, a small, brave band of delighted travelling Chelsea aficionados saluted their heroes, especially their goalscorer from the Ivory Coast, who, yet again, had turned their dreams into reality, a player whom many of them had been jeering only months before. Now a different sound greeted him on his glory trail, a dance song that had, with a slight alteration, become his anthem with its throbbing 'woof, woof, woof' chorus: 'Who Let the Drog Out?'

Who indeed, and how had he got there?

# CHAPTER 1

# Trouble in Paradise

In the late 1970s the people of the Ivory Coast – La Côte d'Ivoire – were living, although few of them realised it, on the brink of economic disaster. Since achieving independence from France almost twenty years earlier, the country – with its complex mixture of religions and more than sixty native dialects – had been one of the few success stories in a corner of Africa continually blighted by poverty and starvation. Unlike many of its neighbours, the country's productivity, based on its one-time seemingly endless cash-crop bounties of cocoa, coffee, pineapples, palm oil and the like, had grown year on year and was hailed as a beacon of success in a part of the world that had suffered for centuries.

So life seemed good for Albert and Clotilde Drogba – both bank workers – when, on 11 March 1978, their first child was born in the country's largest city, Abidjan, then considered one of the wealthiest and safest capitals on the continent with its superhighways, skyscrapers and elegant, affluent suburbs.

The proud parents named their boy Didier Yves Drogba, a

member of the Tébily family, a generic name roughly similar to those of the Scottish clan system. Soon, however, like all small boys in the city, he was given a nickname, Tito, a name still used by some of the people in his homeland to this day. Like all mothers and fathers, especially those enjoying the wonder of parenthood for the first time, they had great hopes for the youngster and dreamed of a better world for him and that somehow his life would be happier, more fulfilled, than theirs.

They cannot have foreseen the heartache that lay not far ahead when their infant son would be saying goodbye to them, along with the other 5 million inhabitants of Abidjan – at that time called 'The Paris of Africa' – who were forced out by the economic nightmare unfolding around them even as Didier lay sleeping in his cot. Less still can the Drogbas have imagined, even in their wildest dreams, that within a generation the small boy to whom they said a tearful goodbye in 1983 would become the most famous person ever born in their country: a millionaire sportsman known in practically every country in the world, a genuine superstar revered with a deference almost befitting a god by his fellow countrymen and women.

To understand the legend or mystique, call it what you will, surrounding Didier Drogba today, it is necessary to look not just at his own background, but also, briefly, at the history of the country where he was born. The reason for this is simple: it has dictated the events of his life through childhood and adolescence and still exerts a daily influence on him as strong as ever.

It was in the 1460s that Portuguese sailors first saw the lush land and forests just north of the equator, on what was to become known as the Gulf of Guinea, and realised that fortunes were to be made ashore. As their ships bobbed in the cobalt-blue waters of the angry shoreline, a trading route for Africans since medieval times, they vowed to bring Christianity to the natives and, in turn, to make themselves wealthy by trading in the area's abundant 'commodities': slaves, gold and ivory. They had heard tales of the vast herds of elephants that roamed the verdant woods and plains inland, which meant a seemingly endless supply of the valuable tusks so sought after for jewellery, art and tools since Greek and Roman times, and they weren't to be disappointed.

Over the next four centuries Europeans established a series of trading posts along the 300-mile West African shoreline, although lack of good, natural harbours meant the area suffered less from the appalling cruelty of the slave trade than elsewhere on the coast. The shallow, dangerous waters were without the major harbour necessary for the loading of human cargo, meaning the early Ivorians were thankfully spared the worst horrors. Those waters, however, were no hindrance to the bounty in tusks that fed an insatiable demand as gruesome, massive quantities of ivory from slaughtered elephants were loaded on board the vessels that were capable of anchoring offshore. Other nations had joined those early Portuguese in the scramble to exploit Africa's great natural wealth and by the Victorian period the French were the dominant force in the area as the European superpowers of the day divided up the 'Dark Continent' between them. Finally, after a merciless war – barbaric even for its time – with one of the region's tribes, the French established a colony in 1893 and officially named it 'Côte d'Ivoire', known throughout the English-speaking world to this day as the Ivory Coast. Other tribes carried on a resistance campaign against colonisation from Paris, but they were fighting a losing battle, and in 1917 the country became part of French West Africa.

After World War Two, Côte d'Ivoire was made an overseas region of France and its first representative in the French Parliament was Félix Houphouët-Boigny, a charismatic tribal chief who was to become president when it eventually became independent in 1960 as country after country achieved home rule after centuries of being ruled by Europe. Under Houphouët-Boigny the Ivory Coast became one of the most successful countries in the region – politically stable, and with countless thriving cocoa and coffee plantations. It soon became the largest cocoa producer in the world as millions of immigrants from neighbouring countries moved in to do the heavy work on the plantations. Many of them were Muslims, who eventually made up a third of the population, most of them in the north of the country.

Houphouët-Boigny retained close links with the West, especially with France – a connection that was to play a vital part in Didier's early and later years – but also, surprisingly, with South Africa. During his time in office, his country was renowned as the most prosperous and most stable in the West African region. It also hosted Africa's largest French-speaking population. To this day French is the language spoken among its population. Didier, as a member of the Bete tribe, would also have heard the tribal tongue spoken.

Although the land young Tito had been born into had an enviable history of prosperity, by the early 1980s, as the toddler first began to kick a ball around, even this isolated pocket of success in Africa was about to suffer – with an effect that was to change his life for ever. Economic recession hit the Ivory Coast during the first few years of the decade as the price of its main exports, including cocoa and coffee, plunged, bringing the reality of the strife that once seemed to exist merely in neighbouring countries. Domestic pressure for the democratic process to end what was effectively a one-party state produced further tension, economically and socially, and when Didier was five years old his mother and father faced the most agonising dilemma that any parents should have to confront: whether to 'lose' their son so that he could have a better start in life.

They knew that opportunities for education and a better quality of life would exist in the sophisticated climate of 1980s France rather than at home in the Ivory Coast, with its struggling economy and internal strife. Their beloved son was already a compulsive footballer on the dusty car park behind the cinema in his predominantly Christian home district of

## TROUBLE IN PARADISE

Yopougon in Abidjan – wearing an oversized replica Argentinian shirt he was given when he was just two. So there was an obvious place for Didier to go and live – with the man who had sent him that shirt, his uncle Michel Goba, who was a professional footballer in France.

This was a golden era for French football: the national side appeared in the World Cup semi-finals of 1982 and 1986 with an exciting team built around the '*carré magique*' – the magic square – of Alain Giresse, Luis Fernandez, Jean Tigana and, above all, Michel Platini, generally thought to be the greatest of all French footballers and one of the finest players ever in the world game. 'Le Roi' Platini – 'The King' – had just moved to Italian giants Juventus by the time that Didier, with no one to accompany him, stepped nervously down from the plane in France after a six-hour flight, during which he later admitted quite openly he 'cried all the way' as he was about to start his new life thousands of miles from home.

Michel Goba may have been, like Platini, a professional footballer, but that was where the resemblance came to an abrupt, and very obvious end. Uncle Michel's lifestyle was in a different universe from Platini's and that of the glamorous Turin millionaires with their massive, fanatical support and the backing of the Fiat car empire behind them. Although Goba too was an international, it was with the fledging Ivory Coast side. Try as he might, he was never more than a workaday player in a career in which he roamed around clubs in the lower reaches of the French divisions. When Didier arrived, his uncle – a forward – was playing for Brest in Brittany, and the town – a port since Roman times – seemed a bizarre place to him. Although, like all Ivorians, he could speak French, the windy football outpost meant that he suffered as near a culture shock as it is possible for any five-year-old to experience. Though delightful in summer, Brittany in northwestern France – famous for its beaches, seafood and endless herds of dairy cows grazing on lush countryside – can be wet and bleak in winter, and the cold winds from the Atlantic must have brought a shiver to the young limbs of the boy used to the steamy equator.

In later years he was to reflect, 'It was difficult, of course, but living with my uncle helped me to develop more, in life and in football. It helped me to grow up quicker.' And he would add, somewhat surprisingly, 'It wasn't as difficult as you might think.' Perhaps this childhood determination to succeed, to adapt to a strange environment and, ultimately, to triumph over initial difficulties, gives an early insight into the character and internal strength that was to become so obvious as Didier developed. More than once in later years, he was to face difficulties that would defeat men with less determination and grit, and that strength of focus meant problems were faced and overcome again and again.

Many observers – especially those from Europe – might think it was a callous move on the part of his parents to let him go, no matter how beneficial they hoped the situation would be for their eldest child, but Michel Goba has defended their decision, explaining how other cultures take a different attitude. 'It's in our traditions that the one who has the best income takes charge of a child in the family,' he explains with simple logic. 'I didn't earn a bad living playing in the French League and Didier, the first of my brother-in-law Albert's family of seven kids, came to live with me and my wife in France. I'll never forget driving to the airport at Bordeaux to pick him up. The little lad was only five and had come on his own.'

It seems inconceivable that Didier's talent would not have emerged in later years, no matter where in the world he played football, but there is no doubt that the years spent living and travelling with his uncle gave him an impetus he might otherwise never have had. Goba reveals, with stunning understatement, 'I had the idea of his becoming a footballer.' A pretty good plan by any standards, although it's possible Didier might have thought of it himself in later years!

But first he had to become accustomed to a vastly different way of life as one of a wave of African arrivals from the former French colonies. His uncle was the one who ensured he kept up with his schoolwork, never an easy task for a youngster moving from school to school and one who, by reason of his colour and new-boy status, would have stood out in rural France, a long way from its metropolitan centres.

As Didier looked out of the car window at the captivating, affluent French countryside dotted with large, chic homes and brightly lit restaurants on the long drive from Bordeaux to Brest he must have wondered what lay in store for him. Little did the small boy who had sat alone and crying throughout the flight realise what astonishing adventures were to come.

# CHAPTER 2

# A New Life

There are some great football clubs in France with traditions that can stand proud in comparison with the famous sides of England, Italy and Spain, but Brest – the side for whom Michel Goba was playing for when his nephew Didier came to live with him – is most definitely not one of them. Officially called Stade Brestois 29, the club had won the French Division 2 title in 1981 shortly before Didier arrived in the area, but their time in the highest division was short-lived; a solitary season in the French First Division was the only one Uncle Michel was to spend. Although the handsome midfield international David Ginola – who later played for Newcastle United and Tottenham Hotspur – and, by a freak coincidence, Didier's future Chelsea teammate Claude Makelele were both briefly at Brest in the early part of their careers, the club doesn't really have a 'roll of honour' to speak of. In fact, to this day that Second Division trophy is the club's only major triumph and their ground, the Stade Francis Ble, has room for just over 10,000 spectators. Somehow Brest's lowly status seems to fit in well in that respect with the town itself.

## DIDIER DROGBA

Although historically a busy port and naval base that once produced warships for Napoleon, Brest was – through no fault of its own – a far cry from 'La Belle France' of the tourist posters. The Germans had a massive submarine base in Brest during World War Two and British and American bombers blitzed the area to destroy the Nazi war effort by preventing deadly underwater killers from attacking Allied ships in the Atlantic. The result was a bombing campaign that destroyed practically every building in the town. Only a handful survived and the subsequent rebuilding after the Liberation and into the 1950s created a landscape filled with street after street of ugly modern concrete offices, flats and houses.

About 100,000 people lived in Brest and twice that in the surrounding region. It was a far cry from the packed streets of Abidjan. For Didier it would undoubtedly have been the first time he had heard his new schoolmates talking not only in the French tongue he spoke, albeit with an accent, but also in an ancient language unique to the area, Breton; a distant relative of the Celtic tongue still spoken in a few areas of Cornwall and Wales to this day.

Due to its proximity to the coast, the area was, and remains, famous for its variety of fish and shellfish, although the young Didier would no doubt have enjoyed the local butter-soaked Traou Mad biscuits (a kind of shortbread) and, of course, the Breton crêpes.

Around the town Didier saw long, sandy beaches guarded by tall, granite cliffs, and although busy with tourists in summer, who relaxed by sunbathing, yachting or windsurfing, even in July and August, Brest could still be hit by storms due to its location perched at the country's corner. For a sports-mad boy there was a lack of activity and the same applies today. In fact one of Brest's few sporting claims to fame is for being the turnaround point in the gruelling Paris–Brest–Paris cycle race dating back to 1891, where competitors battle nonstop for about ninety hours with hardly any sleep to cover the 750-mile round journey bike.

But none of that mattered too much to Didier as he waited for his Uncle Michel to return home from away games in far-flung corners of France. When he came through the front door, often in the dead of night, he would invariably have with him a shirt he had been given by an opponent after the game. As Didier's shirt collection grew, like all soccer-crazy boys, he dreamed of emulating the feats of his heroes, who, he was later to reveal, were all legendary goalscorers who played in France: Jean-Pierre Papin, Rudi Voller of Germany and Croatian goal machine Alen Boksic. All of the trio scored goals throughout their careers for their mighty clubs in the great stadiums of Europe – although by the time Boksic made his brief, but highly paid stay in England with Middlesbrough, he was past his prime. However, they had other things in common: at one stage or another they had all pulled on the white and pale blue shirt of the wealthy and successful Marseilles. It can be no coincidence that the players Didier has confessed to admiring most as a boy all played for Marseilles, a club that was to play a major role in his own life and career. But all that was light years away as Michel Goba packed and unpacked his bags and moved around the provincial towns and cities of France trying to earn enough money to keep his family together.

After Brest he tried his luck at Angoulême, a town of 100,000 people that was sixty miles from Bordeaux, where the local side had experienced only three years at the top. During that halcyon period they had what is still their biggest attendance even to this day. In August 1969, when FC Nantes were the visitors, the gate that day was 10,820 – small-time football doesn't get much smaller than that. In fact, the club continually veered between amateur and professional status.

Goba's next stop was Dunkirk – Dunkerque – whose only claim to fame was that in 1929 the club reached the semi-finals of the French Cup. And that was that. In the half-century that followed they achieved very little. The area does, of course, have its place in history, as almost 350,000 British and French servicemen were rescued from its beaches in May and June 1940 by a flotilla of 600 small boats under intense attack from the Luftwaffe, but in football terms it really was the back of beyond. Didier must have often wondered what a strange life his uncle led, travelling from one small town to another to play in front of sparse, begrudging crowds for just enough money to keep going. But he was now eight, he'd been in France for three years and it was time to go home.

What a joyful reunion it must have been! On one side was the small boy, who had bravely got on with life without his 'mama' and 'papa' while his doting parents longed to hear the sound of their eldest child noisily coming home after school before quickly hurrying out again for the inevitable kick-around with his pals. Life picked up where it left off: Didier was often the leader in organising kick-arounds in the Youpogon district of the city and he and his friends would choose a deserted or not-so empty car park and throw their tops down to make goalposts on its brick-red, dusty surface.

At least as Didier and his young pals kicked their scruffy ball around they didn't have the worries of their parents. The country's economy, which had been shaky throughout the 1980s, was now in such a fragile state virtually the whole population was affected.

There were 30,000 French citizens, including a battalion of marines, in Abidjan, but they formed a tiny part of its diverse population with no one ethnic group holding complete control. In this vast melting pot where tribal differences were still of great importance there was constant arguing. Although in theory the country was a democracy, it was that obvious contradiction – a one-party 'democracy' – and, with the government controlling the press, civil liberties were limited and criticism suppressed. Corruption, so widespread in other parts of the region, was now obvious too – student unrest was growing and while a small, privileged class of bureaucrats and landowners prospered, the hardships of the masses were made all the more apparent. By September 1989 vast changes to the country's political structure of the country allowed all major ethnic groups to be represented in government, but the economy continued its inevitable downward spiral.

World prices for coffee and cocoa were low and exports of timber – the country's third-largest source of foreign cash – fell because of overexploitation. Two offshore oil fields projected to be the saviour of the country's economy by making it self-sufficient in petrol failed to reach their targets and had to be capped while foreign loans had to be repaid. All these factors hit every section of Ivorian society, but as always it was the poorest who suffered most as drug abuse and crime began to rise.

The Drogbas felt the pain, too. They lost their banking jobs and the future looked bleak. One thing was for sure: now eleven, Didier had to be sent back to France.

## CHAPTER 3

# The Tour of France

It would have been wonderful for Didier to return to France and discover that his uncle's footballing career had prospered in his absence, but that was far from the case. During the years Didier was back in Africa, Michel Goba's pilgrim's progress through the lower divisions of French football had taken him to the mountainous Jura region in the east of the country near the borders with Switzerland and Germany for an undistinguished spell with Besancon Racing Club. When Didier, of course by now much taller than when his uncle had last seen him three years earlier, returned, however, Michel was back at Dunkirk.

Dunkirk was, by any standards, an impoverished club a million miles away from the bright lights of the big boys of French football. But, like all such clubs in the smaller provincial towns of France, it played a larger role in the town's cultural and sporting life than its English counterparts might have done. Perhaps it is the large distance between French town's that encourages this cooperative relationship between club and town, especially for youngsters. It was there that Didier began his first games for a 'proper' club, one of Dunkirk's boys' sides. And the boy who was to become one of the world game's most feared strikers regularly ran out to play – at right-back. That didn't last long, as Michel Goba immediately saw the madness of wasting his young nephew's talent. 'The kids coach there played Didier at the back because he was such a big lad. I wasn't having that and, as I was the first-team striker there, I pulled rank and ordered the coach to play him upfront' he explains.

Uncle Michel wasted no time in passing on to his nephew some of the facts of football life. 'I told Didier, "You are a striker from now on, like me. You are made to score goals, not stop them. What are you doing stuck back there? Get upfront! In football people only look at the strikers."' Didier was not going to argue with this, even if he wanted to, although he was later to say, 'When I started in youth football at Dunkirk I was a right-back, but a modern one. I used to get up into attack as often as I could and score goals.' He hung onto his uncle's every word and, as Michel explains, 'I was his idol in those days, so he listened to my advice. Seeing what has happened since, I'm glad about that.' While he might be happy about this, a generation of defenders could have a different point of view.

Night after night, uncle and nephew would sit in front of the television, like men and boys throughout the world, as football games were beamed into their living room. But in their household it was different: it wasn't simply a case of enjoying the game or supporting a particular side. Those hours in front of the TV formed part of Didier's education, a kind of school after school, where the lessons weren't history or geography. Instead he was learning how to score goals.

'I'd tell him to note the runs the strikers made,' says his uncle. 'He learned quick.' In their front rooms in that semi-desolate part of France they might have been living a dream, but outside, in the real world, football was far from glamorous. It was around this time, coincidentally, that Dunkirk's football club were about to play a role, albeit in a manner they can't have envisaged at the time, in events that were to change football for ever and indirectly play a part in the glamorous lifestyle that Didier and a whole generation of players were soon to enjoy. Jean-Marc Bosman was an undistinguished player with Standard Liège in the Belgium Second Division, who wanted to move to Dunkirk because his contract was running out. The Belgians refused to let him go, saying his transfer fee wasn't high enough, however. Bosman's wages were reduced because he was no longer in their first team and so he began a long legal battle that was to end in 1995, when the European Court of Justice gave all EU players the right to a free transfer at the end of their contract.

Another effect of the famous 'Bosman Ruling' was the end of the restriction on the number of foreign players clubs could field. Although few people fully realised it at the time, the massive repercussions from Bosman soon enabled the financial bargaining power of footballers to soar and to herald within a few short years the multinational sides seen throughout football today.

All that lay in the future, however, as Michel Goba's next move took him and Didier to Abbeville – a drab town just south of Calais – for a season that ended with the club going bust. Even the world-weary Goba today admits, 'It was a disaster.' It was at Abbeville, however, that Didier completed the transformation from attacking full-back to striker. Goba continued: 'The one good part was Didier won a big regional competition with his team and he scored a stack of goals.' Didier himself has his own take on it: 'It was an unusual progression. Players usually start in attack and move back into midfield and defence. I've never done the orthodox thing.'

The next stop on the never-ending tour of France took uncle and nephew to Tourcoing, yet another town of around 100,000 inhabitants, this time in the very north of France, practically on the Belgium border, twinned with – among several places – Rochdale in England. As always, Michel earned a living playing for the no-nonsense local club while Didier continued to score for one of their junior teams, but problems were occurring, on and off the field. 'I went to Tourcoing and they gave me such a hard time I felt I was the worst player in the squad,' is Didier's amazing summary of his time there.

Michel casts further light on the situation: 'Didier fell into bad company. His football suffered and he wasn't in the team. There was a bit of bother over some things that went missing and I had to go to the police station. When they sorted it all, they found he had done nothing wrong.'

The separation from his parents and the 'gypsy' lifestyle he was leading could not have helped Didier feel comfortable or settled. About half his life had been spent surrounded by the terrible poverty of Africa and the other half as a semi-itinerant boy traveller across provincial France.

As he entered his teens in 1991, uncle and nephew returned to Brittany. This time it was to the southern part of the area: the beautiful medieval town of Vannes, built around an inlet just north of the Bay of Biscay. Vannes was, and is a delightful spot for tourists to visit, but the local side – the grandly named Olympic Club of Vannes – was yet another step down the football ladder with a ground that held when full (which it never was) a mere 6,000 spectators.

A massive change was to occur in Didier's life that year. As his uncle's playing career drew to a close in sleepy southern Brittany, events thousands of miles away were to impact on his life. A year earlier austerity measures imposed in his Ivory Coast birthplace caused nationwide unrest and strikes, which were violently broken up by police and troops. By May 1990 French troops were on alert as army conscripts went on a rampage and two days later Ivorian Air Force personnel seized control of the airport for a brief spell. Highlighting the chaos, the ageing President Houphouët-Boigny had made his home town of Yamoussoukro the country's administrative capital and in three years had built there – at a staggering cost of £200 million – the largest place of worship in the Christian world, the Basilica of Our Lady of Peace. It was modelled on St Peter's in Rome, which took over a century to create, but it was even bigger. The massive building was filled with Italian marble and 7,400 metres of French stained glass, including depictions of Christ and his disciples dressed in white, with the President himself in black depicted as a thirteenth follower of Jesus. The 7,000 seats inside this building in the middle of the African jungle all had individual air-conditioning ducts to keep worshippers cool. Pope John Paul II reluctantly consecrated the controversial building as the President was re-elected in the country's first multiparty elections.

By 1991 continuing strikes by students and teachers led to repeated clashes with the security police. The country was in chaos and Didier's parents bowed to the inevitable: they would have to leave for France. To many it would seem a simple decision to leave a country of poverty and confusion for the beauties of one of the most sophisticated civilisations in the world. But to Albert and Clotilde, and many like them, it would be a case of saying goodbye to their homeland, family and friends and becoming immigrants – black immigrants at that – in a country that had a reputation in some quarters for not welcoming refugees with open arms. This time they had no choice but their decision would mean that they would be near their beloved son Didier. And, if truth be told, it was a fortunate time for them all to become closer again.

Didier had originally been near the top of the class as he moved around France, but the combination of continually starting new schools with different teachers and the arrival of his teen years had brought an end to those early successes. His parents' arrival coincided with the realisation that the initial reason for his coming to France almost a decade earlier – to better himself and to receive a good education – might have been futile. It didn't take long for his parents to assess the situation and to realise that action had to be taken, and quickly, when he failed his examinations and had to lose a year to take them again.

With customary succinctness Didier sums it up: 'I was falling behind at school and failing my exams, so I gave up football for a year. It was horrible – football was everything to me. All I wanted to do was play. I was doing badly. My family saw me playing football all the time and thought this was the reason. It was a very hard time.'

It seems – and indeed it is – astonishing that in his mid-teens Didier devoted time to resitting examinations rather than playing football. Most gifted boy footballers are, by the time they are fourteen or fifteen, already being targeted by the major clubs and wooed with promises of fame and fortune. Didier was having none of that. The family had already seen that the life of a professional footballer could be soul-destroying and not particularly rewarding, and like all caring parents they knew there was no substitute for a good education. In effect, the Drogbas banned their son from the so-called 'beautiful game' for a year and he was sent to live with his cousin Kriza in the historic town of Poitiers in central France and told in no uncertain terms to get on with his schoolwork. At one stage a career in accountancy was even considered.

It was another year before he was reunited with his parents and his six brothers and sisters in the sprawling suburb of Antony, seven miles south of the centre of Paris and home to a mix of native Parisians and struggling immigrants from the former French colonies. Didier was now fifteen and a tall, athletic boy with a massive gift for basketball as well as football, although his talents weren't always appreciated by his neighbours.

'When I played beneath the tower blocks, there were guys round the pitch with dogs ready to leap,' he recalled in later years when he was beginning to terrorise defenders in the French professional game. 'They used to tell me, "Hey you, stop touching the ball or we'll set the dogs on you." Next to that, I have found it very nice playing in the French championship.'

## CHAPTER 4

# Hamburgers, Chocolate... and a Wife

Uncle Michel wasn't the only one to take notice of Didier's talents. An observant coach, Christian Pornin, had seen him play as a youngster and realised there was potential to be explored and, hopefully, expanded. He persuaded Didier to go for trials at Levallois Sporting Club in Levallois-Perret, a suburb in northwest Paris, the opposite side of the French capital from the Drogba family. Didier had a long journey across town by bus and Le Métro, the underground system for the city, to reach their ground, the Stade Louison Bobet, but it was worth it. The club liked what they saw, invited him to play for them on a regular basis and Didier came under the instruction of the small amateur side's grandly-named 'technical director', Srebencko Repčić, a former professional with the fine Red Star Belgrade side in the 1980s, who won one international cap with Yugoslavia before the country was splintered into several different nations due to the Balkans turmoil.

His ability to turn the raw material undoubtedly possessed by the strapping teenager into something more substantial was a major stepping stone. 'I was lucky to meet him,' Didier now says. 'He gave me encouragement and invested hugely in my development.' Didier's dedication was apparent, too. He'd snatch a snack or meal before, after or even during his cross-town journey and although a handsome young man by this time, he didn't let his natural desire to enjoy himself interfere with his will to succeed. 'He didn't go out to nightclubs on the nights before matches like his mates,' says Repčić. 'He was a very sensible lad.'

The club's Under-17 side was coached by Christian Pornin and Didier was soon in the starring role. In two seasons – 1994–5 and 1995–6 – the young centre-forward started to score consistently. All the time Didier and his parents were writing to professional clubs for trials that invariably led to nothing. Rennes didn't see anything special in him and Guingamp – whom he was to join a few years later – also rejected the teenager. The mighty Paris Saint-Germain (PSG) eventually showed an interest, but Didier, showing the focus he has displayed throughout his career, felt the club was not for him: it was too large and he thought he would be lost among the host of other teenage players at its famous academy. The chances of breaking into the first team would be limited. 'I was offered a trial with Paris Saint-Germain, but they had a terrible reputation for ruining players so I turned them down', is how he sums it up with stunning simplicity.

Didier has been a thorn in their side ever since. One of the first of his controversial on-field antics for Chelsea in later years was when, less than a decade later, he scored twice in their Champions League away win over Paris Saint-Germain. The PSG fans had been cruelly barracking him throughout the game, and after each of his goals in a decisive 3–0 victory he ran to them and cupped his hands against his ears to mock them, mimicking the goal celebrations of their Portuguese striker Paulette. As if that wasn't bad enough, he then began to blow kisses towards them! Afterwards he said, 'I did wind them up but they wound me up a bit as well, didn't they? It was important for me to come here to Paris and score, and to do things in style.' All that lay years ahead as Didier graduated from the Levallois Under-17s and was chosen for their first team, then playing in the French Second Division.

Coach Jacques Loncar recalls, 'Didier lived over fifty kilometres from the club and it was hard for him to get to training. He had to catch a lot of trains and buses, was often late and it wasn't easy for him to train. He would eat McDonald's on the train on the way to training. He moved to Levallois and his lifestyle changed. I made sure he was there on time and encouraged him to eat properly, not sandwiches and burgers. He improved quite rapidly after that, scoring twenty to twenty-five goals each season between the ages of fourteen and eighteen.' However, first-team appearances weren't easy to come by in that Second Division, although Didier managed to score in a brief ten-minute run-out against Fontainebleau.

Nevertheless, scouts from French clubs such as PSG, Lens, Le Mans and Guingamp were noticing the boy and it was only a matter of time before he would move on. That was all put on hold, unfortunately, when he suffered the first serious injury of his career. Bizarrely, it wasn't as a result of a thunderous tackle from one of the growing number of defenders who were beginning to realise it needed something special to stop young Didier, but from a water-sprinkler head concealed below the turf. Didier tripped over one during a match against Caen and fractured a bone in his foot so badly it needed to be put in plaster.

That injury merely delayed the inevitable: Jacques Loncar had watched Didier grow as a footballer and he liked what he saw. He knew he was ready to step up a level, and so he recommended Didier to Marc Westerloppe, the coach at a professional club, Le Mans, who decided to sign him as an apprentice. This time there was to be no refusal: 'The same day I said no to PSG, I got a phone call from Marc Westerloppe, then trainer of Le Mans in the Second Division. He became my spiritual football father. He got me on the right track, though I think I gave them problems because I was such a late developer.'

So, by early 1998, aged nineteen, Didier packed his bags and moved out of Paris to try for the big breakthrough at the fledgling club founded only in 1985, some 120 miles southwest of the capital. In later years he was to continually pay tribute to Westerloppe, so it would be logical and handy to complete the rags-to-riches story if he had become an instant star in the town, more famous for its twenty-four-hour road race than its football, but this wasn't to be the case. Injuries began to dog his career and during his two years there as an apprentice he was constantly suffering from physical setbacks, breaking two metatarsals, a fibula and an ankle. Nevertheless, he made his first-team debut at twenty, and in the season 1998–9 managed one more match.

Westerloppe and his deputy Alain Pascalou realised, however, that there was a great talent waiting to be discovered and in 1999 at the comparatively old age of twenty-one and sixteen eventful years since he had arrived alone at Bordeaux, Didier Drogba signed the forms that meant his apprenticeship had ended and he was now a professional footballer. The young man who had been struggling to pay his electricity bill went out to celebrate by buying a Mars bar and some sweets!

The next year, his first as a full-time pro, was respectable, if hardly headline-making, and he managed seven goals in his thirty outings, although, disappointingly, the following year his eleven games were all goalless. That meant that the man who within a short time was to become a goalscoring phenomenon had failed to find the net in two seasons out of three. Injuries and being played on the wing in some games didn't help, but it must have been galling for a player theoretically in his prime to look around and see some players of his age were already well-established internationals. He couldn't afford to run a car and had to ask his pals for a lift to the ground. Many French clubs have youth setups with severe, almost academic-style, tuition and streaming, with the inevitable consequence that the vast majority of talented players have been spotted in their early teens if not before and marked out for success from a very young age. Didier must have wished many times that he had been given the benefit of this 'silver spoon' football education.

Nor was he helped at this time by the fact that his 'spiritual father' Marc Westerloppe, had been replaced as Le Mans coach by Thierry Goudet, a man with whom he rarely saw eye to eye – and an injury to Didier allowed the Gabon-born Daniel Cousin to take over the striker's role. His career was at a crossroads as coach Pascalou admitted in a newspaper interview years later when Didier was rampaging across Europe.

'Didier didn't have a clue what being a pro meant and that went on for almost four seasons with us,' he told the *Sun*. 'He ate anything and everything without a thought of whether it was any good for his life as an athlete. He sometimes went to a McDonald's just before a match. Unlike most of today's stars, he had never been with a pro club as a kid.

'I had shouting matches with him to try to get him to see reason, but it just didn't seem to sink in. We couldn't believe it. His life off the field was holding him back. It wasn't booze – he never touched the stuff – but he'd go out with mates and get to bed at all hours. He couldn't take anything seriously. That's why he spent most of his time with us shuttling between the first team, bench, reserves and treatment room. Once, when he was complaining about yet another injury, I told him, "Didier, either take your parents to court because you are so puny or change something in your life." He was incapable of being consistent or even finishing every training session. He was explosive, but lacked endurance. He'd arrive late for training. It wasn't a job for him, more a bit of fun. He did annoy a lot of people. It was heart-breaking to see him wasting his potential.'

At least off the field there was to be a major change in his life, greater than anything happening on the pitch. Didier had met one

## DIDIER DROGBA

Lalla Diakite, a beautiful young woman from Mali – a West African state bordering the Ivory Coast – in Paris and she was destined to become his wife. It was at Le Mans in 1999 that their first child, Isaac, was born, and, like all first-time fathers, Didier realised he now had responsibilities. He was later to assess this crucial stage in his life: 'At twenty-one I knew it was my last chance. Everybody told me, "If this doesn't work out, you'll have to earn a living doing something else." I could have been an accountant – I had the qualifications.'

When, in autumn 2001, the new season began, Didier managed to force his way back into the side and in twenty-one appearances managed to score five goals. Nevertheless, his time at Le Mans couldn't by any standards be called a great success and so, when in the transfer window in January there was a chance to move up a division to Guingamp – a club with whom he'd had a trial as a youngster in his old stamping ground of Brittany – Didier decided to take it, no doubt also taking into account his parental duties. The move was recorded, very briefly, in a story transmitted by Agence France-Presse (AFP) on Sunday, 27 January 2002, in its English-language sports round-up after items about defender Bruno Ngotty's transfer from Marseilles to Bolton and British Olympic champion Linford Christie's warning to youngsters about the dangers of a gun culture. The story read,

> Striker Didier Drogba has secured a move to the French first division with Guingamp from second division Le Mans. The twenty-three-year-old, who has scored five times this season, will help fill the gap left by Fabrice Fiorèse's loan transfer to Paris Saint-Germain.

The move to Guingamp was to change his life dramatically, as Westerloppe was to reflect in years to come: 'Didier had tremendous ability but he was used to training three times a week so it was difficult for him to cope with training every day. He was always tired and frequently injured, but once he learned to cope physically his qualities shone out. He wasn't committed to life as a footballer. It wasn't clear he would become a professional and he didn't know what he was doing. He had many injuries at Le Mans and we feared they may ruin his career. When he arrived at the youth centre you could see he was too tall for his body. He was clumsy and not very well proportioned but now his height matches his weight. He looked clumsy on the pitch because something was missing. It took him four years to build up his strength and get over his injuries but by twenty-two he was ready for the top.'

Alain Pascalou, too, was later to recall, 'Didier finally saw reason about six months before he left us. He suddenly started to listen and change the way he lived. It improved him enough to get a move. He probably got a rise because he earned under £500 a week with us. In fact, that's one of the arguments I used to make him see the light. He had kids and I told him he had to think hard about providing for them.

'I was talking about him perhaps doubling his wages. I never even thought about the amazing money he must be on now.' Pascalou remembered the reports he had received from Paris on the young Didier: 'Players I knew in that area all confirmed his potential but said he was arrogant. He had his pride even with us and would stand up to older players.'

As his twenty-fourth birthday drew near, Didier was at last to play in the First Division, the Championnat Ligue 1, albeit in a side struggling for survival. In fact one of Guingamp's claims to fame is that its ground has a capacity greater than the entire population of the town it represents: the Stade Roudorou has room for 18,040 spectators while the town has only around 8,000 inhabitants. The core of its fans, therefore, came from the surrounding area, and they knew their team had a battle on its hands to stay in the top league of French football. Didier must have felt his confidence boosted by the knowledge that the manager there, Guy Lacombe, had insisted that the chairman buy him and that he could solve their goalscoring problems.

# DIDIER DROGBA

Within a few days of being transferred, he ran onto the pitch at FC Metz, the capital of the Lorraine region of northeast France, in front of a crowd of 14,000 on Wednesday, 30 January, for that long-dreamed-of Division One debut. But, as with most dreams, there were some worrying moments involved, too. Guingamp went behind after just seven minutes and were still trailing at half-time. The handful of supporters who had travelled across France to see them play must have feared yet another defeat was imminent. But all that was to change four minutes after the break when the name 'Drogba' was flashed around the news agency reports of the game – as it was to be countless times in years to come – when he scored the equaliser. Goals from Guingamp's Guillaume and Algerian international Hakim Saci followed in a short space of time, and, although Metz pulled a goal back and pushed hard for an equaliser, another goal in the last minute by Saci meant the team from Brittany triumphed 4–2, their first away win of the season.

If only the rest of the season could have maintained that high level of success. Didier played eleven times in all, but injury and suspension cut back his number of appearances, although he did manage to get consolation goals in defeats at Montpellier and RC Lens. Still, a 1–0 victory at home over Troyes on the last day of the season meant that Guingamp managed to hang on to their cherished place in Division One and Didier could look to a summer break with the prospect of a full season of top-flight football ahead of him.

When the fixtures for 2002–3 were announced, however, the fans of Guingamp must have thought they had drawn the short straw: they were at home to the new champions of France, the mighty Lyon, and it seemed they would start a fresh campaign with an almost certain defeat. Didier Drogba, however, had – as usual – different ideas.

## CHAPTER 5

# The Goals Begin

The summer of 2002 should have been a vintage one for football in France. The country's national side were the holders of the World Cup, won in Paris four years earlier by a defeat of Brazil, and two years later they had also triumphed in Euro 2000. So 'Les Bleus' were favourites in many people's books to retain the world title as they headed for Korea before the tournament started.

Confidence was boosted by the fact that manager Roger Lemerre had a squad full of household names at his disposal: Fabien Barthez of Manchester United was in goal and the Arsenal group of Thierry Henry, Patrick Vieira and Robert Pirès oozed class. David Trezeguet of Juventus was rated one of the best strikers in Europe and the jewel in their Gallic crown was Real Madrid's Zinédine Zidane, a player rightly regarded as one of the greatest of all time. All in all, a squad to be feared. As is often the case in football, however, results didn't go to plan, as their three games produced not a single goal. The first shock for the French was a 1–0 defeat by Senegal, then an uninspired goalless draw against Uruguay deepened the mood of despair. Their third, and final, game was a 2–0 defeat at the hands of unfancied Denmark and so France became the only holders of the World Cup to be kicked out after the first round in the competition's history. It had been a disaster.

So the crowd of more than 18,000 who packed the stadium for Guingamp's home game against Lyon some weeks later on the night of Friday, 2 August, for the curtain raiser to the new season, needed something to cheer them up that summer evening. And they got it in style.

Olympique Lyon were one of the slumbering potential giants of French football who had won the title on the last day of the previous season, the first time they had claimed the championship in its fifty-two-year history. They had beaten close rivals Lens 3–1 at home in what was virtually a 'cup final play-off' for the title. And before the Guingamp game their Brazilian star striker Sonny Anderson said confidently, 'We are right up there now. Lyon are now one of the big clubs in France and we have to live up to that billing this season.'

It didn't take them long to show they meant business. Didier started the game on the bench and he and the other substitutes watched as Lyon's Brazilian midfielder Juninho slotted home a brilliant twenty-five-metre lob with the game just three minutes old. Guingamp fought back when striker Stéphane Carnot volleyed in a good cross by Hakim Saci but Lyon defender Jean-Marc Chanelet put his side back into the driving seat, heading home a free kick from the right side by Juninho seven minutes from the break. Captain Anderson took advantage of a defensive blunder to net Lyon's third goal. In the fifty-first minute the match looked over.

With twenty minutes left, Didier came on as substitute and the entire complexion of the game changed. Striker Cédric Bardon reduced the deficit, thanks to an eighty-eighth-minute goal, but it still looked as though Lyon would triumph – but they had reckoned without Didier. Even though the ninety minutes were over and the game was well into injury time he refused to accept defeat. Somehow he managed to squeeze the ball home for a late equaliser – a taste of things to come, perhaps – to send the home crowd delirious with delight.

'It's a perfect start for us,' enthused Guingamp coach Bernard Marchand. 'The guys were brave and they never gave up. It's a good point for the future. We have played ninety minutes at the highest level as Lyon are one of the best sides in the league. We proved we have a great potential and a great will.'

As he got changed after the game in the home dressing room, Didier wasn't to know that not only would he finish the season with more goals to his name than the Brazilian Anderson across the corridor, but the next few months were to be his breakthrough into the big time.

He was on the scoresheet soon after when he headed home a free kick in the third minute of Guingamp's 2–0 win at Ajaccio and, although an injury to his foot kept him out of the side briefly, there was no doubt that once he was fit he'd be in the starting line-up. So he was back upfront and scoring in another 2–0 away win, this time at Troyes, by the beginning of November 2002.

Little Guingamp, a club founded in 1912 but with no great tradition to speak of and who had escaped relegation only by a miracle the previous season, were now proving to be the surprise package of the French First Division, and Didier was the leading their charge up the table. Another goal followed in a win at Bastia and he was on the scoreline in home victories over Nantes and Sichuan – all of them by that familiar 2–0 margin. He scored twice in a 3–1 league win over Ajaccio and January 2003 saw him notch his first hat trick at the highest level in the 5–1 French Cup romp over Seyssinet. By this time there was no stopping him and he was among the leading scorers in the French First Division.

Next to suffer that winter were the mighty Paris Saint-Germain. A run of six consecutive defeats had seen Guingamp drop dramatically down the table after their bright pre-Christmas, so there were only 6,000 fans at the home ground to see PSG take a two-goal lead, one of them a brilliant solo effort by Brazilian star Ronaldinho, who would soon be on his way to Barcelona and glory, as well as a series of epic encounters with Didier. With less than half an hour remaining, the game seemed beyond the home side, but led by Didier – showing a determination never to concede defeat that was to mark his later career – they managed to pull one goal back.

After sixty-nine minutes a powerful shot by Didier from the edge of the area levelled the score and, as the game moved into injury time, Guingamp's Hakim Saci mis-hit a shot that bobbled over PSG keeper Lionel Letizi. The Paris side's Argentinian defender Mauricio Pochettino failed to clear the ball but Didier calmly ignored the mayhem and carefully guided the ball over the line for the winning goal. The few away fans who had travelled to Brittany for the match booed their team off the field – as always, music to Didier's ears.

Another goal followed soon afterwards in a 2–0 win at Troyes. As Didier reflected somewhat immodestly, but accurately, later, 'We had to win to stay up. I had a bruised knee, which was really hurting, but the coach decided I was better on one leg than anyone else on two and I scored the first goal in our 2–0 win.'

By the start of April Guingamp were safely in mid-table, although no one expected them to improve their position when they travelled to Olympique Marseilles, who were vying for a place at the top of the division. But the 40,000-plus supporters in their Vélodrome ground – the vast majority of them home fans – were soon stunned by what happened.

Early on Marseilles failed to clear a corner and Guingamp midfielder Lionel Bah picked up the ball, controlled it nicely and unleashed a shot that hit the post and ended up in the back of the net. The Vélodrome crowd are famous for the vocal support they give their team, but silence fell over them in the fifteenth minute when Didier was picked out by teammate Cédric Bardon. After rounding the Marseilles defence, Didier's angled shot beat Croatian keeper Vedran Runje, making it 2–0. No matter how hard Marseilles tried to get back into the game, they couldn't breach the visitors' defence. How their management – and fans – must have wished they had a striker like Didier, a dream they were soon to turn into reality.

More goals followed for Didier against Nantes in the Brittany derby and against Bastia so that when the season ended Guingamp were seventh in Division One – the highest position in their history – and Didier had scored seventeen League goals in just thirty-four matches, making him the third-highest scorer in the division that year behind only Shabani Nonda of Monaco with twenty-six goals and Pedro Pauleta of Bordeaux, who hit the back of the net twenty-three times.

His success that season wasn't observed just by rival clubs, however, as the men in charge of the Ivory Coast's national side realised they had a great find waiting in the wings. No record of the remarkable season he experienced would be complete without reference to 8 September 2002, when Didier made his international debut in an important Africa Cup clash.

The young man who had spent as much time in France as he had in Africa ran out in front of an excited capacity crowd of 40,000 in the national stadium in Abidjan, named, inevitably, after the late president, Félix Houphouët-Boigny. Ivory Coast (the Elephants) were slight favourites to win over South Africa (the Boys) because the visitors, although rated higher in world football, were depleted through injury, and the *enfant terrible* of their country's football, midfielder Jabu Mahlangu (formerly Jabu Pule), was also absent as he had missed the flight from Johannesburg!

Ivory Coast also had pre-match problems with Marseilles striker Ibrahim Baraboo – who'd had a brief, unimpressive spell at Everton – dropped after saying he was unhappy that the recalled defender Cyrille Domoraud was being made captain. With South Africa ranked fourth in Africa and Ivory Coast eighth, the group they were both in – Group 11 – was generally agreed to be the most difficult of the thirteen in the competition. Qualification for the finals in Tunisia in 2004 was even harder as only the winner of each group had a guaranteed place in the finals.

The Elephants needed all three points from this home game with a tough return leg to come, and once the match began they often looked like scoring on a cloudy, but still hot, day. It was South Africa's first competitive match since their exit from that summer's World Cup, but most of the action was in their half. French coach Robert Nouzaret, beginning a second spell in charge of the Ivory Coast, realised after forty-five minutes that the Boys were going to be a tough side to crack and he took Bonaventure Kalou from Dutch side Feyenoord off at half-time and replaced him with Kandia Traoré, who played his club football in Tunisia – an illustration of how widely spread around the world the Ivorian players actually were.

Nine minutes into the second half Didier came agonisingly close to breaking the deadlock, beating veteran goalkeeper Andre Arendse with a low shot that flew just wide of the post. Marc Guei, another of the many France-based Ivorians, also came on and was a constant menace down the right flank as desperate South Africans conceded a succession of free kicks. Although they were by far the better side, and even got the ball into the net in injury time only for the 'goal' to be disallowed, the Ivory Coast had to settle for a draw.

At the end of the match the smiles on the faces of the South Africans showed their delight at the point they had grimly won. It was a disappointing debut for Didier, and he probably couldn't have guessed that it wouldn't be long before he was to become a national hero.

So, as the 2002–3 season ended, it was becoming increasingly obvious that Didier Drogba's talent was too large for Guingamp's small stage. Didier even appeared in a British newspaper in May 2003 when the *Independent*, in a routine story about transfer news and rumours, had the following passage tucked away near the end of the round-up: 'Meanwhile, Spurs have been linked with Didier Drogba and Florent Malouda of French club Guingamp. Striker Drogba has scored seventeen league goals this season, while attacking midfielder Malouda has hit 10.'

A few days later the *Sun* decided to chip in with its own version of which Premiership side Didier might appear for. The tabloid paper said that Portsmouth manager Harry Redknapp was interested in veteran forward Teddy Sheringham and also went on to say,

> Redknapp is also in a £2 million battle with old Pompey rivals Southampton to sign Ivory Coast striker Didier Drogba from French club Guingamp. Redknapp watched Drogba, twenty-five, score twice during Guingamp's 2–0 win over Lyon last weekend. 'Didier Drogba is a big, strong lad with a good eye for a goal. But I know Southampton are also very interested in him,' he said.

What wasn't reported at the time was that Didier was in discussions with West Ham United after being spotted by their then European scout Paul Montgomery, and would have gone to them for a mere £1 million – but only if they stayed in the Premiership. As it was, the East End side, then managed by Glenn Roeder, were relegated in May 2003.

Roeder has since revealed, 'Paul was convinced Didier would make it in England. We checked him out three or four times and also watched him on tapes and everything we saw suggested he had the potential to score goals in the Premiership.

'I have to say that the Drogba you see now is much more the finished article than he was then – but he had that special something you look for in a striker. Nobody else in England seemed to be on to him and he would only have cost around £1 million. But in the end we weren't able to make it happen.

'He's got the type of character you look for in a player,

dedicated to his game with a real determination to succeed. Sometimes it crosses my mind what might have been but it's no use worrying about that now. I don't suppose he's bothered about missing out on the move, given what's happened to him since.

'He's up there on the world level now. Drogba is good as part of a front two but doesn't mind being on his own. He's a real handful for two centre-backs, never mind one. I don't think I ever saw his like in my playing days. I'm pleased for Didier how things have worked out for him. He deserves his success.'

Montgomery adds, 'Didier was really keen on moving to West Ham. He gave me his word he would join that summer as long as West Ham stayed in the Premiership...

'But unfortunately they went down and he felt that, at the stage his career had reached, he could not risk playing in a second tier of football. He was hardly known in European football ... Didier was a humble lad who just trained and then relaxed at home and obviously the thought of playing in the Premiership was a big thing for him.

'He was earning about £2,000 a week and was looking at £15,000 a week at West Ham, so that was an attraction in itself. He was all over the pitch for Guingamp, back in defence one minute, beating the last defender the next. He was like Captain Marvel. I told him he would be a big player in England and you could tell when you talked to him he had that burning desire. I knew he would succeed over here.'

Southampton, Portsmouth, Spurs, West Ham. The one thing these reports had got correct was that Didier was off to a team based in a port, but it wasn't to be London or either of those two famous south coast cities. Instead he was off to Marseilles, the cosmopolitan city of 1.5 million people on the Mediterranean, the team all his boyhood heroes had played for, a side with gates of nearly 60,000 for sell-out games and a fanatical fan base.

Didier explained why he made the move he did when other clubs, including champions Lyon, were knocking on his door.

## THE GOALS BEGIN

'Marseilles were always in my head, but I was hesitating all the time. Then one day I said to myself, Didier, you have five minutes to decide. I chose Marseilles, called my agent and a big burden was lifted. The money wasn't important. If it was I could have gone to Lyon or England. But Marseilles have a glorious tradition and they are coming back anew.'

Just eighteen months after being a second-division reserve and signing for Guingamp for £100,000, he had rocketed in value by July 2003 when he signed for Marseilles and packed his bags yet again for another club. This time, however, he was not a bargain-basement signing, in fact it was a French domestic record: Didier now had a £4million price tag around his neck.

# CHAPTER 6

# Marseille - and Glory

If Didier Drogba's arduous and at times disappointing journey through French football had taken him to a series of thinly supported, nondescript clubs, all that was about to change in the most dramatic fashion. Marseilles, founded by Phoenician Greeks around 600 BCE, is thought by many to be the oldest city in France. Its position at the mouth of the Rhône and overlooking the Mediterranean Sea has, in the intervening 2,600 years, welcomed Italian, Spanish, Armenian, North and West African communities. The Italian descendants make up the largest ethnic group, and in the 1950s wave after wave of immigrants arrived from France's North African colonies of Algeria, Morocco and Tunisia. The cosmopolitan, thriving and dangerous port – captured in films such as *The French Connection* – likes to think, with some justification, that it has the only football club in the country to truly hold a city in its grip.

Olympique de Marseille, known simply as OM, and occasionally Les Phoceens after the founders of the area, is a standard bearer for the city itself. So, when Didier arrived, he found a metropolis yearning for a repeat of that glorious period ten years earlier when they dominated the French championship and became the first French club to win the European Champions' Cup.

Formed in 1899, Olympique de Marseille – Olympic Marseilles in English – were pioneers of the French game, competing in the country's first amateur and professional league and cup competitions. They would become cup specialists, winning six trophies between the wars, and by the late 1930s Marseilles were playing at the impressive 60,000-capacity Stade Vélodrome, built for the World Cup in 1938. After the war, the club went into the doldrums until Marcel Leclerc took over as president in 1965 and revitalised its performance on and off the field. Leclerc brought in top stars from the stunning 1970 World Cup in Mexico, men such as the Brazilian legend Jairzinho – whose goal had beaten England in a memorable clash famous for Gordon Banks's superb, 'impossible' save from Pelé's header – and Swede Roger Magnusson to appear alongside prolific Yugoslavian Josip Skoblar, and the club captured the league and cup double in 1972.

A new president, the colourful Bernard Tapie, followed Leclerc's lead and, after his arrival in 1985, the club scaled unprecedented heights at an astonishing speed – and plunged to the depths even faster in a fall from grace probably never known in world football before and certainly never experienced in France. With future World Cup winners in young Frenchmen such as goalkeeper Fabien Barthez, defender Marcel Desailly and midfielder Didier Deschamps – the last two later to play for Chelsea – OM won four French titles in a row and lost out on the 1990–1 European Champion Clubs' Cup final only on penalties to a Red Star Belgrade side rated one of the best Europe has ever seen. During their reign their goalscorer *par excellence* was one of Didier's boyhood heroes, the diminutive Jean-Pierre Papin, who in his 244 games for the club scored no fewer than 185 goals – an astonishingly high ratio, even taking into account the poor quality of some of the French defences he came up against.

## MARSEILLE - AND GLORY

In 1993 came Marseilles' greatest moment when they won the ultimate trophy on the European Continent in the first season of the Champions League, beating a fabulous AC Milan side – containing players of the calibre of Paolo Maldini, Franco Baresi and the Dutchmen Frank Rijkaard and Marco van Basten – 1–0 with a Basile Boli header. It was the first time a French side had triumphed in the competition and, historic as the victory at the neutral ground in Munich was, the celebrations in Marseilles, especially around the Old Port area of the city, became, if anything, even more legendary and are still talked about to this day. Not only were the fans wildly celebrating a major trophy but it seemed to be the dawning of a new era: the club was ready to take on the traditionally great sides of European football: the Real Madrids, Milans, Manchester Uniteds and Bayern Munichs.

But, when the partying stopped, there was barely time before a domestic match-fixing scandal broke a few days later. Marseilles were stripped of their 1993 national title and status, although they were allowed to keep their European title. The man at the heart of this sensational story was Tapie – a politician, singer and part-time TV personality who was equally admired and reviled. He was eventually jailed for his part in ensuring that a weakened Marseilles side, who had decided to leave their star players on the sidelines for a League match, still managed to triumph against lowly Valenciennes.

The club quickly managed to get back to their former level, aided by the unlikely figure of one-time Millwall striker and Eire international Tony Cascarino. Its new owner, Adidas boss Robert Louis-Dreyfus, was determined the glory days would return quickly. By the end of the decade the club was able to attract big-name players again, helped by the likes of defender Laurent Blanc – famed for kissing goalkeeper Barthez's bald head for luck before important games and who was later to play for Manchester United. Marseilles managed to be runners-up in their domestic league in 1999 and that same season reached the UEFA Cup Final only to lose 3–0 to Parma of Italy.

The ground had been upgraded for the World Cup in France in 1998. With its pre-match fireworks displays and massive flags rolling down over the crowd, no club ground in France is as colourful as the Vélodrome, nor as ferocious. It is generally considered that perhaps only Lens or St Etienne have a grip on the pulse and emotions of the local population to the same extent as Marseilles, who, even within their own fan base, have rival groups with their own banners, songs, merchandise and clubhouse. Among their number are the 'Yankees', the 'Winners', the 'Dodgers' and the 'Fanatics', and the most fervent, the 'Ultras', who sit behind the south-facing goal popping firecrackers and waving scarves that proudly proclaim they are 'Fier d'être Marseillais' – proud to be from Marseilles.

The support at away games is also large – remember vast distances need to be covered in France from Marseilles' home on the Mediterranean – and many bars in the city run supporters' buses for league, cup and European games. Although Monaco are near neighbours, the biggest rivals are undoubtedly Paris Saint-Germain, whose supporters are on the receiving end of many of the Marseilles fans' chants.

So it was into this powerhouse of French and European football that Didier arrived, determined to prove his worth. Marseilles had finished third in France at the end of the previous season behind League title winners Lyon and runners-up Monaco. That did at least mean they were in the Champions League, albeit having to play in the qualifying round, so their fanatical supporters had some European clashes to look forward to. Didier had no hesitation in saying, 'When I was young Marseilles was the team of my heart, the team that got me going. Players such as Jean-Pierre Papin, Chris Waddle and Abédi Pelé made me dream. I really want to play here and I'm sure I've made the right decision.'

He may have wanted to relax in the club's summer period and

to prepare himself for the battles to come, but there was to be no respite that year. No matter how great club pressures had been on Didier, they were almost nothing compared with the expectations of his Ivorian countrymen, for whom football is one of the few distractions from their difficult lives. The summer of 2003 was to see Didier personally experience this phenomenon first hand.

A few weeks after his international debut in September 2002, civil war had broken out in the Ivory Coast as rebels seized control of the largely Muslim northern part of the country. French troops were protecting their citizens and, to complicate matters further, there were several other rebel factions fighting across the country. So Didier must have been grateful that he didn't have so far to travel for his next cap in a friendly against Cameroon, played in February 2003 in the freezing-cold French town of Chateroux. Although both sides were a long way from home, many of the players earned a living either in France or in other Western European countries, so it made sense to hold the fixture in the centre of the country away from the fighting in West Africa. About 5,000 spectators – many of them immigrants from the two countries – braved the cold to see the Ivory Coast's Elephants impressively beat Cameroon's Indomitable Lions, who were playing their first game since the previous year's World Cup finals. The highlight of the Elephants' 3–0 victory was – as it was to be many times in the coming years – a goal from Didier, for which he latched onto a pass from Kanga Akalé on the stroke of half-time and shot spectacularly into the far corner of the net. He even managed to hit the woodwork in the second half as his side comfortably beat one of the best sides in African football.

All the time, however, the Ivory Coast political situation was worsening and the next month police were firing in the air and using tear gas to disperse hundreds of demonstrators who took to the streets of Abidjan in protest at alleged atrocities during the civil war that had been raging for six months by this time. Witnesses said many people were hurt as they fled the shots and gas, some trampled as they fell, and others were beaten by police. But at least there was a break from the terrible news at the end of March 2003, as the Ivory Coast managed to beat the third team in the tiny Group 11 of the Africa Cup when FC Lens player Daguy Bakari scored the only goal of the game in Burundi in front of a 'packed' crowd of 5,000. There were a lot more in the crowd for the June return 'leg' of the game against Burundi, however. 60,000 shirt-sleeved, sweating fans were packed into the Félix Houphouët-Boigny Stadium in Abidjan as Didier – still with Guingamp at this time – and his teammates, mainly players with French clubs, ran out to a rapturous reception. Within forty-five minutes a country scarred with poverty and violence had a new hero.

Before half-time Didier scored a hat-trick and the crowd went delirious with delight. The Ivory Coast ended cruising to a 6–1 victory over Burundi, but it was Didier's three goals that captured the hearts and heads of the nation. A country that had only a generation earlier been a beacon of prosperity and stability yearned for the good things in life once again, and they glimpsed it in the handsome six-foot-two striker who destroyed the opposition that day.

Sadly, as in all fairy stories, there is a wicked witch. The 'witch' in this case being South Africa, and so it was that Didier and his countrymen ran out just before 3.30pm on 20 June at the 40,000-capacity Peter Mokaba Stadium on the outskirts of Polokwane, the capital of the Limpopo region in the north of South Africa. To stand a realistic chance of qualifying for the finals of the tournament, which, unlike the World Cup, is held every two years, they had to beat the home side. The game was a sell-out and for days fans had been told not to bother turning up if they didn't have a ticket. Those who did – the stadium had at the time grass banking on three of its sides – were, of course, virtually all home fans and they saw Charlton Athletic striker Shaun Bartlett open the scoring in the twenty-first minute with a header from Delron Buckley's cross, which was completely missed by Ivory Coast goalkeeper Daniel Yeboah. But South Africa's defence was caught out four minutes before half-time when goalkeeper Andre Arendse spilt a free kick from Serge Die and the Elephants' captain Bonaventure Kalou was able to turn and strike the loose ball into the net for the equaliser.

In the sixty-fifth minute, however, South African striker Siyabonga Nomvethe marked his first match in almost a year with the winning goal. Although he had missed the entire Serie A season through injury for his Italian club Udinese he came on as a second-half substitute to grab the winner. For once Didier wasn't able to come up with one of his last-minute miracles as, with a half-chance beckoning, he headed over the bar.

That meant South Africa needed only a point in their final game against Burundi – in fact, they won easily 2–0 – to qualify for the tournament finals in Tunisia, so Didier's dreams of appearing on a world stage would have to wait, for the time being at least. Days later he admitted, 'I am enormously disappointed. I am really finding it difficult to get over this loss. We lost at a time when we really didn't expect to. Barring a miracle we will not be going to the Nations Cup finals.' Still, there was the forthcoming French season and the Champions League to look forward to. 'I never set myself precise targets,' he said, 'but if I managed to score the seventeen goals that I got last season it wouldn't be bad, would it?'

Didier wasn't the only new boy at the Marseilles training ground before that August 2003 kick-off to the season, however. The club had also bought Egyptian striker Ahmed Hossam – known to everyone as Mido – from Ajax in Holland, and he'd arrived with a fiery reputation. He was also five years younger than Didier. Not for the first time or the last, the boy from Abidjan had a rival for the starting role upfront. Even coach Alain Perrin was a fairly new face, having been at the club only since the previous year, but his mission was simple: he had to stop Lyon making it three successive French Championships and ensure that it was highly fancied Marseilles who replaced them.

## DIDIER DROGBA

So everyone had a lot at stake as the first game of the new season kicked off. The computers that today produce the fixtures in every major league in the world somehow have a habit of throwing up some strange clashes. So it was that fate decreed Didier's first match in the Marseilles colours should be at the club he had been a sensation at the year before – Guingamp.

18,000 spectators crammed into their Breton ground for the visit of mighty Marseilles, many of them hoping the striker they had cheered such a short time before would fail. He, however, had other ideas. Although Guingamp were on the back foot for most of the match, they held out until the game entered its last minute. Then Didier began one of those powerful yet elegant runs that strike fear into the best of defenders. As the Guingamp defence struggled to keep him out he slipped a pass to Ibrahima Bakayoko and the ball ended up in the net. 1–0 to Marseilles.

Later that week, on the Friday night, 60,000 roaring Marseilles fans gave their new signings a rapturous welcome – and visitors Auxerre a hostile one – at the Vélodrome for the first home game of the season. The result was the same, with the solitary goal of the match coming from Marseilles. Yet again Didier was the creator rather than the scorer, although this time he didn't wait so long. After fifty-eight minutes he swung over a pinpoint cross from the left wing that Mido headed home and minutes later the twenty-year-old Egyptian left the field to a standing ovation.

The third game of the season saw Marseilles take an early lead when Didier bravely burst through a packed penalty area to head home a corner in the eleventh minute at Lens – one of the few clubs to rival the fanatical support of Marseilles – and power home a header in what was quickly becoming his trademark style. But the vociferous 42,000 Lens crowd were not the type to leave their side unsupported and, as they bayed for revenge, they didn't have to wait long until they quickly equalised through Senegalese midfielder Papa Bouba Diop. Then, in extra time, Olivier Thomert netted a left-footed power drive that meant Marseilles left for the long journey home pointless.

As the French season began, however, Marseilles were desperate to progress in 'The Big One', the Champions League, and recapture the glory of ten years earlier. Their qualifying round meant they had to travel north to take on Austria Vienna. They managed to overcome that hurdle comparatively easily, beating the Austrians 1–0 thanks to a fourth-minute goal from Russian teenager Dmitri Sytchev on the day that Chelsea confidently beat Slovakian champions MSK Zilina 2–0 virtually to ensure a place in the next stages of the Champions League with goals from Icelandic striker Eidur Gudjohnsen after forty-two minutes and a sixty-sixth-minute own goal by Michal Drahno.

Back in the French League Didier shrugged off the Lens defeat by scoring at the Vélodrome after thirty-four minutes to give Marseilles the lead against Sochaux and the home side ran out comfortable 2–0 winners. Already their fans were warming to this newcomer, a man they felt could bring back the attention and drama their side had lacked for so long. Four days later Marseilles completed what should have been a routine task against Austria Vienna in the second leg. They managed to qualify, but a nervous performance marred by a brawl, niggling fouls and some uncharacteristic misses by Didier meant the game ended 0–0, enough to see them through to the first round proper for the first time in four years. The bad news was that when the draw for the round came out, Didier and his new pals were paired with Real Madrid, the previous season's UEFA Cup winners Porto – coached by a certain José Mourinho – and the always-tough Partizan Belgrade.

## CHAPTER 7

# Mission Europe

The debate over which is the most famous football club in the world is a never-ending one, but there is always one name that appears on everyone's list as a contender for the title and invariably tops most neutrals' assessment: Real Madrid. Even the game's organising body, FIFA, voted it the twentieth century's best club. The side from the Spanish capital had won twenty-nine national titles and, more importantly, on an astonishing nine occasions had captured the European Cup and its successor, the Champions League. The legend that is Real Madrid today was really created in the 1950s when, in their glamorous all-white strip, the side won the first five European titles with a team that showcased the talents of Alfredo di Stéfano and Hungarian maestro Ferenc Puskás, bringing glamour to football as the misery and drabness of World War Two faded into memory. Their white strip gave them their obvious nickname *Los Blancos*, but in recent years it had changed to *Los Galácticos* to reflect the endless supply of the game's superstars who were brought to Madrid to try to recapture the glory of half a century earlier.

So all those years that Didier had dreamed of soccer glory, from boyhood kickabouts to half-empty French grounds, must have flashed before his eyes on 16 September 2003 as he arrived at one of the great citadels of football, Madrid's Bernabéu Stadium, for Marseilles' first game in the Champions League after the qualifying round.

The Bernabéu once held 120,000 fans, but recent legislation insisting on all-seater stadiums had reduced that to a 'mere' 80,000. If Didier and his teammates felt pressure to succeed at Marseilles, it was nothing to the expectations that the fans have of Real Madrid. Quite simply, they have to win every competition they are in; anything less is failure. To that end, at around the time Didier was moving to Marseilles in the summer, they had spent £24.5 million in one of the most publicised transfers in history when they signed England captain David Beckham from Manchester United on a four-year contract.

Many cynics felt that the transfer had been generated by economic, not football reasons, saying that Beckham and the merchandising he attracted provided a massive boost to Real Madrid's, and his own, coffers. But the handsome Essex-born player who provoked a media frenzy when he and his singer wife, ex-Spice Girl Victoria, hit Spain had already responded in the best possible manner: on the field. It was hardly surprising. As well as Beckham, Real had three players who had all won the coveted FIFA World Player of the Year crown: Frenchman Zinédine Zidane, Portugal's Luis Figo and Brazilian Ronaldo, who was destined to become the highest goalscorer in the history of World Cup Finals. If, for some reason, any of these failed to deliver the goods, they also had the man who was to become the most prolific goalscorer in the history of the Champions League, Spanish striker Raul.

Beckham had scored with a rare header in his debut in the Spanish SuperCup curtain raiser against Majorca and scored on his league debut against Real Betis, so he was answering any critics in the best way possible. He had another fine game a few days later before the Marseilles match when Real trounced poor Valladolid 7–2 as Raul helped himself to a hat trick and Zidane, Figo and Ronaldo all scored a goal apiece.

Marseilles too had a comfortable win before the Tuesday night battle, crushing Le Mans – another of Didier's old clubs – 5–0. Didier had set the ball rolling with a thirteenth-minute goal and Mido grabbed two more. But Le Mans looked what they were, a poor side struggling to cope at the highest level; the same couldn't be said of mighty Real, however.

Ironically, the great Zidane was born in Marseilles and supported them as a boy although he never played for the club and he spelt out a chilling message for OM fans before the kick-off: 'I am looking forward to the game and, although I have a soft spot for Marseilles, I will still take every opportunity I can to score against them, as a Real professional must.' He was generous in his praise of Beckham too: 'It's not surprising David has fitted in so quickly. He immediately got down to working for the team and has been a hard worker. He will get better.'

So it was looking ominous for Marseilles as they began their first Champions League game 'proper' in four years. To make matters worse they committed the cardinal sin against a Real Madrid side who, if they were in the mood, were capable of tearing any opposition apart: they took an early lead, and it was, of course, Didier who scored.

Early on, Marseilles tried to strangle the talented Real midfield as Camel Meriem and Fabio Celestini snapped at the heels of Zidane, Beckham et al. Raul even seemed surprised to receive Luis Figo's centre and waste a good chance. That might have made the optimistic among the French fans think it was going to be their night, especially when, after twenty-five minutes, a Mido mishit shot bobbled around the area and then broke loose to Didier, who slotted it past the young Madrid goalkeeper İker Casillas.

Marseilles celebrated going ahead, but the reality was that they had just woken a dozing tiger by jabbing it with a sharp stick.

Zidane began to move into top gear and soon a Beckham centre was volleyed home by another of the *Galácticos* – Brazilian full-back Roberto Carlos, he of the unstoppable shot. Somehow the result seemed a forgone conclusion after that. Inevitably, Ronaldo scored and then increased the lead still further before Figo completed the all-star scoresheet with a fourth as the ecstatic 75,000 crowd shouted '*Olé*!' with every dazzling passing movement. Daniel van Buyten pulled a late goal back for Marseilles, but by then Didier – who had been doubtful for the game – had limped off midway through the second half. Four–two to Real Madrid.

'It was a tough first twenty minutes,' Beckham said, but he also emphasised the harsh reality of the match by adding, 'Once we'd gone 2–1 that was it, though. Real Madrid are expected to win every competition they enter.'

It was a view echoed by Ronaldo: 'We knew with all our technical skill we could outrun them. But having said all that, it was still good to return to the changing rooms with a scoreline like that.' At least Zidane had words of hope for the Marseilles followers: 'I think this Marseilles team will hurt a lot of teams when it plays at the Stade Vélodrome. It's true, I'm a bit disappointed for Marseilles, but that's soccer.'

As for the Marseilles supporters with whom he had stood as a youngster, he added, 'I think they were very good toward me.' He had good reason to say that. Three and a half thousand fans had travelled from France to Spain for the game and they even managed to break into prolonged chants of 'Zizou, Zizou' – Zidane's nickname – as Real ran amok.

If Real and their superstars were happy, the same couldn't be said for Didier and his new companions. Their performance was summed up by one newspaper, admittedly a Spanish one, as 'insipid' and even Marseilles coach Alain Perrin admitted his side had suffered from the fear factor, despite taking the lead through Didier. 'I think we played with some fear. We didn't have enough time to digest our lead. It was the fear factor. We leave with a feeling of frustration.' Didier, as always, had a very succinct, and yet insightful version of events: 'We just couldn't cope when they came back at us so quickly. They have a lot of excellent players who are all internationals but they're not extraterrestrials.' And just to show that in no way had he been intimidated by the occasion, he had the temerity to say, 'I didn't think so much of the atmosphere in their stadium. I'd expected worse and I'm used to worse.'

By the time the players reported back for training that Thursday in preparation for a tough league match at Nantes, he was still reflecting. 'We didn't give a proper account of ourselves,' he said. 'We played with fear and hesitation. We gave the ball away too quickly and at the end we were given a harsh lesson. We now need to make sure that we redeem ourselves on Sunday.'

Sadly, they didn't. A third-minute goal by Nantes was the only one of the match and Marseilles slumped to two defeats in five days. The season's bright start seemed to be fading fast. It looked to be going downhill even faster at the Vélodrome that Saturday, as unfancied Nice walked off the pitch at half-time in front of 55,000 unhappy fans after veteran striker Lilian Laslandes opened the scoring with a rocket, the first goal Marseilles had conceded at home so far that season. Those unhappy fans might even have rioted had it not been for Didier coming to the rescue. A fifty-ninth-minute shot on the run brought his side level and four minutes into injury time he was the man who calmly walked up to the penalty spot as the referee awarded a spot kick after spotting that Mido had been pulled back in the area. Initially, he played advantage but then changed his mind and gave a penalty.

The Nice players were furious and surrounded him as the delirious home fans realised they had been give a 'get-out-of-jail' card. All the surrounding mayhem didn't seem to affect Didier in the slightest as he confidently hit the ball home, becoming joint top scorer in the French First Division in the process.

Afterwards the side's experienced defender Sébastien Pérez said, 'A team was born in that second half. You could tell the squad were changing and some personalities emerged. At half-time, the coach asked us to do the briefing and express ourselves. Everybody talked and it was very interesting. There was a real burning desire for revenge. Didier Drogba showed a lot of character and so did Mido. This is going to take us far.'

But there still lay ahead a visit in the Champions League from the sturdy Partizan Belgrade side who had drawn their opening match against UEFA Cup holders Porto 1–1. Midfield player Pascal Johansen knew that although Marseilles were joint top of their own league now, in the tough Group F of the Champions League they were bottom, and had a lot of ground to make up. 'This is a different league and in this one we're bottom-placed. We cannot afford to be inconsistent for one half like we were against Nice. At Champions League level, it's just not possible.' Anything less than a victory would be disastrous for OM.

The Partizan coach, former German great Lothar Matthäus, added to the build-up for the game when he said, 'We won't be favourites against Marseilles but it's a situation which suits us fine. We can cause an upset.' One of the few players not to be talking about the game, not publicly at any rate, was Didier. It was to be an ironic silence, because just twenty minutes of the match was all that was needed for the Didier Drogba life story to take yet another unforeseen turn.

It wasn't the easiest run-up to the match as two of the successes from Madrid, Senegal defender Habib Beye and midfielder Brahim Hemdani, were almost certain to be ruled out with a broken rib and thigh injury respectively. Although Partizan were the outsiders in the group, their home draw with Porto had shown they were no pushovers.

The club's European traditions were minimal, with their defeat in the 1966 European Cup Final to Real Madrid being the highlight. Due to its black-and-white strip, similar to that worn by funeral workers in their home country, the fans had the rather gruesome name of 'the Undertakers', and their coach – Lothar Matthäus, a former World Footballer of the Year – was one of the most famous players in postwar football, winning 150 caps for Germany and appearing in a record five World Cup final stages. But that was all in the past. What pleased the Partizan supporters was the way he had helped the side beat Newcastle United in the qualifying round to guarantee a place in the Champions League that season.

58,000 fans were packed into the Vélodrome hoping their beloved side would forget the nightmare of Madrid and put the upstart visitors in their place, but it didn't turn out like that. The home side's best chance invariably fell to Didier, who hit the post early on and after forty minutes the game was still goalless. But then Partizan striker Andrija Delibašić was booked for a foul and, in first-half injury time collected another yellow for diving. Italian referee Domenico Messina showed him the second yellow card, and then the inevitable red, within a second of each other with a typical Latin flourish. So, to the screeching delight of the packed stands and the disgust of Matthias, a tearful Delibašić was sent off, leaving Marseilles to face only ten men in the second half. If truth be told, the home team would probably have triumphed anyway, but Didier was taking no chances.

After sixty-two minutes Mido broke away down the right wing and he sent in a low and hard cross. Didier decided to add to his repertoire of goalscoring technique by back-heeling the ball into the net. Minutes later midfielder Camel Meriem's wonderful centre into the area was powered home by Didier. Game over. Six minutes from time, Didier swapped passes with Russian Dmitri Sytchev before running through on goal and clipping the ball neatly over goalkeeper Radakovic. A legend was born that night in just twenty-two minutes in Marseilles: the fans had a new hero to adore, the defenders of Europe knew there was a deadly new kid on the block and several coaches decided to pencil the name 'Drogba' onto their wish list of players.

Still covered in the sweat of victory, Didier told millions watching on French television, 'This win shows the desire we have had since the start of the season. When we play like this not many teams can stop us. We are very ambitious.'

He added, 'Personally I had nothing to prove. As a team, yes, we did, because we needed points. Of course I was delighted to score a hat trick. That doesn't come to every player, even every striker, in the Champions League. But it was one game. Now we have to play Porto and they're a very different sort of opposition again. There is a lot of learning to do in the Champions League. We demonstrated a great desire to win today. If we play like we did in the second half, there are not a lot of teams that will be able to stop us.' A little later he added, 'I reached another level coming here and I feel I'm getting better and better. Now I've got to learn to vary my game, try to find different ways of losing my markers and make them as scared of me as possible.' And, after his hat trick, he said, 'I don't know what to say when I hear all these superlatives. This rise to prominence, it's not mine, and this victory, it wasn't all because of me. We must be ambitious while remaining as humble as possible – then we can get somewhere.'

In the excitement of that victory, Didier probably didn't devote too much time to other results from around Europe that hectic week. One of them, though, was to play an indirect part in his future...

At Stamford Bridge, fancied Chelsea had lost 2–0 to the Turkish champions Beşiktaş. One agency report summed up the game thus: 'Chelsea, with a huge squad of thirty pros since Russian billionaire oil tycoon Roman Abramovich took over ownership two months ago, were expected by their fans to have no problems dealing with Beşiktaş, which had never won a Champions League game away from Turkey.' Results like that were to have reverberations around world football as mega-rich Abramovich sought to create a team that could conquer Europe.

## CHAPTER 8

# The Hero of the Vélodrome

The impact the hat trick Didier had recorded against the side from Serbia and Montenegro on Thursday evening was still reverberating around Europe as the Marseilles players prepared to get back to a home domestic league game against Bastia on the Sunday. Didier's four goals in two games in the Champions League meant he was the leading scorer in the competition and his five in eight matches placed him joint highest scorer in the French Championship too.

Coach Alain Perrin must have felt relieved that his decision to break the French transfer record for Didier was being justified so early in the season when he said, 'His effectiveness and physical power is beginning to pay for us.' Didier, as often the case, refused to become too excited by the hysteria. 'Let's not get carried away with the victory against Partizan. We have to keep our feet on the ground for the match against Bastia.'

He kept so focused on the game, in fact, that it took him only sixteen minutes to open the scoring in front of 53,000 at the

## DIDIER DROGBA

Vélodrome as Marseilles cruised to a comparatively easy 3–1 victory. No wonder one British newspaper reported that weekend,

> Sir Alex Ferguson and Arsène Wenger have been keeping tabs on £6 million-rated Marseilles hitman Didier Drogba. Both have sent scouts to watch the Ivory Coast striker, twenty-five who has already banged nine goals this term – including four in the Champions League. He could now spark a bidding war.

Not everything in the garden at Marseilles was rosy, however. Alain Perrin had been in negotiations to bring back to the club one of the heroes from the golden era a decade earlier, goalkeeper Fabien Barthez. He had been the youngest ever goalkeeper to collect a Champions League medal in the Marseilles side that beat AC Milan, but now, at thrity-two, he was third-choice goalkeeper at Manchester United and without a first-team appearance in the past six months. He had struggled to fill the gap left at Old Trafford by the departure of Peter Schmeichel, one of the all-time goalkeeping greats, and United's manager Sir Alex Ferguson had finally lost patience with him.

The move was eventually delayed by UEFA but the news of his return on loan – even though he would not be eligible for Champions League games – dominated talk in the bars and clubs around Marseilles and perhaps the players were distracted as they were surprisingly handed a 4–1 thrashing by Strasbourg.

Croatian goalkeeper Vedran Runje wasn't to be blamed for any of the goals as Strasbourg simply outplayed Marseilles. 'He will have to show he is better than me,' Runje said afterwards, 'I didn't come to Marseilles to sit on the bench. I am not going to be frightened, even if I respect him a lot.' The discontent was spelled out more clearly by Marseilles' French midfield player Steve Marlet, once of Fulham, who said, 'This announcement was perhaps a little clumsy. Making headlines on the day of the match isn't great on a strategic level. We're players and this is the bosses' choice. We have no further comment to make on the subject. Having said that, we can be happy to have a high-quality goalkeeper joining the squad.'

Belgium international midfielder Daniel van Buyten joined in the argument when he said, 'Vedran has a lot of character and it takes a lot to bother him. So there will be competition between the goalkeepers, just as there is among other players.'

Runje himself insisted he would not sit back and let Barthez take his first-team place. 'The coach said to me that they had to make a play for Barthez. The choices are clear. I will fight to keep my place. It is up to Fabien to prove he is the best. Leaving here would not be my choice.'

So, in spite of their promising place in the Champions League and high position in the domestic table, all was not well behind the scenes at Marseilles when they kicked off in their home Champions League clash with the one side they hadn't yet met in their group: Porto of Portugal. It was about to get worse too.

The game started in an almost predictable fashion with a goal from Didier. He gathered a pass from strike partner Steve Marlet and used his pace and power to squeeze past two defenders inside the penalty area and inch-perfectly slotted a shot low into the bottom left corner. So far, so good. The happy fans dancing with delight at the Vélodrome as Didier and his teammates returned for the restart almost certainly weren't thinking at that moment about the qualities of the opposition they were beating, but they should have been.

The previous year, Porto had not only won the double in Portugal, capturing both the league and cup titles, but had also won the UEFA Cup in the dying minutes of extra time, beating Celtic 3–2 in a dramatic final in Seville. An estimated 100,000 Scotsmen had flown into Spain for the game and the day before the match an estimated 1 per cent of all the world's air passengers were Scotsmen en route to the game. So their victory in what was almost a 'home' game for Celtic showed the metal running through the Porto team and their brilliant coach, a handsome forty-year-old by the name of José Mourinho.

Only seven minutes after Didier's strike, livewire midfielder Nuno Maniche thundered in an angled drive equaliser and another four minutes after that Brazilian striker Derlei put Porto 2–1 ahead when he reached the edge of the area and drilled a low shot just inside the post. Coach Perrin switched to a more attacking formation in the final ten minutes but the home side were once again punished for poor defending in the eighty-second minute.

Portugal midfielder Deco was allowed too much space on the edge of the area and picked out substitute Dmitri Alenitchev, who converted easily from 10 yards. Moments later Marlet pulled a goal back for Marseilles with a firm header from Camel Meriem's cross from the right, but it was too little too late. Frustration had built up during the match. Didier and fellow striker Mido received two of the seven yellow cards handed out as the referee played an extra five minutes to make up for all the time lost to the theatrical displays of injury by the Porto players. In the second half the stretcher was used three times to carry Portuguese players off the field only for them to return quickly as they hung on for their win, even though Didier went close in the final minutes but was, for once, unable to come up with his almost customary last-ditch goal.

Straightaway the inquest began. Coach Perrin, in the timeless fashion of defeated managers, said, 'We could have led 2–0 – we had chances, and I thought we deserved a draw at least. I think we will have an interesting game in Portugal when we go there.' Didier was more realistic about his side's chances and his own performance. 'It is a great feeling scoring so many goals in my first experience of the Champions League, but it will be heartbreaking if we go out. Losing to Porto at home has left us with a big task, but it's not impossible. I am delighted but not surprised at how well things have gone for me at OM. I had many clubs interested in me, but Marseilles were always my choice. They are the club of the people in France with so much tradition and passion, and when I was an eighteen-year-old kid playing in the Second Division I used to dream about what is happening now. I just needed a chance and for someone to believe in me.

'I got that chance at Guingamp and I responded. Marseilles is another level and I have responded to that also. I have belief in my own ability. I am so happy to be at this club it is showing in my play.

'I know the fans expect me to score every game but I enjoy that feeling. I want to be the main man here and I know I will get better. I had eighteen league goals with Guingamp last season but I'll score more in this team. There is a lot of competition for places with myself, Sytchev, Mido, Bakayoko and Marlet and that's not something I faced at Guingamp. But I've waited a long time to get here and I want to start every game.

'I can't believe it is twelve years since OM were champions – it's time to change that.'

He set about it the best way he knew, by scoring again in Marseilles' 2–0 home win against Stade Rennes after coming off the bench having being rested by coach Perrin. But it was a struggle and the fickle home fans were growing restless with the team and its coach.

Marseilles captain Fabio Celestini later blasted the spectators who jeered both him and his team's performance. 'It's the first time in ten years as a professional that I've been targeted like that. Even when we lost 3–0 against Paris last year I didn't hear a fraction of what I heard,' said the Swiss international. 'I don't know what would happen if we were tenth in the championship. Would we have to arrive in armoured tanks?'

One thing for sure, the media frenzy was by now growing over the young striker, but Didier shrugged it off with a mixture of modesty and awareness of his own increasing ability by saying, 'I reached another level coming here and I feel I'm getting better and better. Now I've got to learn to vary my game, to try to find different ways of losing my markers and make them as scared of me as possible. I don't know what to say when I hear all these superlatives. This rise to prominence, it's not mine, and this victory, it wasn't all because of me. We must be ambitious while remaining as humble as possible – then we can get somewhere.'

Another goal followed in what looked like, on paper, an impressive win at home to Monaco 2–0 in the French League Cup three days later. In truth, their local rivals fielded what was virtually their reserve side and, once a two-goal lead was established, Perrin brought Didier and other key players off and sent his youngsters on too.

As Marseilles's vital return game with Porto neared, they had what should have been a routine league match at Bordeaux – where they hadn't won for twenty-seven years – to cope with first. But for the first time in his Marseilles career, Didier was sent off. As they trailed to lowly Bordeaux at half-time, matters got out of control in the second half and, after the home side's Bruno Basto fouled him, Didier retaliated with what one report of the game called 'a slap'. Off he went, and, to make matters worse, minutes later Marseilles were reduced to nine men when new signing Philippe Christanval was red-carded for a foul.

It was hardly the best preparation for the big game a few days later: the return leg of their Champions League group match with Porto early in November 2003. A win was vital for OM, while a draw might just have given them breathing space, but it was not to be.

A twenty-first-minute goal by Russian striker Dmitri Alenitchev pushed Porto up to second in Group F, their seven points placed them behind runaway leaders Real Madrid, and with just two games left it meant that Marseilles' chances of progressing had virtually vanished. As always, Didier's determination to fight to the end was there for all to see and he almost rewrote the script in injury time when his free kick curled around the defensive wall, beat goalkeeper Vitor Baía but then bounced off the bar.

Porto's manager Mourinho was so impressed with Didier that as they went onto the pitch for the second half, he said 'Tell me where I can find a striker like you – but not dear.' Didier laughed and replied, 'There are lots in the Ivory Coast.'

Back in the real world Marseilles coach Perrin said, 'We're disappointed at losing – a draw would have been a fair result. We played well in the second half after a first half that was more like a friendly than a Champions League game.'

The suspended Didier's absence was felt as Marseilles were hammered 4–1 at home by a rampant Lyon in a shock defeat at the Vélodrome, although he was quickly back on the goal trail and in touch with their fellow title contenders with a convincing 2–0 win at Lille at the end of November 2003 after Didier opened the scoring in the twenty-second minute.

'We would have been happy with a point but it's great that we managed to win convincingly here. We need to start winning more points away from home,' he said after the match. It would have needed a home victory over Real Madrid and all the other subsequent results to favour them too for Marseilles to progress in the Champions League, but the superstar duo of David Beckham and Ronaldo ended that dream when the two teams met again for their second clash.

A Beckham free-kick 'special' gave Real the lead and although Mido headed an equaliser, a classic, flowing move from the *Galácticos* ended with the Brazilian scoring the winner. The move read like a who's who of world football: Luis Figo passed to Raul, who exchanged a one-two with Zidane and Raul ran to the byline before pulling back to Ronaldo, who slotted the ball home. The match was noticeable, too, for the ovation the disappointed Marseilles faithful packed into the ground gave to one of their own, Zidane, who as a boy had stood on the terraces to support the side.

Despite the defeat, Didier had a good game – in fact the entire side's performance was an improvement on the drubbing they had received in Madrid – but it was the end of their Champions League dreams that year. The UEFA Cup was the best Marseilles could now hope for.

## DIDIER DROGBA

'I am really disappointed by this defeat, even if we played better,' Didier said. 'I hope that this will serve as a benchmark for the game against PSG, a game we absolutely must win.'

The game against PSG, Paris Saint-Germain, was a few days later at the Vélodrome. The rivalry between the two clubs – and their supporters – is legendary and the Paris fans are infamous for their right-wing, racist element. Police presence was trebled for the match between the two great rivals, which was eventually decided by a last-minute goal, but this time it wasn't from Didier. Instead, it was scored by the visitors' Fabrice Fiorèse, leaving Didier and his teammates shaking their heads in disbelief as they trooped dejectedly down the tunnel, having lost a match they had dominated for long spells.

So far the season had been a triumph for Didier, and managers around Europe were eyeing his goal tally with envy if they were in charge of cash-strapped sides, or with growing interest if they had enough money to buy him. In three short months his value had rocketed and his ability to destroy the best defences in Europe was now there for all to see.

## CHAPTER 9

# Joy at Anfield

If the season was a triumphant one so far for Didier, the same couldn't be said for Marseilles or their beleaguered coach Alain Perrin. Admittedly his side had been in arguably the toughest qualifying round in the Champions League, but the Marseilles faithful found their early exit from the competition hard to swallow. There was still the possibility of a UEFA Cup place to placate them, but it did not have the glamour and prestige of the senior competition. As with all former winners of the title, there was a hard core of supporters who remembered the glory years and would accept nothing less than a repeat of that triumph.

To make matters worse for Perrin, the club's results in the top domestic league, Ligue 1, had been disappointing and after an early spell at the top of the division the subsequent slump meant they were hovering some points off the leaders. The affair of Fabien Barthez hadn't helped either. When UEFA eventually cleared the shaven-headed international to rejoin Marseilles in the forthcoming January transfer window, it meant the club had four goalkeepers, including the unsettled Croatian Vedran Runje, who was vocal in his criticism of Perrin's tactics at times. So perhaps it was no surprise when he was dropped for Marseilles' final Champions League game at Partizan Belgrade and twenty-year-old Jeremy Gavanon was given the keeper's jersey instead. At least that game gave some relief to the under-fire Perrin. The 1–1 draw in a bitterly cold Belgrade, thanks to a Mido goal and a brilliant late save from young Gavanon, meant Marseilles would have the consolation of a UEFA Cup competition to look forward to. Belgrade boss Lothar Matthäus – who was to resign soon afterwards – said, 'We were the better side and created many chances tonight, but it all came to nothing in the end. I can only salute my team for playing their hearts out – you can't ask for more than that. Marseilles scored against the run of play and it was always going to be an uphill struggle for us from that point. We've been punished severely for not taking our chances.'

Coach Perrin, naturally enough, had a different view of the night: 'I am really happy that we will keep playing in Europe after the winter break, even though it will be in the UEFA Cup and not the latter stages of the Champions League. I believed this was the least we could achieve when the groups were drawn and it is no less than we deserved. It was a spirited performance in a very difficult away game.' He may have sounded bullish, but the overwhelming feeling was that Perrin was living on borrowed time.

More difficult days lay ahead. A home game against basement side Toulouse – who were reduced to ten men early in the game – should have been simple, but the unhappy fans had to wait until Didier's solitary sixty-second-minute goal broke the deadlock. The majority of the observers at the game reckoned poor Toulouse deserved a point at the very least. Welcome as the three points were, they left Marseilles sixth in the table, a massive twelve points behind runaway leaders Monaco, and trailing the title holders Lyon, too.

Nevertheless there was some good news for Didier when he was surprisingly named as one of the five candidates to be African Footballer of the Year, along with the likes of Bolton's Nigerian Jay-Jay Okocha and the eventual winner, Mallorca's Samuel Eto'o, who would soon be heading for Barcelona. Both were established players whereas Didier had really been in the headlines only since the summer. It was an astonishing climb to fame.

Meteoric though Didier's ascent had been, it couldn't save the man who'd brought him to Marseilles, Alain Perrin. In mid-January 2004 it was announced that he'd 'resigned' as coach, although many reports simply said that he'd been sacked and had been replaced by youth coach José Anigo. Perrin, then forty-seven, was to emerge briefly in English football when he took charge of Portsmouth – where he was immediately nicknamed, rather depressingly, 'Reggie' after the doleful hero of the BBC comedy series *The Fall and Rise of Reginald Perrin* – only to be axed seven months later following a string of poor results. 'I have given him more support than any Marseilles president has ever supported a coach, but the drive had gone,' club president Christophe Bouchet said.

Thankfully for him the drive had not gone from Didier. New coach Anigo, Marseilles-born and associated with the club all his life, watched gratefully as Didier scored twice – his tenth and eleventh league goals of the season – in Marseilles' 3–2 home win over a Lens side that was reduced to nine men in the final minutes due to two sendings-off. Didier even provided the service, via a free kick, for the late winner from Russian international teammate Sytchev.

If new coach Anigo thought he would have the traditional honeymoon period of many bosses, he was soon jolted back to reality when Marseilles lost – for the fifth consecutive time – to deadly rivals Paris Saint-Germain in the last sixteen of the French Cup. The winner came in extra time and Marseilles' goal, inevitably, came from Didier.

After they'd gone behind in the opening minutes, after just twenty-two minutes Didier bore down on the goal having intercepted a pass from PSG's Argentinian Gabriel Heinz – later to play for Manchester United – and, with two defenders about to tackle him, for once completely mis-hit his shot. Goalkeeper Lionel Letizi had been expecting a typical thunderbolt from the striker and so was caught unawares as the ball bobbled nervously past him and slowly crossed the line. Even when he didn't strike the ball properly, Didier just couldn't stop scoring!

A few moments later the game exploded into a mass fight that even Fabien Barthez joined in with – albeit to calm it down. Didier went close several more times and was by far Marseilles' best hope of scoring. But no one could break the deadlock and after the Cup Tie went into extra time a disappointed Vélodrome crowd saw PSG snatch the winner.

A scrambled 1–0 win over lowly Montpellier in the league – Didier, of course, was the scorer – did little to calm the growing unrest at Marseilles. With the win, Marseilles climbed to sixth place in the league with thirty-seven points, eleven behind division leader Monaco, and three behind fifth-placed arch rivals Paris Saint-Germain. An agency report of the February match summed up both Didier and his club's season. One line of it read, 'Drogba, Marseilles' shining light in a largely disappointing season for the south coast giants, scored the only goal of the game, scoring for the away side with a wonderful sixty-fifth-minute right foot half-volley.'

It is important to analyse the season so far for Didier. He'd joined Marseilles, a team he had yearned to play for since boyhood, in his hunt for glory and ironically he was almost drowned in plaudits by teammates, opponents and fans alike while the side was struggling with poor results, internal strife and discord among the fans. By this time he must have been thinking that perhaps the Vélodrome and Marseilles weren't the promised land after all.

If he was, however, it wasn't noticeable on the pitch as Marseilles tried for Euro-glory in the UEFA Cup against their far-from-glamorous opponents, Ukraine's Dnipor. Despite home advantage, Marseilles had to rely yet again on Didier – and another fumbled goal. This time it was a penalty, and just as he was about to strike the ball he slipped on the wet turf. As his 'standing' leg gave way, though, he still had the athleticism and power to send the ball spinning past the visiting goalkeeper. Unheralded Dnipor – hardly a household name in European football circles – seemed content to soak up any pressure that came their way in preparation for taking Marseilles back to 'their place'.

A goalless draw at Nice in the league on the last day of February was the next game for Marseilles, but afterwards Didier at last acknowledged the strain he was under.

'Against Nice, had I been fresher, I would have converted the two or three chances I had', he admitted in an interview with the prestigious French sports daily newspaper, *L'Équipe*. 'There were times I would have liked to rest a little but it was impossible because Ahmed Hossam Mido's departure to the African Nations Cup was not foreseen, we did not react when Steve Marlet was injured and we did not anticipate Dmitri Sytchev's transfer.'

At the time Marseilles were still sixth in the standings with forty-three points and Didier had scored an incredible forty-seven per cent of his team's goals with fifteen goals in twenty-five Ligue 1 games. Tellingly, he added that he had expected more from the club when he joined them. Whether the remark was a deliberate 'come and get me' call is irrelevant, but it sent out a clear message to the growing number of clubs who admired him that his contract would not be an insurmountable barrier in enticing him to leave the Vélodrome. 'I'm a newcomer and it is unusual that a single player has so many responsibilities', he said, just to hammer the point home. 'It's been improving in the past couple of weeks but it does not erase what happened before.'

For once Marseilles achieved a good result without a valuable contribution from Didier as the defence were the key when Marseilles managed a goalless draw in front of 25,000 Ukrainians in the second leg of their UEFA Cup tie.

## DIDIER DROGBA

The indifferent season that OM were having in the domestic competitions was temporarily forgotten as their struggling triumph over the Ukrainians meant they would be playing two games against one of the greatest names in European football: Liverpool. The Reds from Anfield had, at that time, already won the European Cup, the Champions League predecessor, on four occasions in a historic seven-year spell in the 1970s and 1980s, and were three times UEFA Cup winners. No matter how fanatical a Marseilles supporter might be, he could not dispute the fact that Liverpool's European pedigree outshone their own.

The preparation for the trip couldn't have been much worse, a 4–1 trouncing – the third time they had conceded four goals that season – by Bastia. Even Didier's late consolation goal couldn't lift the gloom, although it did mean he'd scored twenty-two of his sides' thirty-nine goals in all contests by this time, a ratio that reflected well on him but it meant that if Didier didn't score, the odds were that no one else in his team would.

No wonder Liverpool's manager, Frenchman Gérard Houllier, under mounting pressure himself to recapture the golden days of twenty years earlier, said before the midweek Anfield kick-off, 'In Didier Drogba they have one of the best goalscorers in the French league. Marseilles are very strong offensively and we will have to be careful. No matter whether you're at home or away first, the first leg is always the most significant. It would be useful if we can keep a clean sheet because if that happens we will be in a good position for the second leg.'

Houllier added, 'We have a lot of players who know about the French league, although the likes of Vladimír Šmicer, Salif Diao and Anthony Le Tallec won't be available for this game because of injury. Bruno Cheyrou will also know about Marseilles, but he's now a Premiership player and different to the player who played in France.

'You must also remember Marseilles have players who know about English football in Fabien Barthez and Steve Marlet. The game is really about the players who are selected tomorrow. I will be picking a team I think can win the game and not thinking about who may know the French league.'

Liverpool's English international midfield Danny Murphy also spoke of the Drogba menace. 'I watched Marseilles play twice earlier in the season when they were still in the Champions League. I saw the game with Partizan Belgrade. They won 3–0 and Didier Drogba scored a hat trick. He looks a real danger, a really good player. He'll be a handful and we'll have to keep a tight hold on him. They also were only narrowly beaten by Real Madrid, where I noticed they showed good technique. We're aware how difficult a tie this will be: the fact that they were in the Champions League and we were not says it all. That tells of their quality. We're very aware that they have quality players, a few we've already played against in the Premiership.'

Murphy added, 'But we must concentrate on ourselves. We are confident in our own ability, this is about us and what we can do. We know we must put on a performance. This is the real nitty-gritty of the competition. We've looked at the draw and there's not a poor team or poor ground. It's tasty now, in big stadiums.'

Tasty indeed if your name was Didier Drogba. For many English supporters it was their first view of this confident, born leader of a forward line. For those who had heard of him it was confirmation that there, on his twenty-sixth birthday, was a special talent on display.

Liverpool's Milan Baroš broke the deadlock on a freezing-cold Merseyside night in March 2004 in front of almost 42,000 spectators when he slid in to nudge the ball home after Steven Gerrard threw himself into a challenge with Marseilles keeper Barthez. But then the inevitable happened: Didier – playing a lonely role upfront – scored.

With twelve minutes left, Camel Meriem crossed and Didier held off challenges by Steve Finnan and Stephane Henchoz to shoot past Liverpool's tall goalkeeper Chris Kirkland, the first goal Liverpool had conceded against French opponents at home since the 1977 visit from the dazzling St Etienne side.

## DIDIER DROGBA

Although Barthez then needed to produce expert saves to deny Gerrard and Baroš and Sami Hyypiä had a header cleared off the line as the minutes ticked past, there was no disguising the fact that the 1–1 draw from a Marseilles viewpoint, given their hot-and-cold form that season, was a triumph. So much so that the entire squad burst into song in their Anfield dressing room as soon as they had run off, much to the annoyance of Houllier and the Liverpool camp.

'They think it's over because they are singing in the changing room,' the normally placid Houllier told reporters as the sound wafted down the corridor. 'They have given my team talk for me. I don't think it is over. The second leg will be played in a fortnight and we know we have to score and we know we can do that. Tonight we didn't play particularly well, to be honest and they frustrated us. It was difficult to break them down and we were flat.'

Marseilles coach José Anigo was unimpressed by Houllier's complaint. 'What you have to realise is that when we do something well we sing about it. I'm sorry if we didn't cry,' he said, with a dry sense of humour. 'We are very happy with the result and even though we were singing in the dressing room we are very aware there is a long way to go and this is only half-time. To come here and get a result against Liverpool is a big lift after our defeat by Bastia at the weekend.'

The good mood continued with a 4–1 home league victory over Racing Strasbourg, the only surprise being that Didier managed to score only one goal! He scored twice in their next game, a surprising 4–3 defeat against Rennes, but one of them was an own goal, although he could claim, with some justification, that the header he was trying to clear would have ended in the net anyway. Still, his 'real' goal at the other end was his eighteenth in the league, putting him level with Auxerre's Djibril Cissé in the race to end the season as top scorer. Ironically, Cissé, a French international, would soon be heading for England at around the same time as Didier, but for

Liverpool, where his undoubted ability never transferred to goals in the same manner as his Ivory Coast rival.

Admiration for Didier was now Europe-wide, and it seemed practically inconceivable that Marseilles would be able to keep him despite his contract, which was not due to expire until 2008. Even if they had recaptured some of their glory years it would have been difficult, but with mediocre league form and a UEFA Cup Winner's medal being the best he could hope for, the chances were slim once the big sides moved in.

If confirmation were needed that Didier would soon be packing his bags, it came with a rock-solid announcement from Marseilles coach José Anigo that he was not for sale. In the way that a 'vote of confidence' in a failing manager has become a cliché for 'he'll be fired soon', so the unequivocal statement that a player will be staying at his present club should be translated into 'he'll be gone in weeks'. So it was with Didier.

Nevertheless Anigo announced before the second Liverpool match, 'He's untransferable. If we lose a striker like Didier Drogba we'd have to replace him, given that the club is targeting a place in Europe. That means putting up money but without the certainty of finding someone of his quality.'

But Didier had a different take on the matter. 'I thought the club was better. If there's no improvement I'll consider my future.' He couldn't have spelled it out more simply. By this time, various clubs had been linked with him ranging from AC Milan to Birmingham City. The likes of Glasgow Rangers and Spurs were also mentioned as admirers of the goalscoring phenomenon.

So, by the time Didier ran out against Liverpool at the end of March 2004 for the second leg of their UEFA Cup Tie in front of a packed Vélodrome, chequebooks were already being pulled out, and the value of the Ivory Coast hit man went up even further.

Yet again Didier was on the scoresheet when he scored from the penalty spot. Liverpool had looked in total control, even taking the lead with a comparatively rare goal from their

## DIDIER DROGBA

England striker Emile Heskey, but in the thirty-seventh minute, Spanish referee Arturo Ibáñez sent off Igor Biscan for pulling back Steve Marlet in the penalty area after the striker had raced onto a through ball, a decision that Liverpool coach Houllier later called 'diabolical'. In the cauldron of a stadium, Didier stepped up and coolly converted the penalty for his twenty-eighth goal of the season. He could have increased the tally when he headed home in first-half injury time only for it to be disallowed for a push on defender Jamie Carragher.

In the fifty-eighth minute, defender Abdoulaye Méïté, another Ivory Coast international, nodded home from a corner taken by Demetrius Ferreira for Marseilles' eventual winner and earned them a tie against another of Europe's premier sides, Inter Milan.

It didn't seem to matter where or with whom Didier was playing, he just couldn't stop scoring. His preparation for the Milan game was a flight across the Mediterranean for a friendly game for the Ivory Coast in Tunisia. In front of a paltry crowd the Elephants won 2–0 and Didier, of course, scored both goals.

He found it a lot harder going a week later, however, when he had to face the mighty Inter at home in the first leg of their UEFA Cup quarter-final. The Italians had master defender Fabio Cannavaro, a future World Player of the Year, at the heart of their defence and a teenage striker from Nigeria, Obafemi Martins – later to play for Newcastle United – upfront. If Didier was looking for a partner in crime to share the workload, he was to look in vain. Injuries meant that he was the sole frontrunner against a side whose very name is synonymous with mastery of the dark arts of defending. Yet after just six minutes a spectacular overhead kick by him almost opened the scoring in front of the capacity 58,000 crowd. Not surprisingly, there was little difference between the two sides in the first half, and, even less surprisingly, it was a bad-tempered forty-five minutes; and when Marseilles's Laurent Batlles chopped down Kily González in the Inter area, both players ended up being cautioned after trading slaps to each other's face.

## JOY AT ANFIELD

After the half-hour mark Marseilles, playing with a reinforced midfield, began to find their feet and a long ball found Didier with his back to goal in the Inter area. He chested the ball down superbly for Camel Meriem, who somehow blasted his shot over the bar. Inter's only real shot at goal in the half was Vieri's shot minutes before half-time, which Barthez was equal to.

The second half was a different affair and should have seen the hosts build up a strong lead for the daunting away trip to Milan. Only seconds after the restart, Didier missed his first-time attempt at a high ball lofted in by Meriem, but then he recovered and fired past Alberto Fontana in the Inter goal from close range as the Italian defence was, for once, all at sea. Then came the bad news: Didier was so excited he couldn't help racing towards the fans to celebrate with them and climbed onto the fencing to do so, promptly earning himself a second yellow card of the tournament and an automatic ban from the return. Unsurprisingly, after the game coach José Anigo said, 'It's a tough blow, especially for stupidity like that. It's part of the game but we'll pay for it dearly. I hope the players will have the heart in the return leg to qualify anyway.'

His anxiety was understandable given Marseilles' reliance on Didier all season, but, as events turned out, he need not have worried. Marseilles managed to keep out everything Inter threw at them the following week and in the seventy-fourth-minute a superb solo goal from Camel Meriem gave them a 2–0 victory on aggregate, meaning the end of the road for Inter, surprisingly the last Italian side left in any European tournament that year. Marseilles immediately announced after the win that they were to extend Anigo's contract for another season and president Christophe Bouchet remarked, 'I just wanted to announce it at the right moment and a victory like this is the right time.'

If Marseilles fans dreamed of recapturing former glory, it was nothing compared with the desire of the supporters of their semi-final opponents. For Didier and the rest were facing undoubtedly the greatest underperforming side in British football, Newcastle United. With a massive fan base and only one club in the city, their trophy cupboard wasn't so much bare as redundant. Their glory years had been in the 1950s, led by their famous centre-forward 'Wor' Jackie Milburn and the last trophy of any significance that they had won was the old Fairs Cup in 1969. Third place in the Premiership the previous season had earned them their UEFA Cup slot and en route to the semi-final their most illustrious scalp was PSV Eindhoven, whom they beat in the quarter-finals. And they had their own 'Didier' in the shape of Alan Shearer, their thirty-three-year-old goalscoring centre-forward, who had notched six goals in the competition so far, compared with Didier's nine. England striker Shearer would need to be on top form for the match at St James's Park as key players in his side such as Craig Bellamy, Kieron Dyer, Jermaine Jenas and Lee Bowyer were all ruled out by injury.

Not that any of that bothered Didier. Throughout the game he was a constant thorn in the side of the Newcastle defence. After five minutes, he shot across the Newcastle goal and, a few minutes later, sent a header wide under pressure from Andy O'Brien. The home side's Irish goalkeeper Shay Given hit his head against the post in pushing away a centre that Didier was trying to reach and then, in the sixty-fourth-minute, Demetrius Ferreira clipped the ball to Didier, who struck the inside of the near post. In the closing minutes, Drogba chipped over the bar and forced Given into a save. The game ended 0–0, thanks to some superb goalkeeping by Barthez, and although Newcastle's veteran manager Sir Bobby Robson made the right noises about the tie still being even, it was a good night's work for Marseilles.

'When Drogba hit the post, nine times out of ten that goes in,' coach Anigo said. 'That happens. We certainly created chances and always looked dangerous. We had four real chances in the game and didn't take them. When we get to the second match, we've got to finish them off. That's going to spur everyone on, playing in a European final. It is a fair result – Didier hit the post. He might have done better with another chance.' In what was probably the understatement of the season, he continued, 'But you can't criticise him.' Indeed.

Anigo added, 'And Barthez's performance was notable. It is easy to see why he is number one in France. It was a fantastic atmosphere. Now it is going to be really interesting in Marseilles.

'We had four real chances and now we must make sure we finish it off in the second leg. The Marseilles people are looking forward to cheering their team on to a European final. We are now only ninety minutes away so that should spur everyone on.'

He wasn't so upbeat after fielding almost a reserve side soon after against lowly Metz in Marseilles and ended up losing 1–0. Though rested, Didier had to be brought off the bench in the second half, but it was too late and Marseilles' hopes of qualifying for Europe by virtue of their league position were getting smaller by the day as they were perpetually stuck on sixth place.

In the few days that separated the Metz disaster from the Newcastle return match, two events took place that were to have a massive effect on Didier. First, he was elected Player of the Year 2004 by his fellow professionals in France. His eighteen goals in Ligue 1, nine in European competition and three in domestic competitions made him the unrivalled winner of the title. This was a remarkable achievement given his brief career at the top and his late development away from the structured coaching system for youngsters of which the French were so proud. That meant nothing to his fellow pros – they knew the real thing when they saw it.

'Winning this award really does me a lot of psychological good,' Didier said. 'It will give me just the boost I need to finish off the season in style.'

The second event was across the Channel. Chelsea's Italian manager Claudio Ranieri as good as admitted that he would soon be leaving the club. Despite the millions pumped into it by owner

## DIDIER DROGBA

Roman Abramovich, success hadn't come the way of the men from Stamford Bridge. Something had to be done – and quickly. Ranieri – liked by many but known as 'the Tinkerman' for his constant habit of tinkering with his team – hadn't delivered the goods. 'I haven't much time left ... I feel I've achieved the maximum I could at Chelsea. I can look in the mirror every morning and feel I've done a good job. That is important to me. My reputation is safe and I think a lot of people know me a lot better. They have seen how I have dealt with the pressure. I didn't think the people in England would show such a Latin-style temperament and give me such strong support,' he said, admitting, in effect, that his days were numbered. He was right: By the end of the month he was gone.

If there was any doubt that these two events would be linked, they were surely ended late on the night of 6 May 2004, as the weary players of Marseilles and Newcastle trudged off the Vélodrome pitch, firecrackers and smoke hissing and swirling behind them. The scoreline officially read Marseilles 2, Newcastle United 0, but it should have been Didier Drogba 2, Newcastle United 0. Didier's goals in the eighteenth and eighty-second minutes won the game for his side, but he was constantly a danger to Newcastle and members of the 'Toon Army' who'd made the journey from the northeast of England. The 3,000-strong Newcastle fans congregated in one corner of the ground looked on as Didier broke the first-half deadlock in a manner subsequently described in an assessment in that weekend's *Sunday Times*:

Drogba was already into his stride, the pass found him and released him like a stone out of a sling. For perhaps forty yards Drogba sprinted with the ball at his blue boots. Two Newcastle pursuers were burnt off without getting near him, and then, inside the penalty area, he faced Aaron Hughes. This was where Drogba 'invented' the game. He used the inside heel of his right foot to flick the ball across his own body, throwing Hughes off balance and gaining a yard of space. Next, Drogba stretched out his left leg and in one motion swept the ball, or rather rolled it, past goalkeeper Shay Given and inside the near post. The Marseilles player had been in possession six or seven seconds. In that time, he had out-sprinted and outwitted a quartet of Newcastle men.

His second goal, as the match drew to a close, came with a crisp volley, from twelve yards.

Yet another manager paid tribute. This time it was Newcastle's Sir Bobby Robson, one of the most respected judges in European soccer: 'You can't knock out good players all the time over ninety minutes,' Robson admitted, 'but you can quell them. You have to keep working the whole time, and the defence has to be on it all the time. Drogba was their match winner. He had two clear chances and scored two goals. He's a very clever player, and I am happy to hold up my hands and congratulate him.' This time Didier managed to restrain his own celebrations on the field, no doubt wary of collecting yet another booking, but after the game he ran screaming into the press-conference room where he managed to spray champagne on journalists' laptops!

The rest of the champagne was put on ice, however, until after Marseilles' UEFA Final clash in Sweden with Valencia, the favourites to win. Under their coach Rafael Benítez, the Spanish side had become one of the major forces in La Liga and had won the title twice in three years after over three decades without a championship triumph. They had also become a force in Europe and had been twice Champions League runners-up in recent times. So it was all the more important that Didier – who had scored ten of his side's sixteen 'Euro-goals' that season – should be fully fit, having nursed a painful hip injury for ten days before the sides walked out on an unpleasant night in Gothenburg on 19 May.

Before the kick-off José Anigo said, 'He took time to recover but finally everything is OK. We hope his presence will give us a maximum chance to win this final. If he's in the team it is because he is 100 per cent. If he wasn't, he would not play. On paper Valencia are definitely a stronger team than us, they are more complete than the teams we have beaten so far. There are no gaping holes but happily for us there are always a few little ones and that is what we have to exploit. Every system has its weaknesses and it is my job to find out what they are.'

But if Benítez and his players were concerned about the threat posed by Didier, they tried to disguise it. 'Drogba is a great player of course but we have been playing in a league that also has some very fine forwards and we have never thought of man-to-man marking or of concentrating on just one player,' said Spanish international defender Carlos Marchena. 'We are better prepared than we were for the other finals because we have essentially the same group of players with two or three years more experience,' he added. 'We are convinced we can win this match but we are up against a really good opponent and a final is a final – anything can happen.' Benítez had no doubt where the main concern for him lay: 'I think it is likely we will see a lot of the ball but there will be phases when Marseilles have the chance to break. If we can stop Drogba from touching the ball at those times, then we will have done our job.'

What he couldn't have foreseen was that Valencia would be given a helping hand by the erratic behaviour of Barthez in goal. He saw red when he was sent off in injury time in the first half by Italian referee Pierluigi Collina for hacking at Valencia striker Miguel Mista in a one-on-one situation. Barthez later moaned, 'The referee should not make stupid decisions. It was a penalty, but not a red card.'

The ten-man side had to be rearranged as the resulting penalty was struck home by Vicente and when Mista himself scored in the fifty-eighth-minute there was no doubt where the trophy would end up. For all Didier's effort upfront, a task that was difficult at the start became impossible as the match wore on. The defeat ended his chances of collecting the first trophy of his career and

## JOY AT ANFIELD

with Marseilles seventh in the league trailing Lyon, who won their third consecutive title, the entire world of football seemed to agree on one thing: no matter how great an affection Didier Drogba had for the side from southern France, it seemed certain he would be starting the next season with a new club.

## CHAPTER 10

# Chelsea and a £24 Million Price Tag

It would almost be easier to list the top clubs *not* named in the chase for Didier Drogba than those linked with him in the early summer of 2004. From England Chelsea, of course, were high on the list, as were Manchester United and the two English sides Didier had seen off in the UEFA Cup, Liverpool and Newcastle United. Both Milan sides were watching him and Juventus were also said to be keen.

The common denominator in all the reports was that as the 2003–4 season progressed the sums mentioned that were necessary to prise him away from the Vélodrome rose. By Christmas they had already reached the £10 million mark and had doubled the season's end it. One thing was for sure: the £4 million Marseilles had paid now seemed a bargain and, importantly, the basic £15,000 a week Didier was being paid was cheap at twice the price. Lesser players were earning far more money elsewhere, and in the world of professional footballer the 'who-earns-what' grapevine was as strong as it had always been.

The only difference now was that it was a worldwide telegraph players were listening to.

It's generally assumed that it was this golden year with Marseilles that placed Didier on the 'wanted' list, but we need to go further back in time to find out the truth. During his spell at Guingamp his goalscoring achievements didn't just earn him his first Ivory Coast cap, but also caught the attention of a charismatic young Portuguese coach who was paying close attention to reports coming out of Brittany and the other French grounds.

In the last week of January 2002, Porto, struggling in fifth place in their domestic league, appointed a new coach with a contract to take him up to June 2004: José Mourinho. Thirty-nine-year-old Mourinho, the son of a professional goalkeeper, replaced Octávio Machado, who was sacked after a string of poor results brought the northern side to their worst position at this stage of the season for twenty-six years. Mourinho's former boss at Sporting Lisbon, Porto and Barcelona, Bobby Robson, hailed him as the 'best coach in Portugal' and a 'very good judge of a player. He's a very intelligent boy and I think he will make a very good principal coach for Porto. I think I gave him a good education. He will not panic. He can speak very shrewdly, very cleverly about the game. He understands football.'

The week that Mourinho's appointment was announced, Didier signed for Guingamp from Le Mans. Successful as he was quickly to become, this was nothing compared to the plaudits Mourinho earned during an incredible, whirlwind spell at Porto. In their first season, 2002–3, under his leadership, Porto won the triple of domestic League and Cup and UEFA Cup titles. The following year Mourinho was well on the way to one better, winning not just the Portuguese League but also the coveted Champions League, knocking out Manchester United and, of course, Marseilles, before meeting Monaco in the final.

It is a tribute to Mourinho that, as well as assessing his own players, he confirmed his opinion that Didier was a player to spearhead any attack. Years later, Didier confirmed just how far back that admiration went. 'He's known me for a long time, since I was at Guingamp, in fact. When he was still manager of FC Porto he wanted me then, but the club didn't have enough money. And then when I was at Marseilles he followed me throughout the time when we were getting excellent results in the UEFA Cup. He knows me through and through.'

Of all Didier's professional relationships it is the one with Mourinho that elevated him to world fame. Mourinho's faith in the striker, even when others were criticising both his standard of play and his behaviour, has been a constant foundation for Didier to rely on. But that was all ahead. First, he had to decide, as the 2003–4 season ended, where his future lay. That decision would be linked to events across the Iberian Peninsula in Portugal, where Mourinho and his team were preparing for their Champions League final against Monaco, and in London SW6, where an expensive set of footballers weren't delivering the results their manager expected.

Probably the worst-kept secret of that or any other recent football year was that Claudio Ranieri would soon be leaving Chelsea. It really wasn't a question of if, but when. Money was already being placed on José Mourinho to replace him, although one of the matters that still had to be resolved was which players he would be able to buy. The question was not so much the price that would be paid – Roman Abramovich had already shown this was a small obstacle to overcome – but who were the best players to recruit to Stamford Bridge. Mourinho was known to be keen on his Porto trio of Deco, Paulo Ferreira and Ricardo Carvalho, Abramovich and his advisers less so. The one name the strong-willed coach and his billionaire future boss agreed on, however, was Didier Drogba. As soon as Mourinho's appointment became official, the odds were that Didier would head for the King's Road, especially as after the UEFA Cup Final defeat Marseilles general manager Pape Diouf said, 'If Chelsea were to offer enough money so that I can buy a team and a half, I'd have to think about it.'

Even Mourinho couldn't keep silent for ever. After his all-conquering Porto side easily beat Monaco 3–0 he spoke publicly for the first time about his impending move, telling Portuguese TV, 'I have some offers in my wallet, but one which I very much want to accept, which is that from Chelsea.' In case there was any confusion, he also said, 'The country where I want to work next is England, and I haven't changed my mind about that. The club I gave my word to I would be favourite to go – I'm not the sort of person to change my mind.' But it wasn't quite as simple as that. Days later *The Times* in London reported:

The most protracted sacking in English football was painfully dragged out once again yesterday when Claudio Ranieri was summoned to a meeting in Milan with Roman Abramovich and Peter Kenyon, the Chelsea chief executive, but not dismissed.

The hitch was that Ranieri would be a free agent when he left, and there seemed little doubt he would soon be able to choose another club and yet still be able to claim £6 million in compensation from Chelsea. Add to that the complication of compensation to Porto for losing their highly prized coach and there was still a lot of wheeling and dealing to be done.

Finally, on 31 May 2004, Chelsea released a statement saying that fifty-one-year-old Ranieri, brought in by former owner Ken Bates, would be leaving. The club said:

Chelsea Football Club today announced that Claudio Ranieri is to leave the club. Claudio has done a first-class job for the club and paved the way for future success. We would like to wish Claudio all the best for the future. We are discussing the exact terms of his departure with him and his representatives.

## CHELSEA AND A £24 MILLION PRICE TAG

Mourinho was expected to sign a deal – spread over four years and reputedly worth £16 million – within days.

One of the ironies of Ranieri's axing was that he guided Chelsea to their best league finish, second, since they won the old First Division title for the only time in their history way back in 1954–5. But, with north London rivals Arsenal running away with the Premiership title during an unbeaten league campaign, Ranieri's fate was sealed in May 2004 when Chelsea lost their Champions League semi-final against a Monaco side soon to be easily beaten in the final by Mourinho's men.

Ranieri had helped steer Chelsea to a famous last-eight win over Arsenal, but was widely criticised for his tactical blunder in the first leg of the semi-final, when Chelsea were all square at 1–1 against a ten-man Monaco late in the second half when he responded to Andreas Zikos' sending-off by bringing on striker Jimmy Floyd Hasselbaink in place of defender Mario Melchiot. It was a brave move to win the game but backfired in disastrous fashion when Monaco added two more goals.

Instead of going into the second leg all square at 1–1, and with a vital away goal, Chelsea found themselves trailing 3–1. Ranieri confessed, 'It's my fault. We completely lost the plot but I was sure it was the best thing for the team.' Still, 'the Tinkerman' wasn't out of work for long, thereby revealing why Chelsea had argued over the amount of compensation to which he was entitled. Within days he had replaced Rafael Benítez at one of his former clubs, Valencia, as the Spaniard moved to Liverpool in place of axed Gérard Houllier as part of a continual, and highly paid, managerial merry-go-round.

Two days later came the announcement that Porto had released Mourinho from his contract after he, and his agent Jorge Mendes proved strong negotiators throughout their discussions with Chelsea. Mourinho especially ensured he got guarantees on the freedom he would enjoy on transfers and on who he would take with him from the European Cup winners. Intriguingly, as part of the deal, the two clubs signed an agreement allowing Porto to effectively act as a feeder club for Chelsea, who would be given first option for five years on their young players in return for financing their discovery and training. Roman Abramovich even broke his habit of saying nothing by informing Russian news agency Interfax that Mourinho was now the only candidate for the Chelsea job. 'He is the only one left. I hope the talks have entered their final stage.'

By 2 June 2004 José Mourinho jetted into London and held his first press conference – and what a tour de force it was! From that day on he would be known – in his own words – as 'the Special One'. He talked about himself, why he wouldn't hesitate to get rid of players no matter how famous they were, how he would handle his mega-rich Russian boss – and why he wasn't afraid of Manchester United boss Sir Alex Ferguson.

'I am a winner because I'm good at what I do and because I am surrounded by people who think the same. When I arrive I will put all my cards on the table and say we have to work with big things in our minds. I don't believe in the idea of old managers and new ones. I just believe in good and bad ones, the ones who have success and the ones who don't. But I will say this: we have top players. I'm sorry that I'm a bit arrogant, but we have a top manager. We want top things. If I turn up in the dressing room and just say, "We will work – let's wait and see if Arsenal can do the same or be weaker," and don't talk about motivation and desire, the players will look at me and feel I am a disappointment. I don't want to be seen as one of the new young managers in the world. I'm not just one out of a bottle. I'm a special one.'

And there was more. To show that he would bow down to no one, Mourinho explained why he had visibly reacted to Ferguson after United's Roy Keane was given a red card for stamping on Vítor Baía of Porto during a tumultuous Champions League clash at Old Trafford in February 2004. Mourinho responded to Ferguson's refusal to shake hands by taunting him: 'Alex Ferguson

Didier Drogba in action for En Avant Guingamp, his second league club in France, in July 2002 at the age of 24. He scored 20 goals in 45 appearances for the Breton club.

*Above*: May 2003, and in action for Guingamp against rivals Lyon.

*Below*: Drogba beams with pride after defeating Monaco 3-1 at Guingamp's Roudourou stadium, May 2003. That season, his talent helped Guingamp to their highest ever league place (7th) in Ligue 1.

Didier became a rising star in France and was often photographed and interviewed for sports magazines, where his clean-living philosophy and match-winning performances made him a popular role model.

*Above left*: August 2003 and Didier makes his presence felt for his new top club Olympique Marseille against his old employers, Guingamp.

*Above right*: Increasingly powerful and athletic, Drogba turns on the tricks for Marseille against Toulouse in Ligue 1.

*Below*: The banners come out for Drogba at Marseille, renowned as one of the most fanatical of European clubs.

*Above*: Also lethal from a dead-ball situation, Didier curls one in over the PSG wall in a January 2004 French cup clash.

*Below*: February 2004, and in action for Marseille against his first club Le Mans, where he'd scored twelve goals over three injury-hit seasons.

Didier has always got on well with his managers.

*Above left*: Didier's mentor at Guingamp, manager Guy Lacombe.

*Above right*: Marseille coach Jose Anigo shows his appreciation at full time after Drogba netted his second goal against Newcastle in the UEFA Cup semi-final, May 2004.

*Below left*: Jose Mourinho was a keen admirer of Drogba long before he brought him to Chelsea. Here Jose congratulates his striker after the Ivorian had scored the third goal against Paris Saint-Germain in 2004's Champions League campaign.

*Below right*: With Elephants coach Henri Michel and team-mate Aruna Kone in World Cup warm-up mode.

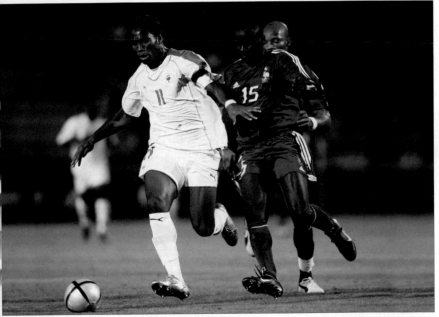

*Above left*: Drogba goes down under a challenge from a Valencia player in the 2004 UEFA Cup final at the Ullevi stadium in Gothenburg.

*Above right*: Still in the top flight of European football but under pressure in the air from Bayern Munich in the quarter-final of the Champions League in April 2005.

*Below*: August 2005 and Didier faces the national team of his adopted home France in an international friendly.

The quarter final of the African Cup of Nations… and the Ivory Coast's nerves are in shreds as Cameroon slot a penalty home. But Didier breaks the tension by scoring the winning spot-kick to make it 12-11 and Ivory Coast go into the last four.

said Baía had overreacted. I disagreed with him and told him to look at the video. I only hope he will apologise to me having seen it. His reaction was not correct but I understand he was emotional because his team were dominated by a side who have 10 per cent of his budget.'

If the press corps were waiting for some platitudes, they were to be disappointed: 'For me it was a normal football situation and his reaction wasn't a personal thing. But I felt my players were not big enough to cope with that kind of pressure and so I had to show that I was not afraid of him and the boss was ready for a fight. At the end of the second leg he came to the dressing room to congratulate me and I have respect for such important people. I haven't come here for fights. I came here to win but at the right moment if I feel my players, my group and my club need my help, it's like family and they will get it.'

He even dismissed the fact that Chelsea had initially wanted England boss Sven-Göran Eriksson at the helm – 'he was the natural choice' – and sent out a clear message to his squad of internationals: 'We only have good players. But the question is whether they can adapt to their manager's way of thinking. Some will not adapt. The biggest issue is motivation. If you have a box of oranges and one is sick and you leave it there, then one month later you have ten oranges to throw into the garbage.' What other manager would talk like this about superstars? Mourinho didn't care. He wanted a squad of 'twenty-one plus three' – twenty-one outfield players plus three goalkeepers.

He added, 'You must try to know every coach's style. I will study them here and try to know them well. I will have scouts looking at the English teams during the pre-season. When you go into battle you must know the strengths and weaknesses of your opponents. To do well you must first of all have a perfect tactical organisation. The second thing is ball possession. You must play how you want to play.' Mourinho was also keen to spell out where he stood with Abramovich: 'He knows what I am and what I want. I understand his desires. He wants to win and I want a close relationship with him. We cannot be separate. We must be a team.'

So now he had the task of getting rid of the players he didn't need and assembling that 'family' of twenty-one plus three. It seemed fairly straightforward that Didier would soon be welcomed into the fold, but the days when transfers were a fairly simple negotiation between two clubs, one player – and perhaps the player's wife – lay years in the past. The average negotiations involved in taking an international star from one leading club to another now have secrecy, denials, financial intrigue and general subterfuge. Chelsea supporters who expected an announcement within days would be disappointed. They'd be confused too, if they read two national newspapers on 14 June 2004.

On the one hand the *Daily Mirror* confidently stated,

Chelsea have been told to forget about making another bid for Didier Drogba.

Stamford Bridge owner Roman Abramovich has twice tried to sign Marseilles's Ivory Coast striker, but the French club have ruled him off-limits to the Londoners. Chelsea's interest has put new Marseilles general manager, Pape Diouf, in a difficult situation. Diouf was Drogba's agent before he took his current job and knows he would face a backlash if his former client was sold just a year after joining the club and helping them to a UEFA Cup Final. 'Chelsea could offer £30m and it would make no difference,' said Diouf. 'Didier is not for sale.' Marseilles' rebuff is the latest in a string of failed transfer swoops by Chelsea, among them Real Madrid's Roberto Carlos and AC Milan's Andriy Shevchenko.

Its rival, the *Daily Star*, had a different story to tell on the very same morning, however:

Arsène Wenger last night confirmed Chelsea are ready to pay a staggering £28m for striker Didier Drogba. But the Arsenal boss insisted he was not shocked by the amazing fee for the Marseilles star. Wenger has claimed two transfer markets exist in European football – one for Roman Abramovich's west London club and another for everybody else. Ivory Coast striker Drogba scored twice against both Liverpool and Newcastle last season to help Marseilles dump the Premiership pair out of the UEFA Cup. And asked on French TV about Chelsea paying 40m euros – or £28m – for him, Wenger replied: 'Yes, but there are two transfer markets – the Chelsea transfer market and the other one for the rest of Europe.' Wenger has a vast knowledge of transfer activities and added: 'For Chelsea there is no limit, even 40m euros. For them it does not shock me at all.'

As the summer dragged on Didier Drogba decided to take his young family on holiday to Florida to escape the pressure, leaving clubs and agents back in Europe to resolve the matter.

Mourinho started as he meant to go on, within days outlining his plans to his players by sending a personal letter out to everyone in the squad impressing on them the need for hard work, tough training and being a close-knit squad. It's not recorded whether Hernán Crespo, the club's Argentinian striker, received one. His imminent loan to AC Milan was an important part of the jigsaw that would bring Didier to Stamford Bridge.

The Marseilles–Chelsea deal over Didier was in fact being brokered by Scots agent Willie McKay – a man with links with French football – who had first suggested Didier to Southampton when he was a Guingamp player, only for the deal to be rejected as the £1.5 million fee was too expensive!

Later that summer, Christophe Bouchet, the Marseilles president, said somewhat bizarrely, 'It is a continuing saga and someone is having a laugh. I have never received a fax from Chelsea about Didier and he will be here next season. I have no worries about that.' It could be that Bouchet was afraid of a backlash from the volatile local fans, who in one year had come to idolise Didier, although OM already appeared to have made plans to replace him with the signing of Habib Bamogo, the Montpellier striker, who scored sixteen goals as his side were relegated from the French First Division.

Mourinho made no bones about where he stood just a day after the pronouncements from Marseilles, stating, 'Drogba is one of the best strikers in Europe. Since my team played against him I started looking at him with different eyes and I felt he needed a better club and a better league to show how good he really is. He can become a good option if in the next days we decide Hernán's [Crespo's] future is away from Chelsea.

'I see the qualities of power and speed. Also his control on the first touch and the way he fights – he's a player who can achieve great success'.

Back to Monsieur Bouchet, who then admitted that despite turning down the original offer of over £18 million, Marseilles were now tempted by a larger one from Chelsea.

'Negotiations have begun between Chelsea representatives and Pape Diouf [the Marseilles general manager]. But we felt their offer of 28 million euros was insufficient and, in the current state of things, I refused', Bouchet said. 'But the situation is extremely complex and it's a real balancing act not only on the human side but also because of our financial state that has to be taken into account as well'.

Earlier in the year Bouchet had said that his club's losses were running at about £10 million a year.

At last the matter was resolved when, on 14 July 2004, terms were agreed between the two clubs: Chelsea upped their £18.5 million bid, Marseilles lowered their £27 million asking price and the deal was done for £24 million. Marseilles' Pape Diouf said, 'Didier is a magnificent striker and it would have been great for us to keep him. But we took the decision in the interests of the club. If we sell him we can buy three international players for the same money'.

## CHELSEA AND A £24 MILLION PRICE TAG

There was still the problem of Hernán Crespo: if he didn't go to Milan the entire deal would have to be put on ice. So Mourinho decided to speed matters up by announcing four days before Chelsea departed for America for a two-week pre-season tour, 'Any new players we want will have to arrive before we go to the United States. I want to go there and begin preparations for the season with my full squad. I will have worked hard to build the squad before we go and it's important I have it in place.

'I want the same group of players until the end of the season and Wednesday is the cut-off day.'

Within forty-eight hours Chelsea announced on their website that they had agreed terms with Marseilles, stating, 'Chelsea are delighted to confirm that we have agreed terms with the French club Marseilles for the transfer of Didier Drogba.'

Even Bouchet couldn't keep his cards close to his chest any longer: 'We reached definitive agreement for Didier Drogba's transfer to Chelsea with [the chief executive] Peter Kenyon at the start of the afternoon,' he said. 'The player will leave for London on Tuesday. Didier leaves a big void but you have to know when to be pragmatic. With this money we are going to build a better team again and bring a healthier complexion to our finances. The long-term future of the club had been in jeopardy.

'What Chelsea offered was double Juventus's offer. Sometimes football can be brutal but we could not let such an offer go, even if we felt torn apart at the idea of letting him leave. Thanks to Didier we can afford to try to create a better team.'

He didn't speak publicly about the transfer at the time, but Didier obviously had conflicting emotions. Later he remarked, 'What Mourinho said was simple but very effective. Marseilles were a good team, yet I had to think of winning trophies first. I had to contest the Champions League every year to make progress. For me, there is Thierry Henry, Ronaldo and you. You belong up there. I said to myself, "Didier, this guy really wants you."

'Mourinho knows how to win. That's why Roman Abramovich

had him come. Quite simply, so he could teach Chelsea to win. Victory feeds the manager's ego. It gives him a boost and he is transmitting this victory culture to the players. Right up to the point where I spoke to Mourinho, I felt like I wanted to stay with Marseilles to the end of my career. Like Thierry, I believed I had found the club of my dreams. I still envy Thierry. He has everything he needs to feel good at Arsenal.

'I felt the same at Marseilles. I shared feelings with the fans and the city. My family had settled in perfectly. I felt so good there. So, when someone told me Chelsea were interested in me in February, I remember my reaction very well. It was, "Chelsea? I will never go there. What would I be doing there?" But all my friends were advising me to go. One player even told me, "Are you sick or what? I'm going to hit you. You don't turn down Chelsea!" I was stunned. I didn't want to leave. I lost my appetite at the table. I was looking for someone to tell me, "Didier, stay."

'Marseilles' general manager, Pape Diouf, used to be my agent. But I was shocked when he came to me and said, "I feel pissed off but Chelsea have made a bid for you." He was very honest with me. He added, "If I was your elder brother, I'd tell you to join them. It's best for you to go." I was astonished. I told him, "Pape, I don't want to go. You're dropping me in the shit. What am I to do?" '

Although the French season had come to an end, Didier was by now a pivotal figure in the emerging Ivory Coast side, and in June and July 2004 they had three crucial matches to play in their Group 3 World Cup qualifying section with Egypt, Benin, Libya, Sudan and, most importantly, Cameroon with only one side to go through to the finals in Germany. That meant long-haul flights from Europe to Africa and back for Didier, plus vast distances to be travelled between games. Cameroon, their biggest threat, had for a long time been one of the dominant forces of African football and were seeking to get to the finals for a fifth successive tournament, even reaching the quarter-finals in Italy in 1990, only to be beaten by England in a thrilling match.

## CHELSEA AND A £24 MILLION PRICE TAG

So, no sooner had Didier packed away his Marseilles kit, perhaps for the last time, than he turned out for the Ivory Coast in front of 60,000 spectators in Abidjan against Libya and scored from the penalty spot to seal a 2-0 victory after his close friend Aruna Dindane of Anderlecht in Belgium put the home side in front. The same two – both Players of the Year in the country where they plied their trade – repeated the act at the end of the month in a 2-1 win over Egypt in Alexandria in front of 16,000 fans.

But the showdown with Cameroon was to be a massive disappointment. In front of a capacity crowd of 75,000 crammed into the dilapidated Ahmadou Ahidjo Stadium in Yaoundé, African Footballer of the Year Samuel Eto'o broke the deadlock after eighty minutes and substitute Guy Feutchine added the second goal a minute later to give the Indomitable Lions a 2-0 victory.

It was to be a depressing end to the first round of games across the Continent, which were to end in joyous celebrations. Didier had to put all that behind him, however, when he returned to the decision of where he would be playing his club football within a few weeks. Once the Chelsea move was finalised, he was understandably, upbeat, although he couldn't disguise his slight disappointment at having to leave Marseilles: 'It is the right choice for me to go to Chelsea. Neither I nor Marseilles could refuse this offer from Chelsea. What truly convinced me that they wanted me was the personal telephone calls I received from Mourinho. I also had offers from Italian clubs but going to Chelsea is an interesting challenge. I want to continue to progress alongside players of the quality of Mateja Kezman, Adrian Mutu, Claude Makelele and Arjen Robben. I will never forget my year with Marseilles but it is their desire that I should leave and mine as well.'

He added, 'I wanted to stay at Marseilles because I have experienced fantastic times there, but financially and in a sporting sense I could not refuse Chelsea's offer. I made my decision on my own, no one influenced me. What convinced me to join Chelsea is that they really showed that they wanted me, and that counts a lot.

## DIDIER DROGBA

I will give my best for them now. I also had offers from Italian clubs but going to Chelsea is an interesting challenge in my career. I am glad to join them and I hope I will live up to their expectations.'

Later he said, 'I am hoping this will be a long and happy adventure. I know a bit about my new teammates because in France we always look for the Premiership. So I know Gudjohnsen, Mutu, Makelele, Gallas – these players are very, very good.'

Questions were already being asked: was this another example of Chelsea's massive buying power outweighing common sense? After all, this was a twenty-six-year-old who had only had one season of success at the top. Would he, and indeed Chelsea's other summer signings, justify such a spree? Mourinho, as always, had the answer when the question was posed to him by journalists: 'I have read a lot about the money that Chelsea have spent. But I hope in a year's time you are here in front of me asking why we are not buying players. I think you only know if a player is cheap at the end of the season or at the end of his contract. Sometimes you pay £5 million for a player, you think the player is cheap and he is the most expensive player in history.

'So it depends. We will see this season, but first of all – and I think I am not wrong – last summer Chelsea spent more money than they did this summer. I am telling you to wait. If players help us to get what Chelsea have been fighting for over so many years, if we become champions, European champions or win an English cup, all is beautiful. If we do something great and a player helps us to arrive there, then I think he is cheap. If we arrive at the end of the season and he has not contributed then I think he is expensive.'

On the day Didier and his new colleagues were to head for American for the pre-season tour, Mourinho said, 'The oldest player in our squad is Claude Makelele at 31. Otherwise we have a very young squad.' All the players were chosen because of their ages, ambition and motivation. He continued, 'So I think we have a very good group and a very good atmosphere. And I hope – I say again – that in a year we will not sign any more players because all the positions are covered. I need a central defender and, if it's possible, another midfielder to complete a twenty-four-man squad. But I am really happy with what I have.

'First of all, I am not wrong in saying that Chelsea spent more money last season than this season. I tell you to wait. If Drogba helps us to get what Chelsea have been fighting for over many years – if we become champions of England or Europe, or an English cup – then all is beautiful. If we go great places and he helps us arrive there, I think he is cheap.'

## CHAPTER 11

# The Challenge Begins

Mourinho's remark that Drogba would be a 'cheap' signing if he helped the club to claim trophies needs to be put into perspective with a brief examination of Chelsea's history and the impact of Roman Abramovich's arrival a year earlier.

The club was founded in 1905. Not even the most die-hard Blues fan could logically argue its trophy cabinet placed it in the highest echelon of English club sides. Only once had Chelsea claimed the old Division One Championship and that was in the mid-fifties, and its three FA Cup triumphs, albeit far more recent, were outnumbered by many other sides. Admittedly there were two League Cup triumphs and two memorable European Cup Winners' Cup victories; also a European Super Cup in modern times. This was certainly not a record to be ashamed of, but nowhere near the tally of other English football powerhouses such as those at Old Trafford, Highbury and Anfield.

Arguably the club's greatest days came in the 1960s and 1970s, when – along with its proximity to the King's Road – Chelsea suddenly became one of the country's glamour sides with teams under Tommy Docherty and then Dave Sexton bringing flair to the game. The side of Terry Venables and Bobby Tambling was replaced by the likes of Peter Osgood, Alan Hudson and Charlie Cooke in a team fondly remembered by all who saw them play.

But by the 1980s the club was in severe financial trouble and businessman Ken Bates took over for just £1. His reign at the Bridge was one of the most colourful in football and the late 1990s and early years of the millennium saw success domestically and in Europe. In the summer of 2003 when Bates sold out to Abramovich the agenda changed dramatically, however.

The mega-rich Russian, orphaned at the age of four, had been looking at several clubs before he decided to take on Chelsea and their £80 million of debts – soon it became clear that he didn't only want qualified success, the club *had* to become one of the kings of European soccer – anything less would be failure. Hence second place in the Premiership, significantly eleven points behind Arsenal, which Ranieri had achieved for 'Chelski', just wasn't good enough.

Didier's move meant he was the last of seventeen players brought in under Abramovich at a total cost of about £200 million in the most astonishing spending spree football had ever seen. It was £55 million more than Real Madrid spent assembling their squad of *Galácticos* in the previous four years and it wasn't far short – by about £20 million – of Alex Ferguson's total spending in eighteen years at Old Trafford. So that is why Didier's transfer fee – making him the most expensive forward in the Premiership and the most expensive African player in history – and his £60,000-a-week salary would be 'cheap' if it resulted in some silverware at the Bridge. As always, Didier put it into perspective: 'First and foremost, football is about pleasure. But I'm very pleased the club and the manager put so much effort into getting hold of me to play for Chelsea and I just hope now I can prove my worth.'

The UEFA Cup games against Liverpool and Newcastle opposition and visits to their historic grounds, allied to regular conversations with his Ivorian compatriot Kolo Touré of Arsenal, meant he already had a taste of the English scene.

'Kolo said English football was very attractive and interesting. He also told me it was physical but it's up to me to adapt. When I was in France I kept up with the Premier League and English football, and I know it's not easy to score against the English-style defence, but I'm sure with the quality of my colleagues I can score goals. My life has been transformed in a very short space of time, but that's why I'm in the job, to savour moments like the last year. I'm looking forward to learning a lot from José Mourinho and achieving great things with my teammates.

'I was surprised about the amount of money but I'm not involved in the financial side of things. I don't wake up each morning and think, Oh, I'm worth so much money. I don't feel pressure. Chelsea may have paid a lot of money for my services but it's only other people who are suggesting there is pressure on me. It's a game and I enjoy it. Even though it cost quite a lot of money I was pleased the club and the manager put so much effort into getting hold of me. Now I just hope I can prove my worth.'

He also made it clear that the Premiership didn't concern him after his Anfield and St James's Park experiences: 'It won't be easy to score but I succeeded in those games and I have the quality of teammates to help me do that at Chelsea.'

A fascinating insight into Didier's awareness of his new fame and, more importantly, how to handle it, came when he met the British press at the Sheraton Hotel in Seattle for the first time as Chelsea's American pre-season tour began at the end of July 2004.

'What is the worst thing to have happened to you in your career?' he was asked.

'There is no worst thing. Even injuries, they are just part of the game,' he replied, by way of a straight-bat response. Then he was asked, 'Can you have the same impact as Ruud van Nistelrooy, your predecessor as Britain's most expensive striker?' Aware that any word out of place would prompt headlines saying he boasted he could outscore Manchester United's Dutch hero, he simply said, 'Oh, no, I only hope to be like him.'

After his signing and draining transatlantic flight Didier was rested for Chelsea's first game of their three in the USA, as they beat Celtic 4–2. But he had a surprise when he turned up for the first training session with the squad wearing a pair of running shoes as he expected to do some straightforward running. Mourinho gave him a surprised look and said, 'You can put those to the bottom of your bag. You'll never need them with me.' From that day on Didier, like the other players, ran with a ball at his feet as the coach insisted that runs in training should be identical to those players have to make in matches.

Like the rest of the squad before the next game Didier heard that his old opponent from Porto, twenty-six-year-old centre-half Ricardo Carvalho, was in mid-air with Chelsea's chief executive Kenyon to join up with the rest of the side, having signed for the Blues for just under £20 million. The deal took Chelsea's summer spending to more than £89 million after the arrivals – before and after Mourinho's appointment – of Didier plus Mateja Kezman (£5 million), midfielder Tiago Mendes (£8 million), Arjen Robben (£12 million), defender Paulo Ferreira (£13.2 million) and goalkeeper Petr Čech (£7 million). Other managers could simply look on in wonder. In fact those transfers made up six out of the top seven moves in English football during the so-called break. The exception was Djibril Cissé's £14 million transfer from Auxerre to Liverpool.

It was on 29 July in the unlikely setting of Pittsburgh, Pennsylvania, in front of a crowd of 25,317 that Didier made his Chelsea debut against Roma at a half-full Heinz Field, with its unique feature of two giant ketchup bottles at one end which pour simulated tomato sauce whenever local American football side – the Steelers – score. Didier scored with what was becoming almost an obligatory goal.

'I hope it's the first of many,' he said. 'There was no pressure.

## THE CHALLENGE BEGINS

Having only one week of training was difficult but it was good for my confidence to score. I have worked really well with the staff for just one week, and to score was good for the confidence. It was very competitive for a friendly but Roma are an Italian team and you expect that from them.'

Joe Cole and Mateja Kezman had already put the Blues in control when Didier opened his account in the sixty-eighth minute of a match that, in the best traditions of comparatively pointless pre-season games, erupted in a massive fight that saw two red cards – one of them to Kezman – and six yellows. Didier, it must be said, was adjusting to his new teammates and missed several chances that in games to come he would take with aplomb. As it was, his goal was a tap-in, but he still, somewhat bizarrely, won the man-of-the-match award. Although Mourinho appeared none too pleased by the fracas, skipper John Terry's comments afterwards gave an indication of things to come when he said, 'It's good to see and shows we've got great team spirit already. These things can happen throughout the course of the season and we've got to stick together.'

His views were echoed by Arjen Robben: 'We have a very strong squad and with this kind of fight you can see that we are a team and we fight for each other – and that's good. We train well together, we know we have a lot of quality in this group and we can win prizes this year. But you have to do it together, everybody knows that. That's why we played so well.'

Another new boy joined for Chelsea's third and final match of the tour: a 3–2 defeat at the hands of AC Milan in Philadelphia – defender Carvalho. Didier made it two goals in two games with a resounding, towering header, but the Italians snatched victory with an eighty-eighth-minute, superbly struck free kick from their Ukrainian centre-forward Andriy Shevchenko.

As they prepared to head home, José Mourinho waxed lyrical about the challenge that faced him and his new team back in England: 'The Premiership is top level every weekend, so what can you do but fight every day to be better? A foreign coach has to show he deserves to be there and I'm ready to cope with it. I hope people respect my past, because my past is more beautiful than many, many, many people working in the Premiership for many years. I hope to deserve to be in your wonderful football country.'

Back at Stamford Bridge, Didier's debut was a fairly friendly one, a belated farewell for Italian Bridge hero Gianfranco Zola in a friendly against Real Zaragoza, which saw him take just eight minutes to tap in Ferreira's right-wing cross at the far post in front of a full house. One thing was certain: the next game at Stamford Bridge would be far from friendly. Chelsea were starting the season with a dynamite fixture, a home game in the Premiership against Manchester United.

Didier seemed certain to start, which may be an obvious statement to make about such an expensive signing, but Mourinho was never one to go for the obvious choice. He had at his disposal rivals in the shape of Mateja Kezman – who won his appeal to the Football Association to overturn a three-match ban after the American sending-off – Adrian Mutu, who pledged his future to the club after a move to Juventus fell through, and Eidur Gudjohnsen.

Manchester United would be without several of their stars due to injury or suspension. The likes of Ruud van Nistelrooy (hernia), Louis Saha (knee), Ole Gunnar Solskjaer (knee), Wes Brown (knee) and Rio Ferdinand (suspended) were ruled out, although Mourinho wasn't too sympathetic to the plight of Sir Alex Ferguson. Before the kick-off he announced, 'Top teams have top squads. He always has eleven top players to play. There are no excuses – in fact they have some very big advantages over us.'

Didier too was in a positive mood for such a challenging start: 'I could not dream of a better start unless we played Arsenal. With Marseilles last year I was already impressed by St James's Park. Everyone says that the atmosphere will be exceptional. That is what's so great in England. What is happening to me is exceptional, it's pure happiness. My only worry is to give my best the same way I did it at Guingamp and Marseilles. I know where I stand. I need to work a lot more and to prove a lot more.

'I also know that Chelsea invested a lot of money and that they are expecting some payment back. But I am not worried. There was a lot of emotion surrounding my departure from Marseilles. But things went very fast. I went for a tour in the United States with Chelsea and I did not have the time to think too much. I realised that something exceptional was happening in my career. I will never forget Marseilles but the chapter is closed now. I was the one who took the final decision of leaving Marseilles. Sometimes you need to make choices and I believe I made the right one.

'I am with Chelsea 100 per cent. I am here to score the same goals I was scoring with Marseilles, to enjoy my life and share my happiness at playing football.'

He told a friend, 'The goals are fine, but they mask a bit the fact that, physically, I do not feel good. I have played quite a few matches this summer with the World Cup qualifying games for the Ivory Coast. I have had very little holiday, just twelve days, and haven't had the time to recover from my last two seasons. I am suffering in training.'

But he admitted he had been 'very pleasantly surprised' by the team spirit at the club. 'There is a great deal of solidarity amongst the players. There is one unmistakable sign. They speak with affection and regret of the players who have just left. There is more than just money at Chelsea. There is a soul in the team. That is reassuring because human relationships are essential to me.

'To give of my best, I need to have the same vibes as my teammates and to share the passion of the fans. United? It's huge. I could not have dreamt of a better start, except perhaps Arsenal. I can't wait to be there and to have the shivers going on to the Stamford Bridge pitch.'

So it was that Didier made his Premiership debut at 4.05pm on Sunday, 15 August 2004, in front of a crowd of 41,813. As the teams came out he peeled away to applaud his new home supporters, only to find he headed straight to the 3,000 United fans at the game who greeted him with a stream of Mancunian catcalls! He was the one who was smiling, however, in the fifteenth minute when he cushioned a header down for Eidur Gudjohnsen to bundle the ball over the line past a hapless goalkeeper Tim Howard and Roy Keane, playing at centre back, to score what turned out to be the only goal of the game.

If Didier had impressed the Chelsea fans, the United supporters were determined to have what they thought was the last word. Deep in the second half, with twenty minutes remaining, a tired Didier was replaced by Mateja Kezman. As he came off the pitch to a standing ovation from the fans in blue, the visitors chanted, with remarkable lack of foresight, 'You should have signed for a big club.'

Mourinho had a very different view. He gave his new striker a very public thumbs-up, saying afterwards, 'It's not easy for him to play like that. We played with two strikers and no wingers.'

It had been a fairly disappointing game, it must be said, and even Mourinho admitted that United were unlucky to lose, although he added, 'We deserved to win.' But both sides must have had their thoughts on the game that had taken place earlier that afternoon at Goodison Park, where Everton had lost 4–1 to Arsenal. It was the Gunners' forty-first consecutive game in the league without defeat after they'd gone the entire season before without losing.

Those were the standards that Didier, Mourinho and everyone else at Stamford Bridge knew they had to match.

# CHAPTER 12

# Goalbound

**D**idier's start to his Premiership career was at St Andrews, home to Birmingham City, one of England's less fashionable clubs. Unkind critics might even say that it was one of the less fashionable sides in Birmingham, given that its illustrious rival on the other side of the city, Aston Villa, could lay claim to seven triumphs in both the old Division One and the FA Cup, and had also picked up a European Cup. The Blues, however, seemed merely to move between the top division of the game and the second tier without ever pausing long enough to pick up any silverware.

Still, Didier's tours of those provincial French grounds must have been useful experience as he ran out against a side managed by former Manchester United defender Steve Bruce, who chose to play with an 'away' formation against his galaxy of star opponents. The five men in the middle and just one upfront had the strange result of providing Birmingham with more chances than Chelsea. As it was, Didier lasted the entire course of this match, but it was Joe Cole, one of the three substitutes used by

Mourinho, who scored the only goal of the match, in the sixty-eighth minute.

Didier could, and should, have scored after a quarter of an hour following a mistake by Mario Melchiot, one of the former Chelsea players in the home side. He shot wide with only goalkeeper Maik Taylor to beat. With just eleven minutes left, and Chelsea holding grimly on to their lead, Didier again had the goal at his mercy, only to slice his shot wide. Two sitters missed in one game was very uncharacteristic. Still, two wins in two games, albeit both rather unconvincing and by just 1–0, meant six points in the bag. All it needed now was for Didier to score – and Blues' fans didn't have to wait long for that to happen.

Though Chelsea's ground is probably in the most glamorous setting of all English clubs, surrounded as it is by multimillion-pound houses, exclusive antique shops, Michelin-starred restaurants and expensive boutiques, the same couldn't be said of Crystal Palace's Selhurst Park home set in south London. The locals decided to greet Didier the following Tuesday night in down-to-earth fashion with the old cry of 'What a waste of money!' They even upped the volume after a mere six minutes when they thought his reaction to a Tony Popovic foul was theatrical, in their eyes at least. It was a taste of things to come.

But an even greater insight into what lay ahead came in the twenty-eighth-minute. Joe Cole – who was in the starting line-up following his impressive appearance at Birmingham – and Claude Makelele combined for the Frenchman to send over a cross from the left that hung in the air. Didier shrugged aside the challenge of his earlier assailant Popovic and then headed the ball powerfully down and wide of goalkeeper Julián Speroni to score his first goal in the Premiership.

Palace bravely stayed in the game for almost another hour, but Tiago Mendes, Chelsea's £8 million summer signing from Benfica, rounded off a good night's work with a goal sixteen minutes from time. It was another Cole-inspired move, and this time Didier was the provider as he moved the ball on to Mendes for the second goal. It would have been fitting if Didier had stayed on the pitch for the entire match, but two minutes after creating the second goal he was the victim of a bad challenge by Mark Hudson – which earned the Palace player a yellow card – and he limped off with an ankle injury to be replaced by Eidur Gudjohnsen.

Two games without scoring could hardly be described as a goal famine; nevertheless, there was a hint of relief in Didier's voice when he said after the game, 'Everyone can expect a lot more from me. I am not physically at my best yet and need more time to improve my sharpness. I'm keeping my fingers crossed that when I'm settled and ready I will take a few more of the opportunities I get. You need to score as a striker, but I can help the team in other ways and I feel I am fitting in well in the Premiership. I love playing here and the team have performed well in the first three games.'

Chelsea's coach, Steve Clarke, put into words what others were feeling when he said, 'It's always important for a striker to get goals. Drogba's a big-money signing which puts pressure on him, but he showed that if we get quality crosses into the box, then he'll be a threat. The quicker Didier got his first league goal for the club the better, so it's nice he has got one. Eidur Gudjohnsen has one and hopefully we can get one for Mateja Kezman on Saturday. He showed tonight that if we get quality crosses into the box then he's going to be a threat.'

One bunch of players who definitely settled down were the Arsenal squad. At about the same time as Chelsea were proving too good for Palace, the Gunners extended their unbeaten run in the Premiership to an incredible forty-three games, spread over three seasons, breaking the top-flight record of Brian Clough's Nottingham Forest side a quarter-century earlier.

Still, Didier's ankle injury had settled down somewhat for Saturday's home game against Southampton at Stamford Bridge and he was named in the starting line-up with 40,864 inside the ground. If the Blues hoped to have a good start to the game, it could hardly have been worse. They were behind to one of the quickest goals in the history of the Premiership when, as many of the crowd were still getting to their seats, James Beattie sent a twenty-five-yard shot over Petr Čech's head and under the crossbar after just twelve seconds. It wasn't quite as rapid as the nine seconds it had taken Ledley King to score against Bradford some four years earlier, but it meant that the Blues were behind for the first time that season.

It didn't take long before Chelsea struck back and Gudjohnsen might have equalised after four minutes when he headed Frank Lampard's inviting left-wing cross wide from six yards. Didier's left-footed shot was dropped by Antti Niemi, but Lampard failed to cash in. An equaliser had to come – the only surprise was that it took thirty-four minutes to arrive.

A Lampard corner was flicked on by Gudjohnsen and James Beattie had the misfortune to put the ball past his own keeper to join the select band of players who score at both ends in the same match. In the forty-first minute, when Didier caused mayhem in the Saints' penalty area and Claus Lundekvam handled, Chelsea's regular penalty taker Lampard buried the spot kick. The only question that remained was by how many Chelsea would increase their lead, but somehow they didn't get there. Nevertheless, four wins out of four was a pretty good start for Didier, Mourinho and the rest.

As Didier's England teammates prepared for a World Cup qualifier with Austria, in September 2004 Didier was off to Abidjan once more, where the Ivory Coast easily beat Sudan 5–0 in their qualifying game, with Didier scoring the first from the penalty spot. The bad news, however, was that an ankle injury meant he had to leave the field before half-time.

After the game he made a remark that illustrated his affection for the country he had been forced to leave as a child. After presenting a Chelsea shirt to the country's head of state Laurent Gbagbo at a luncheon reception the next day he said, 'I was in France since the age of five but I have always kept my love for the

# GOALBOUND

Côte d'Ivoire. That is why, despite French nationality, I chose to play for my country.' The audience was part of a series of meetings initiated by Gbagbo with Ivorian professionals who 'honour the country through their performances'.

Earlier in the year Didier had been due to meet the country's leader in Paris, but schedules meant the meeting didn't take place. 'To make up for that miss, I decided to meet Didier Drogba following the Elephants' brilliant victory against the Falcons of Sudan,' Gbagbo said. And he praised Didier's choice in plumping for the African side: 'With his talent and renown, he could have tried to play for the French national team.' He could indeed, but he chose the Ivory Coast – one of the main reasons why his reputation in the country was soaring, as the population closely followed every move of his career. Indeed he would often wear an Ivory Coast wristband in English games.

Back in England, the first dropped point of the season came when Chelsea could manage only a goalless draw at Aston Villa despite being the better side. But the match was memorable for one thing: it was the first time Didier was thought by the referee to have dived.

Players going to ground in the area after the slightest of touches in the hope of winning a penalty was hardly a new phenomenon in football, but somehow the slur on Didier's behaviour was to follow him for the rest of the season in almost unprecedented fashion. There were just ten minutes left at Villa Park when Didier – who had earlier hit the bar – went to ground under a challenge from Ecuadorian defender Ulises de la Cruz. Referee Rob Styles refused to give the penalty and the only action he took was to book Didier for the 'dive'.

There was almost more action off the field afterwards than during the ninety minutes on the pitch as practically everyone seemed to agree that not only had Didier not dived but the decision should have been a penalty instead. Somewhat predictably, Mourinho made his view of the incident clear: 'The

Man of the Match was the referee because of that decision. If a similar situation happens in the future to Thierry Henry or Ruud van Nistelrooy we will see if a similar decision is given. I do not believe it will be. It was more than a penalty. I think in some countries it would have been two penalties. It was ridiculous. But we speak about points and, today we lost two points here.'

Villa boss David O'Leary, somewhat more surprisingly, agreed with him. 'I think we got lucky with the penalty,' he said. 'From where I was standing, it looked a penalty to me. I think if that had been at my end, I would have been expecting it. We've had a few decisions that have gone against us, but that one went for us today.'

Mourinho controlled his anger long enough to hold out an olive branch to referees, though. 'I have to say, to be fair, that I love the way referees do it in England. They believe in fair play and work the advantage law fantastically – better than any country in the world. Their philosophy of refereeing is fantastic. But there are crucial decisions that, in terms of points, become really crucial.'

The one person who agreed with the decision, not surprisingly, was the defender. 'The referee was absolutely correct. I didn't touch him. A dive like that belongs in the swimming pool.'

Tellingly the yellow card was rescinded a few days later after the referee viewed videos of the tackle – ample justification of both Didier's surprise at receiving it and the anger displayed by his coach. Even referees' boss Keith Hackett, head of the Professional Game Match Officials Board, apologised to Mourinho after the blunder. Hackett said, 'Referees are human beings but when we get it wrong we do get disappointed, so I have some sympathy with managers who walk the tightrope.'

Another tightrope was to be walked by Didier the following Tuesday: a return to France for a clash with Paris Saint-Germain, one of the few teams in France who had actually prevented him from scoring during the previous season. The PSG fans didn't let him forget it. He was barracked for his Marseilles connection from the moment he ran out onto the Parc des Princes pitch as the home fans unwrapped banners proclaiming '*Ce soir, c'est Hastings*'. In fact the fighting spirit of 1066 came from the English side, not the French.

After John Terry's straightforward header put Chelsea in front in the twenty-ninth minute Didier silenced the boos on the stroke of half-time. Mateja Kezman's effort had been blocked and Didier elegantly stroked the ball into the PSG net – and promptly ran towards the crowd with his hands cupped to his ears, defying them to continue their jeering. More was to follow when, with a quarter of an hour left, Kezman was tripped on the edge of the box and Didier curled a free kick around the wall and into the top of the net. After his second goal he celebrated by wheeling behind the goal in front of the Kop du Boulogne end of the ground with its notorious racist fans, his arms outstretched in the trademark style of PSG striker Pauleta.

After seventy-nine minutes Mourinho decided to being replace Didier with Damien Duff. As he left the field, he couldn't resist sarcastically applauding the crowd for the treatment meted out to him all night. Not perhaps all that laudable an action, but, given the animosity they had shown towards him, it was perfectly understandable.

He explained it in his customary straightforward manner. 'I did wind them up but they wound me up a bit as well, didn't they? It was important to come here to Paris to score and do things in style. I lost three matches against PSG last season and it was good to win this time. I feel better every day with my new team and my new partners.

'It has taken a while for my second goal to come along, but it came in the Champions League, and so much the better. It's important to get off to a good start in the Champions League, but it's not always easy when you start away from home.

'It's the first time I've come to the Parc des Princes and not lost. People whistled me above all because I used to play for Marseilles. They got at me so much that, after my two goals, I could allow myself to have a go back. But you know how it is in France.'

## DIDIER DROGBA

Mourinho was obviously worried that Didier – who had missed a Marseilles match in Europe the previous season because of his goal celebrations – might be punished. 'It was a fantastic game. Didier was Man of the Match and UEFA ought to give him an award for being fantastic. It's always better to look on the bright side.' In fact he was so pleased that he gave Didier some time off in Paris as a gesture of thanks. Normally he would have been expected to return with his team, so this was an exception for once. It was a generous gesture on the part of the Portuguese, especially as the flight to Paris had been delayed as Didier was stuck in traffic en route to the airport! He was due to receive an award for being the best African player in the French league last season and Mourinho gave special dispensation for him to stay, stating,

'I like my team to be together from the moment they leave London to the moment they arrive home, but Didier received an award for being the best player in the French league last season. He asked me if the two goals he scored were enough and I said yes, it was enough for me to change my mind. He was the top player in France last season and if you love football – even if you support PSG – you have to appreciate his performance. He'll be very well received and it will be a great day for him. He deserves it as a player and a person. Didier was the Man of the Match. He scored two goals and respected everybody.'

His view was echoed by Frank Lampard: 'He reacted in the best possible way by scoring. If you're a player and getting that sort of stick you can be excused some exuberance when you score.'

There was more good news the next day when UEFA ruled out any punishment for Didier after match reports from referee Manuel Mejuto González and their own referees' delegate failed to mention his celebrations. A spokesman said, 'There was nothing mentioned in the reports so there won't be any action against Didier Drogba.'

## CHAPTER 13

# Life in the Premiership

There's an old saying along the lines of 'After the Lord Mayor's Show comes the dustcart' – and the next Saturday, the 42,246 inside Stamford Bridge got the footballing equivalent of that sad rubbish lorry.

Tottenham Hotspur were the visitors, but if the home fans were hoping for a continuation of the goal spree from Paris five days earlier they were disappointed. Spurs had only three draws to show from their previous eleven Premiership visits to the Bridge, and it showed. Throughout the game the feeling was that they would be more than satisfied with a point, so for the second successive Saturday Didier battled his way through a 0–0 draw, meaning Chelsea had scored only six goals in six domestic games – hardly Championship-winning form, especially as the standard bearers Arsenal had scored no fewer than twenty-one times. Mourinho again made three substitutions, but this time kept Didier on for all of the ninety minutes in the fruitless hope that he would break the deadlock.

## DIDIER DROGBA

Nevertheless, the Blues were in second position when they travelled to Middlesbrough, potentially a difficult match on paper. The result, another 1–0 in Chelsea's favour, seemed to prove this was the case, but the fact of the matter was that the Blues should have won by a far greater margin. Such was their domination that there were only five minutes left when the home side managed their first shot on goal and that was blocked. Petr Čech didn't have a save to make throughout the game. The goal, when it came, was from Didier, but Chelsea left it late too, as it wasn't until the eighty-first minute that he latched onto a free kick from Frank Lampard and broke the deadlock with what was, surprisingly, his side's first domestic league goal in 310 minutes of football.

In truth Didier had some chances to clinch the match early on, but the solitary goal was enough to maintain Chelsea's pressure on the top aided by a defence that had let in only one goal in seven competitive matches. It was that defence, rather than any goalscoring bonanza, that had held the secret of Chelsea's success so far in the season, but it was obvious that pretty soon the goals would start to flow. Although Didier hadn't repeated the sensational start he had at Marseilles, it was obvious to many knowledgeable observers that once he became more accustomed to the different pace and physical challenges of the Premiership, he would be a threat to any defence.

Perhaps it was that newness to the English game that made him feel more comfortable in European games such as the Paris Saint-Germain match and he soon had the chance to show just how at ease he was in the Champions League. In the middle of the next week, Chelsea were at home to the side José Mourinho had plucked from obscurity to become champions of Europe, Porto, as – in one of those ironic twists that always seem to happen in cup competitions – Chelsea were drawn in the same group as their coach's old side, the current holders of the trophy. As always, Mourinho was bullish in his approach to the match, both in dismissing criticism of his new club and in making it perfectly clear that there would be no room for sentiment when he came up against his old one.

First of all he wanted to get rid of the 'Chelsea one-nil' tag that some were trying to attach to his side. 'In Portugal, they called me many things but never a defensive coach,' he said. 'Don't ask me why the ball won't go in the net. It's not as if we don't try. When you are unpopular, sometimes it makes you stronger as a group. And I have to say that my group are really strong. Criticism does not worry me. If you don't feel you get the protection, the sympathy and the credit that you deserve, it makes you stronger.

'When a team are playing as we are and getting the results that we are after only three months together, I am not worried. People who don't like us to win, they are the ones who should be worried. Porto are the defending champions and everyone wants to beat them, but also everyone wants to beat Chelsea because of the players we have and the power we are showing.'

In case people still hadn't got the message, he spelled it out clearly: 'We only focus on the team. Now, I face my old club Porto, but for ninety minutes I will feel no emotion. The only thing that will matter is the three points ... And one day, I will play against Chelsea and the feeling will be similar ... It is just one more match, no more than that. Emotions? Nothing at all. This is the true nature of football.'

Even Mourinho, though, couldn't have reckoned with one disgruntled Porto supporter who, as the coach was signing autographs for some of the 1,500 travelling contingent shortly before kick-off, spat at the Chelsea boss in a vile show of his twisted feelings towards the man who had, after all, brought great success to the club in a very short space of time.

At least the 39,237 turn-out at Stamford Bridge didn't have to wait too long to see the 'true nature' of their team, as Russian international midfielder Alexey Smertin gave them a seventh-minute lead with his first goal for the club. Didier then took a hand and in the second half scored his fifth goal for Chelsea, a goal he both created and scored. Five minutes after the interval a clever flick with the back of his heel so confused Ricardo Costa that he had to foul him. Damien Duff, anxious to stake a regular place in the Chelsea side, floated over the free kick from the right-hand side of the pitch and the Porto defence, who should have known better, allowed Didier to climb without obstruction and head the ball home past the helpless goalkeeper. Mourinho punched the air with visible delight. South African Benni McCarthy – later to play for Blackburn Rovers – pulled a goal back for Porto, but John Terry soon restored order with a thunderous near-post header from a Lampard free kick. Job done.

Mourinho could have been resentful over the disgraceful behaviour of some of the Porto fans, but instead chose to concentrate on the virtues of his new side. Of course Porto weren't the team they had been twelve months earlier: they lacked Mourinho and several of the players who had bought them success. In fact only five of the winning side from the previous year's final were on the field. Still, that wasn't going to deter Mourinho from enthusing. 'The mentality of my players is absolutely fantastic,' he said. 'We play as a team, every minute, every second of the game. In most of the big teams in Europe, where the big players are, they think a little bit more about themselves. What is amazing is the way my big players played as a unit for the result. That's the reason why we have played nine matches and not been beaten. We have the right personalities and characters. We have beaten the European champions, who were unbeaten in the competition for twelve matches. Also, we had not won in the Champions League for four games at home, so we have broken through a few barriers. We are in fantastic condition. The result is great. We have six points and we are in a fantastic position to go into the next round.'

Didier was receiving praise both privately and publicly from his teammates, but perhaps a better analysis might be one from an opponent, albeit one he hadn't crossed swords with yet. Arsenal's talented French midfield player Robert Pirès assessed him in the following fashion: 'Drogba is very impressive. He had a very good season with Marseilles and now he is confirming his status. He showed it by scoring two against Paris Saint-Germain. It proves he is a player with enormous qualities and someone we need to keep our eye on.' Praise indeed.

By now Didier had three young children, two boys and a girl, and so a home was important. The poor boy from the Ivory Coast who had been brought up in a tough housing estate in the Paris suburbs was to move, so London's *Sunday Times* revealed, into one of the most prestigious and exclusive areas of Britain – the St George's Hill area of Weybridge in Surrey. His neighbours would include singing legends Cliff Richard and Tom Jones and veteran comedian Eric Sykes. Past residents were Beatles John Lennon and Ringo Starr. Not bad for a boy from Yopougon. Importantly, the area is also close to the new Chelsea training ground at Cobham in Surrey and virtually all the squad live nearby.

Didier, however, didn't have all that much time to help unpack as he would soon be facing his adversaries from the previous UEFA Cup season, Liverpool. Chelsea were second in the league table, but it didn't seem to impress the Reds' Czech striker Milan Baroš, who said before the Stamford Bridge clash, 'They do not contribute anything to football. I do not like the way Chelsea play under Mourinho because it does not contribute anything new to soccer. They are concerned with the result too much and I don't like that type of game. Yes, they win, but that does not bring them fans. I am convinced that in the next few weeks Chelsea's performance will drop and we will raise our game. Didier Drogba is very opportunistic. The danger is if he scores a goal with his first shot. But if we can cut his supply line he will be left on his own. Chelsea's defence have made errors in all their games and I will be there to take advantage.'

He might have thought that before the kick-off, but he was to be sadly disappointed. It turned out to be another 1–0 for Chelsea, scored by substitute Joe Cole, but the bad news for Didier was that he was the man being replaced. The reason was a severe groin injury in the first half and Chelsea backroom staff soon realised it was a serious problem – so serious, in fact, that Mourinho revealed, 'It's a muscular injury and there are no miracles with those. Drogba will be out for two, three or four weeks. I don't yet know exactly how long. But it's completely impossible that he will be able to play for his national team next weekend.'

For once Mourinho got it wrong because it was the final week of November before Didier was able to return to first-team duty. It was a massive blow for Chelsea and even more so for him. Among other things, it meant he would miss the Ivory Coast's World Cup qualifier in Benin, a game they were to win 1–0.

With every game in the Premiership Didier had been finding his feet with his new colleagues, as well as adjusting to the different pace and physicality of the English league. With five goals, he was their leading scorer and there was strong evidence that he was poised even to go up a gear. As it was, he had to sit and watch as Chelsea tried to survive without him. It has to be said they didn't do too badly.

They overtook Arsenal – whose astonishing run of forty-nine consecutive league games without defeat was ended by Manchester United – to take pole position in the premiership, and they also won by that now familiar 1–0 margin in the Champions League at CSKA, thanks to a goal from a man whose recovery from injury had been one of he catalysts of their continued success, Dutch winger Arjen Robben.

Robben had been one of Claudio Ranieri's final signings from PSV Eindhoven in March 2004, but an injury picked up in pre-season against Roma meant he missed the big kick-off.

Didier's injury, the poor form of former PSV teammate Mateja Kezman and the absence of Adrian Mutu, subsequently banned for cocaine use, had pessimists saying Chelsea didn't have the quality to cope, especially when they suffered their first defeat of the season at Manchester City through an early Nicolas Anelka penalty. But Robben changed all that after he made his competitive debut the next week at Blackburn Rovers. He then starred in a 4–1 win at West Bromwich Albion, got the goal in Moscow that ensured Chelsea would be in the final sixteen of the contest and on 6 November scored the only goal of the game at home to Everton, a victory that took Chelsea to the top of the Premiership.

He followed that with a goal in Chelsea's 4–1 win at west London rivals Fulham, which had Mourinho counting his blessings that the player had been brought to the club when he said, 'The Premiership is always difficult and sometimes individual players can open the door for you, and Robben is that kind of player. It wasn't my responsibility but I have to say it was a fantastic decision to buy him.' Unlike with Didier, for the flying Dutchman there was no long, hard trawl through the lower regions of soccer. He made his professional debut as a sixteen-year-old for Groningen and might have gone on to the famed Ajax of Amsterdam but as they failed to spell his name right when they wrote to him and so his father decided that PSV Eindhoven – who spelled it correctly – would look after the boy better!

After a fine tournament in Euro 2004 he would almost certainly have been in the starting line-up but for that injury in America. 'I won the Championship in my first season at PSV and it would be great to do the same again here,' was how Robben summed it up. Unfortunately for the Blues, their last game before Didier returned was far from a title-winning performance. They led 2–0 at home to Bolton Wanderers but were pegged back by two goals, including an equaliser three minutes from time. It was 20 November and remarkably it was the first time they had let in two goals in a competitive match that season. This was an even bigger shock for Mourinho, who in all his career had never seen one of his teams let a two-goal lead slip.

'It has never happened before. No, no, no, never. It is the first time, the first time. It is always a surprise to lose a two-goal lead

– but that is football. If anyone is guilty it is the manager, not the players. That is the way I see things. Since the first day I've been here, I have been in reality and I know that every game is difficult. But I trust my team. You cannot get three points in every game.'

So the return leg that week of the match against Didier's old foes Paris Saint-Germain seemed the ideal time and place for the Ivorian to reappear on the scene. There have been some great evenings at Stamford Bridge, but sadly this was not to be one of them. To begin with, there were rows of empty seats for the clash as, with Chelsea already assured of progressing, some home supporters felt they would watch the 'dead' match from the comfort of their living rooms or the nearest pub. Second, the game itself was far from a classic. From Didier's point of view the highlight came after sixty-two minutes, when he stripped off and came on as substitute for the disappointing Mateja Kezman. It could all have ended in glory in the eightieth minute when Eidur Gudjohnsen put him clean through on goal, but instead of planting the ball in the net in the manner the home fans had come to expect, he simply blasted it at goalkeeper Lionel Letizi.

There is no such thing as a sure thing in football, but the odds are that Didier at his fittest and sharpest would have had no trouble in converting such an easy chance. Even his coach quickly pointed it out. 'Drogba could have won us the game near the end. He is not back to his explosive best just yet and he is not running at full pace. He did some good things for the short time he was on, although you can see he is not quite 100 per cent. But, within a week or so, he will be there. Our team performance was up and down and I'll admit that it needed a bit of salt and pepper added. I'm disappointed to lose our own 100 per cent record in the group. But the first objective is to go through to the next stage and deliver when you are there.'

Didier was being eased back into the action and 'easing' doesn't come much more casual than his next outing. Chelsea were cruising 4–0 at Charlton when he was sent on for the final thirty minutes of the match without any problems arising. It was the third consecutive away game in the league in which the Blues had scored four in and the only problem seemed to be who would make way for Didier. Gudjohnsen seemed favourite, in view of Robben's stunning form, although he had been scoring in Didier's absence. Either way, it was a nice problem for Mourinho to have.

It was Didier's turn to start when Chelsea travelled down the New King's Road and were fortunate to beat Fulham 2–1 in the Carling Cup, courtesy of a late goal from substitute Lampard. But Didier didn't last the distance as he came off after an hour to be replaced by – who else? – Gudjohnsen.

This game of revolving doors was reversed for the next match – the twenty-six-year-old Icelander was on the field for the start of the home game against Newcastle, but Didier replaced him at half-time. Chelsea's recent habit of scoring four goals a game seemed to have come to a grinding halt as the hour mark was reached without score. Mourinho had thrown Didier and Mateja Kezman on as well as the attacking defender Wayne Bridge, meaning that the Blues, criticised so recently for all those 1–0 victories, had four men upfront.

So, when Lampard's sixty-third-minute icebreaker at last beat gallant Newcastle – who at one stage looked as though they might snatch their first victory in eighteen years at Stamford Bridge – it came as no surprise that they fell apart at the seams. The man who clinched it for Chelsea was Didier, who had at last got back on the scoring trail in the sixty-ninth minute, when Lampard picked him out with a superb through-ball and he carefully sent his shot around goalkeeper Shay Given. Normal service was being resumed. Arjen Robben's mazy run brought him a third and then, following suit, Mateja Kezman achieved his first Premiership goal in the final minute when he scored from the penalty spot.

Next stop was Porto for the second leg of their Champions League match. Although Chelsea were assured of taking part in the later stages, there was no such luxury for the holders. The Portuguese side had to get a result, and that was exactly what they did, albeit by the skin of their teeth. After the disgraceful spitting incident in the first leg, there were worries that Mourinho would be targeted again, yet he received warm applause when he walked out onto the pitch. There was no such bonhomie for Didier, unfortunately, as he and William Gallas were constant targets for racist taunts. An unpleasant element in the Porto crowd made monkey noises as Jorge Costa was booked for fouling Didier and then the two tangled almost immediately afterwards. As always, Didier was not one to back down in any confrontation. It must have made it all the more rewarding then, in the thirty-third minute, he laid the ball off to Lampard, who then fed Duff. The Irishman beat full-back Pedro Emanuel and bent his shot into the far corner of the net.

So far, so good, but when Diego equalised on the hour with a stunning volley the home crowd burst into life. They greeted every Porto challenge with a roar and howled displeasure at every Chelsea challenge. So it was predictable that they should erupt with delight when, with just minutes left on the clock, McCarthy rose at the far post to head home what turned out to be the winner. The goal from the South African – who had also scored twice in the ties against Manchester United the previous year – meant Porto would be in the hat for the next round.

If McCarthy was pleased with the result, he wasn't so happy about the taunting Didier and William Gallas had to endure. He spoke about it openly after the game: 'In this life people have to grow up a little bit and I don't see why people make those kinds of noises. They do it to one black player but our team also has black players so we feel it, too. People need to be more mature and think about these issues. We all want a better world and these things can start on the football field. We should show respect for all people whether they are a black guy, a white guy, Indian, yellow or blue, or whatever.'

## LIFE IN THE PREMIERSHIP

At least Chelsea had an extra day to recover from the Euro-jaunt as their next game wasn't until Sunday. The problem was that the game was already being labelled Judgement Day – it was against Premiership champions Arsenal at Highbury.

## CHAPTER 14

# Chelsea on a Roll

Arsenal had won the 2003–4 Premiership title with football that even their detractors – of whom there were quite a number – found it virtually impossible not to praise. Under the reign of the man who had managed them since 1996, Arsène Wenger, they had eventually perfected a brand of high-speed passing football and movement off the ball that was, at times, breathtaking. They had gone through the previous season's thirty-eight league games undefeated – something that had happened only once before in English football, and that had been over a 100 years earlier. Arsenal had scored more goals that year than Chelsea (seventy-three against sixty-seven) and let in fewer (twenty-six compared with thirty) and ended up eleven points ahead of the Blues in second place.

Their side oozed class with the likes of Dennis Bergkamp, Patrick Vieira, Robert Pirès and, above all, their centre-forward Thierry Henry running riot in a league that was, and is, often called the best in the world. Yet in the run-up to that Arsenal-Chelsea match of Sunday, 12 December 2004, if the Arsenal train hadn't exactly gone off the rails, it was certainly in need of refuelling. After losing their magnificent unbeaten run of forty-nine league games to the men from Old Trafford, they had started to leak goals in a very un-Arsenal manner, and before kick-off had conceded twenty-six league and Champions League goals, compared with Chelsea's miserly nine. Chelsea had overhauled them and Arsenal weren't even second at the time, that slot being occupied by Everton. To stop the rot Wenger had dropped his controversial German goalkeeper Jens Lehmann and replaced him with Manuel Almunia, and he too had been criticised for his performance in the Champions League midweek against Rosenborg, although the Gunners' 5-1 victory had seen them, like Chelsea, comfortably through to the next round.

Even though it was still early in December, it was obvious that the result of the Sunday match would have repercussions on who would hoist the winners' trophy in six months' time. But it wasn't just in England that football fans were excited about the clash. Due to the global nature of the game today and satellite transmission's ability to beam matches worldwide, thousands would be glued to televisions in the Ivory Coast, some roaring for the Blue of Chelsea, others supporting the Red of Arsenal and their Ivorian star defender Kolo Touré.

Touré, it transpired, had been one of the key people in the decision Didier made to come to London from his beloved Marseilles. The two were friends from a long way back and during the transfer negotiations had spoken on the phone about the pros and cons of leaving France. Touré, an army officer's son who had been in the Ivory Coast national side for over four years, urged Didier to move to Chelsea, praising both the club and life in the Premiership. The men subsequently often met up for dinner and had even arranged to go out on the Sunday night after the match.

'I was happy because I didn't want to be the only player from the Ivory Coast playing in the Premiership,' said Touré. 'It's good to have him around. Didier is my best friend. He's a great man as well as a great player. I'm not surprised he's doing so well at Chelsea. If he hadn't picked up that injury so soon he would be up near the top of the goalscorers, closer to the likes of Thierry Henry in the table.

'But he will get lots of goals. I know this because I know him very well. I just hope he has a bad day when we play each other on Sunday. I hope he doesn't score any goals.'

Unlike most Ivorians who have succeeded in European football, Touré played for a club in his homeland until the relatively late age of twenty-one before Arsenal's spying system picked him up for an initial bargain fee of £350,000. He had subsequently become a highly rated member of their defence, although he admitted that the one time he had ever played against Didier – in a trial game for the national side – Didier had managed to score. 'One half of the country will be red, the other half will be blue,' said Abidjan-born Touré.

Frank Lampard had, not surprisingly, a different view of the match given Chelsea's place at the top of the league table: 'It's important and it's nice mentally to be at the top. We weren't there last year and we were always having to win games to try to stay with Arsenal. It won't make the game any easier but it's nice to know we're above them already. We want to win everything. We're lucky to have a strong squad so we can rotate and still put out a very strong team. Didier Drogba's back and he will score goals. All the strikers are getting goals and the midfield is as well. John Terry scored two against Charlton. We need the goals to come from everywhere.'

They certainly did, but one thing was certain as the teams ran out on the pitch: Didier wouldn't be an early scorer, as Mourinho surprisingly decided to have him on the substitutes' bench. Despite his recovery from injury, the long lay-off after surgery obviously meant the coach had doubts about his being in the starting line-up.

## DIDIER DROGBA

There was no question about the man leading the Arsenal charge being slow out of the blocks, however. It took Thierry Henry just seventy-two seconds to head the ball towards Cesc Fàbregas and, as Paulo Ferreira and Ricardo Carvalho were drawn to the ball, receive it back quickly and swivel to fire Arsenal into the lead. Lesser teams faced with an Arsenal side with all guns blazing and behind so quickly might have folded, but not Chelsea.

Manuel Almunia had to tip a Lampard shot over the bar but he was helpless soon afterwards when John Terry burst into the Arsenal box and powered home a header after just seventeen minutes. A tendency to let in goals from set pieces had been one of Arsenal's faults so far in the new season, and Chelsea began to take a grip on the match. Almunia denied Gudjohnsen and Tiago headed over the bar from a splendid Arjen Robben cross. Arsenal set about rectifying it in the manner they knew best – scoring at the other end – and after Henry uncharacteristically missed his kick in front of goal he managed to put them back in front with a controversial free kick.

Robert Pirès was pressured by Lampard and Claude Makelele took a tumble. While Čech organised his wall, the referee – Graham Poll – asked Henry if he wanted to take a quick free kick. He agreed. Gudjohnsen was desperately telling Čech to move, but the blond striker moved away from the ball and, as he did so, Henry chipped his inside the unguarded far post helped by a deflection off Tiago.

Chelsea were furious, and Robben was booked for dissent, although with the benefit of hindsight, they should have been aware that it was a trick Henry had successfully performed before and their concentration had been found lacking for once. It was the Frenchman's eighth goal in ten games against the Blues, and one that, if not exactly gifted to him, should have been prevented.

At half-time, Mourinho decided it was time to send for Didier, and he came on in place of Tiago – a clear attempt to exploit Arsenal's problems in the air. Within a minute that chink in their armour had been exposed as Lampard's free kick was met by William Gallas and the unmarked Gudjohnsen headed in. It was now a pulsating match for the 38,153 crowd and Lampard put a free header over which Almunia denied Robben after a fine run after sixty-eight minutes.

But Arsenal might also have won it. Henry, unexpectedly and totally out of character, shot wide after a Fàbregas pass, but it would have been unfair if either side had lost. John Terry summed it up when he said, 'We're top of the league for a reason – because we're playing the better football and getting better results. We have an edge over Arsenal now. We showed that when we were 2–1 down against a side who have been great for so many years and came back again.

'I've been too close to winning something too often and I'm fed up with it. I desperately want to win something this year. The Premiership will be fantastic, but we're also in the Carling Cup and we want to win everything we are in. You can see that determination in the lads. If we keep performing the way we did against Arsenal, we will be fine. This squad on paper is as good as anybody.'

His boss Mourinho for once didn't attempt to vent his spleen over that controversial goal, but he managed to get his message across when he said, 'If you can forget the way Arsenal scored their second goal – if you can call it a goal – the result was correct. But it's difficult for me to forget Arsenal's second goal, so I don't think the result was fair. If I speak about it maybe I would have to go to the FA and be sent to the stands for a few weeks or pay a large fine – and I should keep my money for Christmas presents. I am more than unhappy, but unhappy is a nice word.

'I cannot say the words in my heart and soul. I just cannot do it. In pre-season, we had a top referee at our training ground who showed us all the rules of football. So I have no doubts about it. One of the things he explained to us was walls, distance, whistle – everything was clear.'

# DIDIER DROGBA

Referee Poll, meanwhile, simply gave his gentlemanly rundown of the incident: 'The whistle doesn't need to be blown. I asked Henry, "Do you want a wall?" He said, "Can I take it, please?" He was very polite. I said yes. I deal with the laws of the game; I deal with fact. I gave the signal for him to take it.'

Such is life in the higher reaches of world football that barely had the dust settled on that epic encounter than a new drama was announced: the draw for the knock-out stages of the Champions League. Chelsea were drawn against one of the superpowers of world football, Barcelona. No matter how exciting the clash looked then, no one can have imagined the astonishing events that would take place during those games, Didier's part in them and the impact the matches would have on world football.

Mourinho enthused on hearing the draw: 'I'm very happy with this. Since I left Barcelona in 2000, I have never been back. I love the club and in every corner I have a friend. It will be emotional to return there. They are a top team, they will want to play football, pure football, and it will be two great matches.'

The teams had last met in the quarter-finals of the European Cup four years earlier, when Chelsea won the first leg at home 3–1 but lost 5–1 after extra time at the mighty Nou Camp stadium. The games would be played the other way around this time, and Mourinho was confident. 'It is the same risk for Barcelona as it is for us. That is the beauty of this stage. I don't like the word *fear*, I don't believe in it, but we will not fear them and they will not fear us.'

Barcelona's £18 million striker Samuel Eto'o opted for a confrontational manner, however, when he said, 'I want to be European Champion, and for that we have to beat the best teams. Currently Chelsea is number one in England and I'd prefer to play them twice than once in the final. But this team doesn't worry me because Barcelona this year is capable of winning against any club in the world. I see Chelsea's defence as slow, which is perfect for my fast pace game. And Ronaldinho is worth half of Chelsea's players. That's our great advantage on the field. Several times I've been close to signing for Chelsea but the deal was never closed. Now they'll have me on the other side of the pitch and they'll come out as losers, because they won't get to the quarter-finals. The Chelsea forwards are good, but in Africa, for example, I've always been ahead of Drogba.'

With his extensive knowledge of English football, Giovanni van Bronckhorst, the Barcelona defender who had until recently played for Arsenal, was far more diplomatic when he said he realised that it was going to be a tough tie for the Catalan giants:

'You only have to see how well Chelsea are doing in their league to see that they have a great chance of success in Europe. Chelsea play in a mature way and have a tight defensive unit, which seems to be what the team is based on. But look at their attacking options as well, the likes of Arjen Robben, Didier Drogba, Damien Duff and Eidur Gudjohnsen. They have so much quality.'

Too much quality indeed for Norwich at Stamford Bridge the final Saturday before Christmas. The three chances that came their way in the first half were all dispatched calmly by, in turn, Duff, Lampard and Robben. The recent good results meant Didier was again on the substitutes' bench – more a tribute to Eidur Gudjohnsen than a criticism of himself, this – but, when they did their now customary swap-over, Didier emphatically announced he hadn't lost his goal touch.

A corner by Duff seven minutes from time saw a massive, athletic leap on Didier's part to power home the fourth goal. The whistle couldn't come quickly enough for brave Norwich, who trooped off knowing they had been outclassed in every department. The win took Chelsea six points clear at the top of the league and it was the sixth time in their last nine league games they'd scored four goals.

Even though it could hardly be classed as too strenuous a game for Didier and his teammates, they were all given two days off to recover – not from any charitable motives on Mourinho's part, but simply because they would be working for the next fifteen consecutive days over the Christmas and New Year periods.

Although Didier was obviously pleased to be part of a successful side, he can't have been too happy that, at times, he seemed to be taking second place to Eidur Gudjohnsen, who gave his view on the battle for the striker's spot in such a talented squad, saying, 'Everybody was talking about the players who were arriving but it is now my fifth season at Chelsea. Look at the strikers that have come and gone and I am still here. I spoke to Mourinho in the summer and he gave me a lot of confidence. He spoke of his faith in me.

'Now, there is competition between me and Drogba. I have got tremendous respect for Drogba. He was unfortunate to get an injury but he has been back for a while now and I know I have to be on my toes. At Arsenal, we were 2–1 down and Didier came on at half-time and I dropped in behind him as a second striker. I was lucky enough to get the equaliser straightaway. There's no reason why we can't both be on the pitch.'

Another admirer of Didier was Aston Villa's Czech defender Václav Drobný – who had played against him the previous year when he was at Racing Club Strasbourg – and he reckoned the Ivorian would eventually become a better player than Thierry Henry or Ruud van Nistelrooy. 'Henry and van Nistelrooy are obviously fantastic but I think Drogba will make the biggest impact. He is big and powerful and has scored goals wherever he has been. I played against him three times when he was at Marseilles last season and he was very impressive. There are many great strikers in the Premiership but I think Drogba will be the man to watch this season,' he said on the eve of Villa's Boxing Day trip to Stamford Bridge.

Poor Villa went the way of many others, losing by a solitary goal from Duff, and the Chelsea defence kept another clean sheet two days later when goals from Robben and Joe Cole were enough to claim all the points at Portsmouth. Intriguingly, Gudjohnsen started the Villa game and was replaced by Didier, but Didier began his first game since his injury at Portsmouth then had to give way to the Icelander not long into the second half. Something wasn't right. Reports of the match agreed that he was a long way short of his best but Mourinho sprang to his defence. In doing so he confirmed what many had been thinking: The 'routine' injury that had kept Didier sidelined for weeks had consequences far greater than everyone had at first realised.

'We have taken specialist advice from other players who have had the same injury, and they say that it is very difficult to recover,' said Didier's coach.

'You know you are OK and are fit again, but it still feels very bad and it makes it hard to move freely. It takes time to trust that your body is OK. The feelings in the groin and abdomen are really bad, and it takes time to recover, to sprint, to be sharp and to jump and tackle. At the moment Didier needs that time, but it's no problem because we believe in him and he will get that time and will show just what a quality player he can be.'

Rather than himself, Didier preferred to talk about the team and its hunt for four trophies that Christmas, a constant attitude he has shown wherever he has played: 'Everything is possible in football and we can win four titles, but we can also lose everything,' he said. 'We have to be very careful and I think to win something you have to carry on working the same way you have always done. You have to be modest and humble if you want to keep on winning.'

## CHAPTER 15

# Who Can Stop the Blues?

It would be uplifting to say that New Year's day, 1 January 2005, heralded a new chapter in Didier's life. Sadly, it was to be the same story at the beginning of the New Year as it had been as the old ended.

He was wrapped up in a substitute's warm layer of clothing as Chelsea's starting eleven kicked off at one of the major shrines of English football, Liverpool's packed Anfield ground. Since it opened for business in 1884 it had seen countless great contests, most of them coming in the modern era from the 1960s onwards when first Bill Shankly and then the men who followed in his footsteps steered a succession of great sides to glory at home and abroad. In fact it was at Anfield a year earlier with Marseilles that Didier had one of his first tastes of European competition at the highest level.

So, no matter how great a squad member he was, it must have been galling to see Eidur Gudjohnsen in the central striking role – the Icelander failed to impress and, minutes after failing to reach a low cross from Damien Duff and with an hour on the clock, Didier came on to replace him. By then he had seen a blatant handball appeal against Tiago – a decision that even José Mourinho later as good as admitted was a mistake – turned down by referee Mike Riley as, for once, flowing football from Chelsea was replaced by the need to grind out a result. Didier almost 'ground down' England's Steven Gerrard with an ugly challenge, but before the incident escalated both men sensibly diffused it by giving each other an affectionate hug.

It was ironic that a display by Chelsea that could be described in no way as one of their most flowing eventually gave them three points. Ironic in the sense that the victims were Liverpool, who – even at the height of their powers – were famous for getting the right result even if they weren't firing on all cylinders. The match winner came from another substitute, Joe Cole, ten minutes from time, and even that was courtesy of a deflected shot. Liverpool pressed to the end, but Čech kept them at bay and they recorded a double over the 'Pool – the first time they had achieved that in a season for eighty-five long years. It really was a massive win for Chelsea in a match in which they could easily have been beaten; the balance of power was definitely changing.

Mourinho had gone on record to say that it can take players from abroad, even the top-ranking ones, six months to settle into Premiership football. If there were any questions about when Didier's six months was up, he went a long way to answering them just three days later when he, at last, began a match when Chelsea were at home to Middlesbrough. Two goals in three minutes before the game had really got under way were enough to send out a clear message to the football world that he was back in business.

Before kick-off Chelsea gave their former striker Jimmy Floyd Hasselbaink an award in recognition of his services to the club and he was also warmly received by the crowd. But the generosity ended there and Didier soon poised a threat when he met a Arjen Robben corner with a firm header that was gratefully held in the arms of goalkeeper Mark Schwarzer. But Didier was just too good for the visitors' defence. Another volley was saved by the Australian goalkeeper and when Lampard put him clear he shrugged aside a challenge from England defender Gareth Southgate and his shot was too good for Schwarzer. Two minutes later, worse was to come for the visitors as Didier showed all the power he possessed as he soared to a Lampard free kick and released a breathtaking header that thumped into the net with the power many a player would be proud to see.

Chelsea could, and should, have scored more and Didier was eventually replaced late into the second half. This time, however, there was no question of the decision being for questionable tactical reasons: it was simply that he'd done his job and in the crowded Christmas and New Year programme that is peculiar to English clubs he fully deserved to watch the final moment of the match with his feet up.

The four games over the hectic holiday programme have often proved to be a quagmire for sides on a roll. Chelsea had no such problems. Four games in ten days had produced a maximum twelve points without even one goal against them, and the Blues were seven points clear at the top. The players had obviously enjoyed their two days off beforehand and decided to say thanks in the best possible way by gaining maximum points.

The newspapers the next day were unanimous in their praise for Didier, something, it must be said, that they had not been for some time. One summed it up by saying that Drogba 'was proving impossible to defend against'; another that, 'Chelsea's record £24m signing destroyed the Middlesbrough defence with a performance of pace and power.' A third reported that his first goal was worthy of anything Thierry Henry could produce, but his second was beyond even the wonderful Arsenal striker in that it was a combination of raw power, unhesitating courage and brutal strength.

There seemed no stopping Chelsea in the Premiership, but perhaps they could be halted in the FA Cup. That seemed unlikely, as their opponents at Stamford Bridge for the third-round tie on 8 January 2005 were deemed by even their most fervent fans unlikely to beat them. The visitors were Scunthorpe, a team who brought new meaning to the words *lowly* and *unfashionable*. 6,000 Scunthorpe fans, 10 per cent of the town's population, packed into the ground. Even they must have had to look twice after eight minutes when the Chelsea net bulged after Paul Hayes' quick turn left Alexey Smertin on the floor and he toe-poked the ball through Carlo Cudicini's legs and into the net for the first goal Chelsea had conceded in eight and half hours of competitive football. They had succeeded where a string of Premiership internationals failed.

Chelsea had, understandably, fielded a weakened side due to both choice and injury, but no matter who was wearing the blue shirt, defeat for the world's most expensive side against the team from England's lowest division would have been unthinkable. Didier was in the starting line-up but, for once, perhaps he wished he hadn't been. It was his first experience of the FA Cup, the oldest football competition in the world, and now he was seeing at first hand what it was all about. He also experienced the caustic wit of the Scunthorpe fans, who realised they had to make hay while the sun was shining by chanting, 'Are you Grimsby in disguise?' followed quickly by 'Can we play you every week?'.

It couldn't last, and Didier's header led to Mateja Kezman's twenty-sixth-minute equaliser, although the Irons defiantly stayed in the game with Carlo Cudicini busier than his opposite number Paul Musselwhite, who, astonishingly, was a survivor from the match seventeen years earlier when Scunthorpe knocked Chelsea out of the League Cup. Someone had to sort things out, and that was Didier. The most surprising fact was that it took him until the fifty-eighth minute to do so. For once he wasn't the scorer, but he outpaced defender Clifford Byrne on the left and drove in a low cross, which Scunthorpe captain Andy Crosby stretched to reach and cruelly turned into his own net. That was the cue for Scunthorpe to fold, but they didn't. Instead they shot back with a vengeance and Chelsea were put under more pressure than they had been for weeks. It had to end eventually, but it took until four minutes from time, when Scunthorpe's veteran goalkeeper twice made saves only for Gudjohnsen to push the second rebound home.

The Scunthorpe players stayed on the field for five minutes taking the applause of their fans, and that of a lot of Chelsea supporters too. José Mourinho stayed on the pitch to acknowledge them and personally congratulate every one of them on their performance. It wasn't quite what Didier had joined Chelsea for, to risk humiliation at the hands of a bunch of workaday professionals, but, boy, had it been a learning curve! The Chelsea players may have reckoned they had been near to an embarrassing result, but at least they finally managed to win, unlike their great rivals Manchester United, who were at the wrong end of one of the most astonishing Cup results of recent years that same weekend. Little Exeter had gone up to Old Trafford for what everyone assumed would be a thrashing. Instead they walked off the pitch heads held high and hailed as heroes for their 0–0 draw, leaving Alex Ferguson to label the Reds' performance the worst he had seen in the competition in his eighteen years at the club!

It all added more spice, as if that were needed, to the confrontation at Stamford Bridge a few days later between the two giants in the first leg of the Carling Cup semi-final.

Didier was again on the subs' bench but came on after the goalless first half for Gudjohnsen as their inevitable change-partners routine occurred again. Although United lacked players such as Roy Keane and Rio Ferdinand, they still fielded an all-international side, but they were overrun by Chelsea. It took two goal-line clearances by United to keep the Blues at bay and Didier soon felt the warmth of their 'welcome' when he was clattered into by South African Quinton Fortune.

Perhaps that was the reason why he reacted so strongly near the end of the goalless match during an astonishing touchline flare-up as the game exploded into a mass brawl. Cristiano Ronaldo and Didier disagreed over a throw-in and Didier kicked the ball away. The tempestuous Portuguese teenager – later to earn notoriety for his complicity in Wayne Rooney's World Cup sending-off – then took what was admittedly a fairly gentile swing at Didier before Quinton Fortune arrived at the scene. There was obviously some ill will from the previous argument and he barged into Didier, causing the striker to grab him by the throat in return.

The referee Neale Barry and fourth official Peter Walton dived in to calm matters down and John Terry hauled Fortune clear. As football fights go it must be pointed out that one observer compared it to jostling in the queue at the Harrods sale! Barry booked Ronaldo and Didier and that seemed to be that. But there was to be an aftermath. Mourinho was convinced that the referee's decisions had gone United's way after the interval and said, 'You saw one referee in the first half and another in the second half.' In what was to be a foretaste of events soon to be the centre of a much larger controversy, he added, with obvious reference to the opposing manager and a conversation with the referee, 'I'm suggesting that the referee didn't walk alone to the dressing room at half-time. What I saw, heard and felt at half-time made it easier for me to understand a few things. Maybe one day, when I'm sixty and have the respect of everybody, I will have the power to speak to people and make them tremble a little. I understand that with a few clever words and a little pressure you can change a few things. If someone from the FA asks me what happened I will tell them.'

Sir Alex Ferguson had a different take on the night's events. 'The referee gave Chelsea an awful lot in the first half,' he said. The matter rumbled on, though as the Scot was to add, 'I think Mourinho has opened a can of worms for himself. But I don't think his comments have anything to do with what happened on Wednesday. It was more about trying to influence the referee for tomorrow's game against Tottenham. What I find more interesting are John Terry's comments when he says the referee wouldn't listen to him. I ask the question, "Why would he listen to him?" '

Didier just had to be drawn into the argument and Ferguson also hinted that the Ivorian should be facing FA action for grabbing Quinton Fortune by the throat. 'The referee acted quite rightly in booking Drogba for kicking Cristiano Ronaldo. But then Drogba reacted by grabbing Quinton Fortune by the throat. So I wonder whether the FA's compliance unit will be thinking about that.'

In a belated attempt to calm matters down, Mourinho said he may have used the wrong word, *cheat*, when, at one stage in his outburst, he had said some of the United players had gone to ground too easily; and he also said he had no criticism of the referee. 'I know I could be punished for pointing out that somebody did something wrong so, if the FA do it, I think it will be unfair. I don't think they should punish Sir Alex for what he did. I think they should just tell referees not to allow it, whether they are the top manager in the country, a guy who has just arrived or a lower-division manager. I always say what I think and feel. I am not worried by the consequences. I live better with the consequences than with my mouth closed and keeping what I feel I have to say inside.'

It should be noted, in this bizarre battle of words, that it isn't widely known that the two managers had actually, as is often the custom, had a drink together after the match in the Chelsea manager's office and the only dispute was that Ferguson hadn't been totally enamoured with the quality of the wine! Mourinho, at least, saw the funny side of that, saying, 'When we go to Manchester United, I will take a very good bottle of wine because the wine we drank was very bad and he was complaining. It is my birthday when we go to Old Trafford, so I will go with a beautiful bottle of Portuguese wine to enjoy with him at the end of the game.' The Old Trafford second leg thirteen days later, where Mourinho was to keep his word by arriving with a £240 bottle of vintage wine, promised to be a night of fun and games.

## DIDIER DROGBA

The weekend's Premiership match was a great deal more predictable. Spurs, who hadn't beaten Chelsea in the league for fifteen years, succumbed again, this time to two Frank Lampard goals, one a disputed penalty. Didier started but didn't finish, as he was replaced by his rival for the centre-forward berth. Still, the weekend's other results meant Chelsea now had a ten-point lead at the top of the table and Mourinho – confident as ever – told Chelsea's TV station, 'There is so much ground to make up for the teams chasing us now. Of course, we cannot go to sleep yet because it is possible for the gap to be reduced. But 10 points is a huge gap and the reality is that, if it goes to twelve or thirteen points clear, maybe then it's all over.'

Didier, lacking his boss's gung-ho attitude, was a lot more circumspect as he considered both the title race and his own first months in England. 'Everything is going great here but a ten-point lead is not enough,' he said. 'We've already seen situations where those kinds of leads have melted. Chelsea are a team who are in control of our football and we are playing intelligently. But we're not unbeatable or untouchable. We know very well that we are going to lose games – but then again, we won't lose many in a row.'

And he was to give the first of the hints that his happiness at Chelsea was not yet at the same level as it had been in Marseilles when he admitted, 'I'm satisfied with my first six months despite the critics. My injury made me miss games, but it did allow me to realise that I needed a break. I've had two very busy years.

'I have a working relationship with my teammates, but when we're in the changing room or on the bus, we also have a good laugh. When we meet up for training, we really get into it. I also benefit from a little more freedom in everyday life in London. At Marseilles, people used to talk about me a lot.

'It's true, though: I'm not yet getting as much enjoyment from living in London as I was in Marseilles. However, you just have to bounce back and get on with things, and that's what I'm trying to do. I could have spent years at Marseilles but in the end my destiny was elsewhere. I do not suffer from my price tag. People often remind me of the transfer fee, even when we play at home. As soon as I miss a chance it's "Why did they spend so much money on him?" There's even a song about it. But I like that, it motivates me.'

The criticism may have been 'motivating' but there was no doubt that, in spite of his success both at playing level and in integrating into a new club in a foreign country, Didier still had reservations about his move. Of course he was being paid more than at Marseilles and his years in the football hinterland, both with his uncle and as a player, had made it clear to him that there was nothing to be ashamed of in earning as much as possible during a short-lived career. But he had been idolised at Marseilles and there was no disguising the fact that he had not yet won over the Stamford Bridge faithful to the same extent. It wasn't just the away supporters who chanted 'What a waste of money!' - some home supporters expressed the sentiment too.

The more astute would have noted that his years of constant football, followed by an injury that had a greater effect on him than many realised, were hardly ideal preparation for the challenges that the constant stream of Premiership, Champions League and English cup contests were posing, but that didn't stop criticism in several quarters. Still, there wasn't much to moan about even for the most severe critics, as Portsmouth were next to be brushed aside due to three first-half goals at Stamford Bridge. Didier scored two of them and Arjen Robben, in devastating form on the eve of his twenty-first birthday, the third. Robben, as always looking older than his years, set up the first for Didier, rounded the goalkeeper when he scored the second and won the free kick that enabled Didier to curl the ball around the wall and into the net for the third. The pair were later taken off, no doubt with the thought of the arduous test at Old Trafford that was looming.

So if Didier was having doubts, or at the least reservations, about joining Chelsea, he can't have had any time for them when he ran out onto the so-called 'Theatre of Dreams' in the starting line-up for once, in front of 67,000 fans for the second leg of their Carling Cup semi-final. And he would have felt he had definitely made the right move when, after twenty-nine minutes, Frank Lampard passed to Robben and the Dutchman fed Didier down the left. Didier worked his way along a congested byline and past Gary Neville in the process then cut the ball back to Lampard, who'd covered a full sixty yards in order to slot the ball home. Ryan Giggs equalised, but Duff's eighty-fifth-minute free-kick winner put Chelsea into the final.

The bad feeling from Stamford Bridge continued. Fortune badly fouled Didier. There was a sixteen-man pushing contest and a ninetieth-minute wonder save by Petr Čech from Ronaldo that kept the crowd agog for the second forty-five minutes, but, apart from the rarity of conceding a goal, it had been another splendid day at the office for the Blues.

As the month drew to a close Didier still had his misgivings, but said, 'I'm very pleased with the goals I've scored because it's my first year in England. It's not easy to come to a new country, to score goals and to adapt. This is one of the best championships in Europe and I need time to adapt. I've also been injured and I am not 100 per cent.'

And he was almost Mourinho-like when he told French *Football* magazine, 'This season we really have the team to go very far in every competition. We are here to win one title at least, and maybe more than one. I don't care how many goals I score or how many matches I play, but I want to know what the feeling of winning a title is like. Our lead over Arsenal and Manchester United is quite big and we are going to face Barcelona in the Champions League. Some say it's a tough draw for us but it's certainly a tough one for them too.'

He was also, very diplomatically, and very truthfully, full of praise for his coach José Mourinho. 'He is one of the best in the world and he is really impressive. He has his own ideas about strategy but he never lets himself get trapped into it. He is capable of changing tactics during the match if it's needed. He is able to anticipate and guess what the scenario of the last five minutes of a game is going to be. He works a lot with the video. When we played the fourth division side Scunthorpe United in a Cup match, he bought a video of our rivals. We watched it and knew everything we had to about them.'

And, speaking from personal experience, he made a telling remark about the standards expected on a weekly basis in England and France: 'The leading team in the French championship would finish in the middle of the table here. Lyon can beat anyone on their day but they wouldn't stand the pace the whole season.'

While Didier may have been frustrated by limited first team appearances, he was at least better off than his German teammate Robert Huth. The big defender had managed only eighteen minutes' first-team football that year, but at least he got on the team sheet, with John Terry, in a routine FA Cup fourth-round home win over Birmingham, who gave them far less trouble than little Scunthorpe earlier in the month.

Didier missed out on the next match completely, a 1–0 win at Blackburn, due, it was reported, to a groin injury picked up in training, and the following disappointing goalless draw at home to Manchester City, the fourth point Kevin Keegan's side had taken off them that season. He was also ruled out of the side's solitary goal triumph over high-riding Everton on Merseyside and the nightmare FA Cup journey to Newcastle United. Nightmare because in the freezing Tyneside weather Chelsea's dream of winning all four competitions eventually came to an end. When the final whistle blew they had lost 1–0 to a Patrick Kluivert goal and, bizarrely, had just nine men on the field. A combination of injuries, Mourinho using his substitutes early and then the sending-off of goalkeeper Carlo Cudicini meant that Chelsea's side was reduced in number, and even some of those were limping badly when the final whistle blew.

It had been a frustrating time for Didier, who, despite having been out for a long time before Christmas, was then on the sidelines again. Still, there were lighter moments. No matter how famous, and wealthy, he had become, he was still aware of the hierarchy that exists in football. Roman Abramovich would often visit the Chelsea dressing room to congratulate players after a match, and on one of the visits he brought his eleven-year-old son Arkady with him, who asked Didier for his sweaty shirt. 'Of course, as it was the son of the boss, I gave it a good wipe, folded it and quickly gave it to him.'

He wasn't going to be restricted to giving away shirts with a smile on his face soon, however. After he missed five games, it was time to reappear on the pitch. His comeback game was to be against mighty Barcelona in Spain in a clash that was to become one of the most notorious in football history.

## CHAPTER 16

# The Battle of Barcelona

Football clubs don't come much bigger than Barcelona. Founded in 1898, it has been one of the major players on the world football scene for decades and its ground, the legendary Nou Camp stadium, holds 98,800 supporters when full. In the 2004–5 season, Barcelona had an incredible average home attendance of 73,360 fans eager to see the stars wearing the famous blue-and-maroon-striped shirts of the club. But its identity goes beyond mere soccer success: the club is a focal point for Catalonia the region in which Barcelona is located. During the Franco years when the Catalan flag and language were banned, the interior of the stadium was one of the few public places where the tongue could be spoken. No wonder its motto is '*Más que un club*' – more than a club.

But if anyone thought the fireworks would have to wait until the night of Chelsea's Champions League match in Northern Spain they were wrong: the action started days before. It had been barely a year since José Mourinho had arrived on the international stage as a comparatively unknown coach who'd stunned the football world when his Porto side triumphed at Old Trafford in the same competition. The intervening twelve months had seen him soar to heights of fame greater than that of many of the players he was in charge of, or who opposed him. So perhaps it wasn't to be totally unexpected when, as the Nou Camp match neared, he launched a remarkable attack on his Barcelona counterpart, a man who had been one of the greatest players of the modern era, the Dutchman Frank Rijkaard.

Mourinho said, in very clear language that Rijkaard could not compete with him as a coach. 'Frank Rijkaard's history as a player can't be compared to my history – his history is fantastic, mine is zero,' he told the world. 'But my history as a manager can't be compared to his, because he has zero titles and I have a lot of them. He just can't be compared to me. I don't have to be jealous of Barcelona because they have a hundred years of history and have won the European Cup once.

'I have only been managing for five years and I have the same amount of Champions League trophies to my name. I have to defend what is mine and, at the moment, the Champions League is mine. I was the last winner as a manager, so at the moment it's my competition and my cup. I have to fight for Chelsea and have to fight for myself and defend my cup until the last. It means a lot to me. Maybe because I won the Champions League I had a big change in my life and I could come to a big football country like England.'

He couldn't resist another jibe at the club, where, it must be remembered, just a few years earlier he had been a lowly assistant coach.

'Barcelona do score a lot of goals, that's true. They have the African player of the year [Samuel Eto'o], the world player of the year [Ronaldinho] and the best player in the Champions League last year [Deco]. They have a lot of super quality in that attacking area, I agree. When it comes to the Champions League, winning is winning. That's very, very difficult to do. There are a lot of fantastic managers in the world who couldn't win one, not a single one. That shows how difficult it is.'

As the clock ticked by until kick-off time and Chelsea's injury-hit squad trained in secret, Rijkaard hit back, albeit in a less loquacious and more diplomatic manner, saying, 'When people talk like this before a match, it is a sign they are not calm, not at ease with the match to come. Manchester United are catching them in the league and they have a few injuries to key players to cope with.'

But he couldn't resist adding, 'They have been in Barcelona for three days and have trained behind closed doors. But now Mourinho has named his team. You certainly don't see that happen very often. But he has the right to express himself.'

Indeed Mourinho had gone public with his side days before kick-off – and that meant Didier would be back in the starting line-up. He didn't stick totally to his word, though, deciding at the last minute to start with Duff instead of Gudjohnsen.

There were almost 90,000 fans in the Nou Camp, including 5,000 from Chelsea as the teams lined up like this on the night of 23 February 2005.

BARCELONA (4–3–3): Valdes; Belletti, Márquez, Puyol, Van Bronckhorst; Deco, Albertin, Xavi, Giuly, Eto'o; Ronaldinho.
CHELSEA (4–3–2–1): Čech; Ferreira, Terry, Carvalho, Gallas, Tiago, Makelele, Lampard, Cole, Duff, Drogba.

No team ever coached by Mourinho could be accused of a lack of confidence and Chelsea soon showed there was no way they were going to be intimidated by the atmosphere. Still, they were up against some of the finest players currently strutting their stuff on the stage of world football and the Brazilian Ronaldinho – an old foe of Didier's from the days in French football – was calling the tune in the opening minutes, twice firing wide and setting up Eto'o, who also shot over the bar. But after that first worrying spell, when Barcelona's stars showed their quality, the teamwork of Chelsea proved to be more than a match for them. So much so that, although on the back foot for spells, in the thirty-third minute they took the lead with a wonderfully worked goal.

Frank Lampard released the perfect pass that found Duff onside and the fair-haired Irish international accelerated down the right wing. He left Giovanni van Bronckhorst for dead and cut the ball back to where Didier was waiting to pounce for what would undoubtedly have been his first goal after weeks of inactivity. But before he could provide the finishing touch, a desperate attempt by Juliano Belletti to rescue the situation saw him merely slide the ball home for an own goal. Two minutes later Chelsea could have increased the lead when a scintillating pass from Claude Makelele enabled Didier to surge in from the right, only uncharacteristically to shoot wide for what was to prove a massive miss. It seems unlikely that if he had been match-sharp such a golden opportunity would have been wasted.

Nevertheless to go off at half-time leading the mighty 'Barça' by a goal was an achievement in itself, especially when the Spanish club's record against English opponents at the Nou Camp was astonishing. They had lost only once and that was to a great Liverpool side almost thirty years earlier. The players disappeared down the tunnel and what took place there and in the catacombs below the stadium in those few minutes off the field was to have massive ramifications.

Soon after the restart Didier was booked for a second foul on Rafael Márquez, although many observers felt the offence for which he received the yellow card was the type of clumsy challenge that would normally go unpunished in the Premiership. They also agreed that Barcelona's Deco's reaction was spectacular. But the warning lights were flashing for Didier, and he had to be calmed down by the Swedish referee Anders Frisk after he clashed again with the giant Márquez, Didier pointing out that he had been raked by the Mexican captain's studs. So perhaps he should have thought twice and erred on the side of caution ten minutes into the second half, when he went for a 50–50 ball with home keeper Victor Valdes after a back-pass from Belletti fell short.

The worst that could be said of the incident was that he was reckless to make the challenge in the first place, as endless television replays showed that it was, at most, a marginal foul – if it was a foul at all. One neutral report of the game stressed that 'he had every right to go for the ball' and described the referee's reaction as 'harsh'. Didier, who was also hurt in the collision, immediately protested his innocence as the goalkeeper rolled around on the ground, but it was to no avail. Perhaps, with hindsight, he should not have made the challenge knowing it might earn him a second booking, but he hadn't progressed from the lower reaches of French football to world fame in an incredible two seasons by holding back when the ball was there to be won.

Perhaps if he was not so 'ring-rusty' he might have made better contact, but the flamboyant Frisk harshly showed him a yellow card followed instantly later by a red one. Didier, with understandable reluctance, left the pitch to the delight of the Barcelona fans to first surprise and then disgust from the Chelsea bench and the blue-and-white contingent in the ground. Frisk was not their favourite man because five years earlier he had been the referee who had awarded Barcelona two penalties in a match they won 5–1 after extra time.

The incident was later put in context by Frank Lampard, who said, 'There was a build-up from their players and fans. There were a few situations when their players were falling to the floor, trying to make a big deal out of them. That set their fans off and their whistling and screaming put pressure on the referee. In the end, Frisk reacted, saying, "One more tackle and you're off!" Yes, Drogba collided with the keeper but there's no way his studs were up over the ball or anything like that.

'But, although their keeper is six foot three inches, he fell down dramatically and all of a sudden they were all around the ref trying to get Drogba sent off.'

But as Didier headed off the pitch it meant thirty-five long minutes faced the Blues if they were to survive in an atmosphere that resembled a bear pit – and a massive one at that. There was no denying the quality of the Barcelona players, and, given the added space that the extra man now gave them, that long half hour was to feel like an eternity.

Ronaldinho, a world footballer of the year, and Eto'o, who had made his full international debut for Cameroon at fifteen, combined with an exchange of passes and young substitute Maxi Lopez pounded in the equaliser.

A draw would have been more than acceptable to Chelsea but they conceded again on seventy-four minutes, when the dangerous Maxi turned goal maker as his shot turned, accidentally, into a cross for Eto'o, who got between John Terry and Ricardo Carvalho to rifle his shot home. By the final whistle, Chelsea had done well to keep a rampant Barcelona side down to two as Terry headed away Deco's shot, which was heading towards the top corner, and in injury time Čech saved superbly from Andrés Iniesta. A sickening defeat for Chelsea in general and Didier in particular, true, but it still meant they trailed by only a goal for that all-important second leg in the middle of March.

If the game had been stormy, however, the heavens really opened for the after-match tempest and the mother of all off-pitch rows. The first indication that there was trouble in store was when Mourinho and his Chelsea entourage didn't appear for the mandatory press interviews. Chelsea spokesman Simon Greenberg would only say a complaint had been sent to UEFA about an incident at half-time, and, until it was resolved, no one would speak to the media.

He gave no details, but Barcelona coach Frank Rijkaard claimed Chelsea was exaggerating. 'I'd like to say I saw what happened, but I can't because nothing did', Rijkaard said. 'They're exaggerating all this.' He added he believed that the complaint was due to his salute towards Swedish referee Anders Frisk as both teams left the field at half-time. He denied rumours that Frisk entered the Barcelona changing room during the break. 'This is what's happening,' said Rijkaard. 'They [Chelsea] are inventing something that didn't happen.' By now really giving vent to his feelings, he said he thought Chelsea's behaviour was 'lamentable' and 'incorrect'. The Spanish news agency EFE, however, reported that the incident stemmed from Barcelona's assistant coach Henk ten Cate challenging Frisk in the tunnel to complain that he thought Chelsea's goal was offside. Chelsea officials intervened to protest, EFE said, citing Barcelona officials.

Back at the stadium one of the rumours starting to circulate was that Mourinho, who had never before in his managerial career been in charge of a side that lost two consecutive games, was kicked up the backside by Henk ten Cate, although thankfully this suggestion was later dismissed by both sides. What wasn't dismissed, though, was that there had been an altercation between the two sides' backroom staff and there had been contact at half-time between the Barcelona hierarchy and the referee, although what form it took and what was said was later to become more complex. The row, which we will return to later, was to rumble on for a long time after that, overshadowing much of the remainder of the season and, of course, the sensational return leg two weeks later at Stamford Bridge.

The Barcelona players were bullish about their performance and their prospects for the second leg, and even suggested that the Chelsea after-match complaints were designed, in some bizarre way, to take public attention away from a 'poor' performance – although a 2–1 defeat, with its away goal, suffered by a side down to ten men could hardly be described as a catastrophe!

Giovanni van Bronckhorst said, 'There may have been some talking in the tunnel but from the way it is being portrayed you would think somebody had been shot. It really doesn't appear that anything important happened and you just have to wonder at why all this hype has been created. We were easily the better side. It seemed to me Chelsea decided they couldn't match us football-wise and so switched to a really defensive performance.' The ponytailed centre-back Rafael Márquez – Didier's arch foe during the match – insisted, 'This is just an excuse. Everybody could see who was the better team. Chelsea are just angry because of the defeat. Drogba's sending-off was not unjust. I'll tell you why there was a battle between him and me. He hit me twice, committing two fouls, and that compelled me to react. I was in despair when Chelsea got their goal, then outright furious.' Match winner Samuel Eto'o couldn't resist joining in, saying, 'The result was not as close as it looks, and we deserved to score more goals.'

It has to be noted, however, that the impending investigation wasn't the only disciplinary matter the club had been involved in during the season so far: before Christmas they had been charged over their fans' behaviour during a clash with West Ham and there was also a probe into a players' fracas at Blackburn. On top of that was the start of the infamous saga over the 'tapping-up' of Ashley Cole from Arsenal. So perhaps it was good that there was actually a game of football for Didier and the team to concentrate on, the Carling Cup final against Liverpool.

There's an old saying in football: 'Show us your medals'. It's often said by players who have achieved not just success but have won titles and trophies to back up their ability.

One of the intriguing – if not downright surprising – facts about the Chelsea line-up was that three of its key players, Didier, John Terry and Frank Lampard, hadn't won one major competition between them. Terry had a medal from the 2000 FA Cup final, but he was only substitute for that and didn't even make an appearance on the field. So the Chelsea centre-half, who had started off as a boot boy whose youthful duties included toilet cleaning, left no doubt about his desire when he said before the Liverpool game, 'Now I'm at the top, the pinnacle. I'm the captain and I want to stay captain and be a successful one. Winning a trophy and lifting it for Chelsea would be the ultimate.'

# THE BATTLE OF BARCELONA

Lampard, who week in, week out, was proving the mainstay of the Chelsea side, echoed that when he said, 'I've not really won anything yet. I did get the Intertoto Cup with West Ham but that's something I don't like to talk about. If I got a medal, I don't know where it is. I've not won anything except the Youth Cup. I came here to win trophies. People talk about money, and of course that's important. But at a club like Chelsea you have to have real ambition to win. You can't just trot along in mediocrity here. You've got to be a winner.'

Didier, of course, had never tasted title triumph of any sort, and there was one other member of the Chelsea setup who had yet to see the men in blue ascend a victory podium: owner Roman Abramovich. Given the countless millions he had spent on players, he too must have hoped that the curse would be broken as the two teams walked out on to the pitch of the Millennium Stadium at Cardiff in front of 78,000 spectators on the afternoon of Sunday, 27 February.

After that rarest of rare events, two defeats on the trot for Chelsea, it seemed that things, as the song says, could only get better. That most definitely wasn't the case, as the Blues found themselves trailing to a goal that wasn't so much early as practically predawn. The match was only forty-five seconds old before Petr Čech – the goalkeeper who had turned clean sheets from a hobby into an addiction – was turning round to see the ball nestling angrily in the back of his net.

Within moments of referee Steve Bennett's signalling the start of the match, Fernando Morientes collected the ball on the right of the Chelsea area, passed William Gallas, and, with no particular exciting options open to him, sent a careful centre towards the far post. The Chelsea defence, for once, were spectators as Norwegian powerhouse John Arne Riise arrived on the scene and his thunderous left foot did the rest. If Chelsea were to avoid making it a catastrophic three consecutive defeats on the trot, they couldn't have picked a worse way of starting.

When the going gets tough, the tough, as they say, get going, and so Chelsea gradually, and remorselessly began their fight back. They started to control key areas of the game and before half-time Didier managed one strong shot from the edge of the area, which brought the best out of Jerzy Dudek in the Liverpool goal. The second half continued with Chelsea dominating, but Liverpool were not ready to crack. It seemed they had enough resilience to keep out the efforts of Didier and the rest. Gudjohnsen came on at half-time, Kezman after seventy-four minutes, but there was still no change on the scoreline. Gerrard could have sealed victory for Liverpool with a quarter of an hour left but a challenge from Ferreira managed to halt him. For all Chelsea's pressure, Liverpool were within sight of the victory line and Chelsea had used all their substitutes when, in the seventy-ninth minute, German international Dietmar Hamann checked Lampard's run down Chelsea's right. Joe Cole reacted angrily as referee Steve Bennett gave a free kick instead of playing advantage. He wasn't so riled a moment later when Ferreira's subsequent free kick went over Riise and Jamie Carragher but then clipped the head of Gerrard, and the Liverpool captain watched in anguish as the ball at last went past Dudek and into the net. Irony indeed, as Gerrard had been, and was to be in the near future, the object of transfer talk about his moving from his native Merseyside to Chelsea. Agony for the red section of the crowd, ecstasy for the blue, where pandemonium broke out.

That meant the game would move into extra time, although José Mourinho wasn't able to give the customary pep talk cum tactical advice to his players. He had been 'sent off' for putting his fingers to his lips indicating a 'be quiet' gesture as the equaliser went in, an action, the police reckoned, was aimed at the Liverpool fans. They told the fourth official to move him from the touchline. Mourinho later said, depending on which report you read, that he was gesturing to his wife Tami or to the media to tell them to stop criticising his side.

Either way, the Blues had to sort it out without his advice – having to rely instead on Mourinho's assistant Steve Clarke – and

# THE BATTLE OF BARCELONA

Didier was the man to do the sorting. The goal that swung the match Chelsea's way may not have been the finest of his career, but it was one of the most important. Extra time was only two minutes old when his header hit the post, only for the ball to rebound away from the goal until, after 107 minutes of pulsating football, substitute Glen Johnson's throw passed over the head of John Terry and fell right at the feet of Didier at the near post. Quickly, and economically, he turned it home. Victory was in sight. The goal may not have been spectacular, but the celebration was. In his rampant joy Didier ripped off his shirt to show his happiness – and earned himself a yellow card for his troubles.

Moments later, Dudek pushed out a free kick that fell to Gudjohnsen on the touchline to the right of the Liverpool goal. He sent the ball in to the near post and Kezman forced the ball just inches over Dudek's line from close range for the third. Surely nothing could go wrong now, could it? But yes, it could, as Nunez forced home the ball for Liverpool with just seven minutes of extra time remaining. Extra time also saw an example of the wit and wisdom of football fans when Gerrard took a corner to a standing ovation and cries of 'There's only one Steven Gerrard' from Chelsea fans delighted by his own goal.

When the final whistle went, it meant that after years of endeavour and criticism Didier had, at last, won a medal. And his thoughts turned to the man who had made it possible, José Mourinho. The coach, having been 'banished' from action, watched the rest of the game from the Sky TV room, but Didier wasn't going to allow him to miss out on the celebrations and hauled him onto the pitch. In the ecstasy of victory he had time to explain why: 'I had to do this for my teammates. I told him that we win together, we lose together and we celebrate together. It was me who went back for him but it could have been any of us. That is the spirit of this team. I always score against Liverpool. I scored in both UEFA Cup games with Marseilles last season. My goal at Anfield was a beauty but this one was more important.

When I saw it cross the line from a yard out, I felt such happiness.'

And, as if he needed to, he expanded on why the goal, and subsequent victory, meant so much to him, coming as it did in the wake of the Barcelona fiasco. 'I had to score in this match. I knew I had let my teammates down in Barcelona by being sent off and I had to make up for that. I know I will not be there for the second match but I am confident the team will win through without me. If I had played one or two more matches before Barcelona then I am sure I would have been quicker and would not have been sent off. I let the team down in Barcelona.

'But this is football and, if I knew before the game I was going to get a red card, I would not have done it. This trophy is very important for us, though. We have not been down in many matches this season and won. This will give us great confidence now to go on in both the Champions League and the Premiership.'

The exultation of the moment even led him to say exactly where he thought the fate of the Premiership lay: 'We are already the champions. We have already won the title, everybody knows we're the best. OK, United play well and Arsenal, of course. But we are the best team and good enough to win lots of trophies, that is our aim.'

As Mourinho reacted with predictable anger to his touchline treatment, there was also a reminder that in football for every winner there is a loser.

Steven Gerrard was musing: 'It's very hard to take. Chelsea deserved the win and we've got to pick ourselves up. We scored early on – maybe a bit too early – but we were happy with the goal and tried to see the clock out. But then they got a lovely own goal by myself. It's very painful. Losing any game is painful, but especially cup finals and an own goal. It's a bad day for me.'

## CHAPTER 17

# The Referee and the Death Threats

If there is one person who is famous for being riled if he thinks his team is coming under attack then it is Manchester United's Sir Alex Ferguson. It was predictable, therefore, that he would be quick to respond to Didier's assertion that the title was as good as in Chelsea's pocket.

'Their players are saying they've won the title already, which is quite bullish with ten games to go,' he said. 'I'm wondering why Drogba is saying these things with ten games still to go. Maybe they're trying to convince themselves. Whether it can unship them, who's to say? But I do think football can be a cruel game and these things can backfire on you.'

José Mourinho's response was simple: 'This is not a lack of respect for Manchester United and Arsenal, or for the teams we still have to play against. It's just how we feel.'

If Didier was to celebrate in style it wasn't to be in that weekend's match. Although he started, he failed to score in a fairly routine 3–1 win at relegation-threatened Norwich and was replaced by Kezman midway through the second half. There were only two days' rest between the trip to Norfolk and the return leg of the Barcelona tie, but, as had been the case in Spain, there was plenty going on before the match even started.

Chelsea upped the stakes by complaining to UEFA about Barcelona boss Frank Rijkaard's half-time contact with referee Anders Frisk, and then Mourinho added to the simmering row by hinting that Frisk might have favoured Barcelona in that ill-humoured first leg. Discussing who would be a good choice to referee the second leg of the tie, he said, 'If you asked me who I would want for this game I would say Anders Frisk. Maybe he would help us the same way he helped them [Barcelona].' He can have had little cause for complaint with the man who was to officiate, Italian Pierluigi Collina, admitting, 'Every manager and player would say Collina is the best in the world and that is because he's the type of referee who doesn't have any influences from the outside.'

Such an astonishing battle of words would make most observers feel that the game itself must be an anti-climax. But for once this wasn't the case. In fact, it was one of the most memorable, nerve-racking, downright glorious soccer nights seen in England for years. Minus the suspended Didier and the injured Arjen Robben, Chelsea, 'boring' in the eyes of their Nou Camp detractors, began with an intensity and belief in their own capabilities that would be impossible to exaggerate. In eleven pulsating minutes early in the first half they breached the defensive wall of Barcelona on no fewer than three occasions.

First, Frank Lampard took advantage of the Catalans' square back line and sent Kezman clear down the right. The striker beat Giovanni van Bronckhorst and passed to Eidur Gudjohnsen, who rounded Juliano Belletti and scored. Lampard then volleyed a John Terry header wide before adding the second with the game barely seventeen minutes old. This time Joe Cole was the playmaker, gliding down the right, again cutting past Giovanni van

## THE REFEREE AND THE DEATH THREATS

Bronckhorst and managing to shoot only for Victor Valdes to half-stop his effort. But Lampard was there to put the rebound in the back of the net and Stamford Bridge went wild again. A mere two minutes later and goal number three arrived when Joe Cole prodded a pass to Damien Duff, who ran clear and rifled the ball under Victor Valdes. What could Barcelona do to get back into the game? Give the ball to Ronaldinho, that's what.

The slender Brazilian with his ponytail and toothy grin began to display every trick in his vast repertoire After twenty-three minutes he sent a header just wide, and soon afterwards Samuel Eto'o had a shot brushed over by Čech. But, after just twenty-six minutes, Paulo Ferreira misjudged a Belletti cross and it hit him on the hand. Referee Collina gave the penalty and, although Čech did well even to get close to the ball, Ronaldinho's shot beat him. And, with a certain inevitability, the game's traffic was now in the other direction.

Ronaldinho's second goal on thirty-eight minutes was the completion of a move that had begun on the edge of Barcelona's own area. When it reached him, however, he was practically stationary by the time he had the ball under control. Ricardo Carvalho was facing him so closely that Ronaldinho must have felt his breath. Then came a moment of brilliance. With hardly a movement of his body, no momentum and practically no backlift, he came up with what can best be described as a toe poke. But it was a toe poke of sublime skill, deliberately done and with the knowledge that it was the only option available that might threaten the Chelsea goal. Threaten it did: Carvalho turned round to watch the ball, as did the stranded Čech, as it powered into the net. A goal to remember from probably the only footballer in the world capable of conceiving it in the midst of such a full-throttle match. Thirty-eight minutes gone, five goals scored, a night of European magic to compare with any in the history of the competition.

What it meant, of course, was that Barcelona were now ahead

on the away-goals rule and the advantage of Chelsea's miraculous start had evaporated. When Joe Cole struck a post and Gudjohnsen wasn't able to steer the rebound home, there were those with faint hearts who thought Chelsea might now be a busted flush. But an inspired performance from Petr Čech in the second half kept the score as it was until the seventy-sixth minute when a Damien Duff corner arrived in the crowded Barcelona penalty area. Carvalho and goalkeeper Valdes connected with each other and John Terry headed home a famous goal. The Chelsea fans in the 41,515 crowd screamed with delight; the Barcelona players yelled with frustration, saying Carvalho had impeded their goalkeeper. Referee Collina was having none of it. As the final whistle sounded, one report was already describing it as 'football of the gods'. Newspapers and television and radio reports were saying it was a game to be rated among the finest ever played and even that most neutral of observers in the media, the *Scotsman* newspaper, was prompted to ask the question, 'Was this the best club game ever?'

And, of course, there was post-match mayhem to add to the cocktail on a night to live on in the memory. Scuffles broke out in the tunnel, Eto'o said he was called 'a monkey' by a Chelsea steward – a claim the club vehemently denied – and Rijkaard reacted angrily when he was blown kisses by one of the Chelsea backroom staff. Eto'o didn't just complain about the alleged insult, he went further saying, 'We were the only team that wanted to play football. Chelsea going through is a disaster for football, and, if this team wins the Champions League, it would make you want to retire. With so much money and so many players, what they do is not football. Mourinho is shameless.'

Rijkaard continued, 'Feelings were running high and some man – I don't know who he is – came over and kind of insulted our bench. I am a little bit more bitter than normal because this was a great opportunity to make a statement after some of the lies Chelsea told before this game.'

## THE REFEREE AND THE DEATH THREATS

At least Frank Lampard's remarks had more maturity about them when he said, 'A lot was said from the Spanish side before the game, but I think that we showed a lot of people around Europe that we have great character and ability. All the talk from Barcelona between matches was a bit strong because it was only half-time. But maybe it gave us that extra edge, which is why we started so well. Our performance shows that we're a top team, but it'll mean nothing if we don't get through to the final.'

Mourinho was busy on the pitch embracing his players and he even had time to blow kisses to the Barcelona fans – who replied by throwing plastic bottles at him.

As if the forthcoming UEFA investigation into the events surrounding the two games were not enough to cope with, there was another, even greater, drama to come from the tie.

That weekend Swedish national news agency TT flashed out a brief item that was to reverberate round world football. 'Anders Frisk has decided to retire immediately from refereeing following a number of threats aimed at him and his family. "I don't want to go into the details, Anders will have to talk about that. But the threats have been serious enough," said Bo Karlsson, chairman of Sweden's football referees' association. "We have spoken and I can confirm that he is quitting."'

The sensational truth was that Frisk, one of the top referees in the world, felt he couldn't go on, given the threats he and his family had received since Didier's sending-off and the criticism from Mourinho. He said the threats from Chelsea fans – coming by phone, email and regular mail – had escalated in the past week. 'I've had enough,' Frisk told the Swedish newspaper *Expressen*. 'I don't know if I even dare let my kids go to the post office. Then it's gone too far. These past sixteen days have been the worst in my life as a soccer referee.'

The forty-two-year-old Swede said he informed UEFA about his decision on the Friday of that week. He declined to describe the threats, but said most had come from England. Some were directed to other members of his family, he said. 'It's made me think a lot about what's important in life. You shouldn't have to be subjected to this, shouldn't have to be afraid to make a decision on the field.'

Frisk had been one of FIFA's top-ranked referees for a decade, and has taken charge of 118 international matches, including the European Championship final in 2000 between France and Italy. It wasn't the first time he had been in the eye of the tiger: in September he was hit in the head by an object thrown by a fan during half-time of the Champions League match between AS Roma and Dynamo Kiev in Rome. Frisk was taken to the hospital with a bleeding forehead, and the game was stopped. Dynamo were later awarded a 3–0 forfeit victory, and Roma had to play its next two Champions League matches before an empty stadium. In Sweden, he was once attacked by a hooligan during a 1995 league match. The fan ran onto the field and tackled Frisk, but he was not seriously hurt.

Frisk's decision to retire caused strong reactions from the Swedish Football Association. He told another national newspaper, *Aftonbladet*, that he received a threatening phone call as recently as that Friday. But he stood by the decisions he made at Nou Camp. 'I still claim that what I did in Barcelona was correct, but I could never in my wildest imagination understand what it would lead to. It's really sad, because I really love to referee.'

In a statement, Chelsea quickly promised to take action if it was proved that any of their supporters had made threats against Frisk.

We would like to make it absolutely clear that both the club as a whole, and our manager and first-team coach José Mourinho, condemn any threats made to Mr Frisk, his family or friends which may have, in any way, influenced his decision to retire as a referee.

If there is any evidence of such behaviour by Chelsea fans

then we would totally disassociate ourselves from them and we would welcome any such evidence to be passed to us so we can investigate and take the appropriate action.

Frisk was to reveal that the calls started on the evening after he arrived home from Barcelona. They were too numerous to count and they came on his mobile, his work number and his 'secure' home number. The calls were quickly followed by emails, faxes and letters. But they continued and turned into threats as anonymous callers, not all with London accents, got through on the phone to his children and claimed they knew what each person in the house was doing in every room.

'I've never had a problem with fanatical crowds, never been afraid to make a decision on any pitch, but this was the worst sixteen days of my life,' said Frisk. He disconnected his phone and, after the retirement announcement, the messages stopped coming. 'In the light of what's happened to me in the past three weeks, I can't go out there and be absolutely certain that I will not be caught out during a match thinking of the consequences of a decision. I can't afford to think like that. It's not about corruption, or about accusations or any outside influence. It is for a referee to make the decision on what he sees, with no thought that maybe that will have this effect or that effect.'

Frisk said that until the grotesque events at the Nou Camp he hardly knew José Mourinho. 'I don't study football outside of matches I'm involved in. I tried not to bring prejudices or preconceived impressions of players or managers into my duties. In the case of Drogba, I gave him a yellow card and at least one warning. I sometimes am surprised a coach does not take responsibility to take off a player who persistently invites a card.'

Didier later tried to calm things down when he said on the *Telefoot* programme on the French channel TF1 that he hoped his dismissal was not the catalyst for Frisk's decision to quit. 'I offer my apologies to Mr Frisk if his decision is a consequence of my sending-off. I hope he reconsiders his decision because we need high-quality referees.'

Even Chelsea's return to the comparatively mundane task of winning three points at home to lowly West Bromwich Albion was overshadowed by the row as it rumbled on. FIFA president Sepp Blatter blasted the Chelsea boss, saying, 'These verbal attacks on referees make me sick. We should remember the one who is attacking referees is also attacking the football environment he is living in. It is this kind of behaviour that leads to problems among supporters and I would strongly recommend all parties show respect for the referees and think about fair play.' UEFA referees' chief Volker Roth dubbed Mourinho 'an enemy of football'. There was even talk of referees across Europe going on strike.

So the change of tempo from Barcelona to the Baggies must have been a welcome change of pace for Chelsea. It certainly was for Didier, who scored the only goal of the game in the twenty-sixth minute, rounding off a superb move when Frank Lampard found Damien Duff down the left and, after making ground, he centred for Didier to score left-footed from close range. The delighted Chelsea players ran to celebrate with Mourinho in a public display of bonding with the manager. One report of the game said that, if he had been on form, Didier could easily have scored 'two hat-tricks' and he was guilty of some appalling – and very uncharacteristic – misses.

His performance prompted Chelsea goalscoring legend Jimmy Greaves – who scored a remarkable 132 goals in 169 games for the club – to say, 'I actually have a lot of time for Drogba. He has all the makings of a great striker bar one – he can't finish! He's quick, strong, good in the air, gets in all the right positions, takes on the responsibility of leading the line and causes problems with his movement and awareness. But he will never be a thirty-goals-a-season player.' And, in case anyone hadn't got the gist of what Greavsie was saying, he put it in fairly explicit terms: 'He couldn't hit a cow's backside with a banjo.'

# THE REFEREE AND THE DEATH THREATS

Perhaps Greaves' verdict was crude and exaggerated, but Didier, too, was aware that there was room for improvement: 'I'm not happy with myself. I've scored nine goals in twenty-one Premiership matches and three in the Champions League. I know I could have done better. When I arrived, I had to put up with the transfer fee and the expectations that go with it. I also had to adapt to a new environment. It was a little heavy to bear and, just when I was starting to digest it all, I got a hamstring injury. I was scoring regularly at the time. We are a united squad – no one plays for himself. The objective is to win trophies for Chelsea.

'Marseilles depended a lot on me. Here, I am no longer the main attacking option. There are other players who can open the match up. But it doesn't mean I have less pressure. I am not forgetting I have signed for the long term here and, for the moment, we are fulfilling our task well.'

While Didier's recent form was somewhat unsure, there was nothing uncertain about how convinced the bookies were on Chelsea's winning the Premiership, quoting them at odds of 40–1 on to take the title. Their record shows why: by the middle of March they had dropped only thirteen points from five drawn games and one defeat, and the fewest points dropped in a full Premiership season was twenty-three by Manchester United in 2000–1, when they won the title with ninety-one points. Chelsea had conceded just nine goals, while the Premiership's most miserly defending in a season was by Arsenal in 1998–9, when they let in seventeen. So far the defence had managed thirty clean sheets in forty-six league and cup matches and, with twenty-two clean league sheets The Blues were one away from equalling the record for a twenty-club Premiership, the Arsenal total of twenty-three six years earlier.

Next came a straightforward 4–1 victory over Crystal Palace at Stamford Bridge. Although Didier failed to score, at least he had some positive news when his website was launched in March 2005. The site meant that the vast army of fans he still had in France, not to mention practically the entire 20-odd-million population of the Ivory Coast, could follow his exploits in full, complete with his own diary of events. But it coincided with a far less pleasant event, as UEFA charged José Mourinho with bringing the game into disrepute over the Barcelona affair. The European governing body stopped just short of accusing Chelsea officials of lying, but said Mourinho had created a 'poisoned and negative' atmosphere at the match. UEFA also opened proceedings against the club itself, assistant manager Steve Clarke and security official Les Miles on the same charges.

There was even the possibility – albeit a very remote one – that Chelsea could be kicked out of the competition before taking on their next opponents, Germany's Bayern Munich, but Mourinho and the others certainly faced match bans or fines.

Mourinho didn't take long to say that he expected UEFA's charges that his team lied about the tunnel incident to be dismissed.

'Obviously, I as well as other people involved, mainly the club, which is much more important than we are, have the expectation of complete dismissal,' the coach told Portugal's SIC television. 'My job is to train, to evaluate, to try to get the best results possible. I have always been this way. Sincerely, I don't want to change and I want to finish up my career twelve, thirteen years from now at most, I want to finish it up this way. That is, to be loved by my own. And right now I am loved by the Chelsea fans and I don't worry hardly at all about other clubs' supporters. That's the way I am.'

Not that Mourinho needed anyone to defend him, but Didier was still prepared to do so.

'People are just trying to make a big villain out of him but he is not a villain,' he said. He was convinced that the riches and success of Chelsea had created a horde of enemies for them to battle and that they were targeting Mourinho because they were envious and didn't like a man who said what he thought.

## THE REFEREE AND THE DEATH THREATS

'People have to admit Mourinho is a top coach. Under him Chelsea are now one of the best teams in Europe. We have a special team spirit here. When someone attacks someone in our group, it is like they are attacking every player. So we will stay close and we will stay strong. I have a very close relationship with the coach. He was the man who brought me here and I really want to show that.'

When the Frisk affair reached its conclusion, the general feeling was that Chelsea escaped fairly lightly – it certainly could have been a lot worse. Mourinho received a two-match ban but the club successfully convinced the UEFA disciplinary panel that Steve Clarke and Les Miles did not deliberately lie about seeing Barcelona coach Frank Rijkaard entering the official's dressing room at half-time in the Nou Camp, but were involved in a misunderstanding. Mourinho's ban was to apply to both legs of the quarter-final against Bayern Munich and he was also fined £9,000. The coach was not to be allowed in the dressing room, tunnel or technical area but could watch the Bayern games from the stand. It emerged that Clarke and Miles saw Rijkaard using an alternative route to his dressing room, which left from the same reception area as the corridor to the referee's room, and they formed the wrong conclusions. The pair were reprimanded and the club fined £33,000.

What a month! And Didier had played – although he in no way had wanted to – a major part in one of the season's most sensational matches with its wide-reaching repercussions. That wasn't all for that March, though, for Didier had also been busy enhancing his heroic status in the Ivory Coast.

# CHAPTER 18

# A Nation's Hero

Didier Drogba is admired in Europe for his rampaging performances in the shirts of first Marseilles and then Chelsea. But that fame is totally eclipsed by the adoration he inspires in the population of the Ivory Coast. By the time he flew to Abidjan at the end of March 2005, civil war had been tearing the country apart for three years and, on top of the military and financial plight the country was in, AIDS was becoming endemic, with at least seven per cent of the population suffering from related illnesses. The life expectancy for men was below fifty. It is at times like these, with existence so hard, that people seek heroes to lift them above their daily torment, and in Didier they had found one. The country's blossoming football talents and the generation of fine players representing the Elephants gave Ivorians a reason to be proud, and none made them walk taller than him.

World soccer experts had for some years recognised the growing influence on African nations in the global power game and many of the top clubs in Europe had Africans in their side, but no national team had yet established itself as a major force. Cameroon were probably the nearest to that category, and they were in the same tough group, Group 3, fighting to get to Germany the next summer as were Didier and his compatriots.

The teams had already met once and in the game at Yaoundé in Cameroon two goals in the final ten minutes from Barcelona's Samuel Eto'o and then Guy Feutchine had been a body blow to the Ivorians. True, they had beaten the other four teams in the group – Libya, Egypt, Benin and Sudan – whereas Cameroon were dropping points in these games, but the loss to Cameroon was a significant one. Didier knew that, as the nations prepared for the second 'leg' of the group ties, there was no room for complacency against little Benin – known as 'the Squirrels' – as only the top team in each group was to go to Germany.

He had spoken to fans shortly before the match, pointing out that his years in both the Ivory Coast and France meant he was 'part of two cultures' and when a few months earlier anti-French rioters spilled out onto the streets the scenes made him 'feel the country had gone back ten years'. The demarcation line between the north and south, and the various religious and tribal differences affected all the Ivorians, but Didier's views were simple: 'The national team is a reflection of what the Ivory Coast should be and what it was. I come from a certain ethnic background, Kolo Touré and Aruna Dindane from another. We don't try to avoid each other, far from it – there's no tension at all.

'We know the image we put out is important for Ivorian people, and it makes you happy that when you are playing for the national team, nobody will be out on the streets. Everybody is in front of the TV and, when you score, nobody is asking which ethnic group the goalscorer comes from.'

The Ivory Coast side were often compared to Holland, both for their attractive, attacking football and the bright orange shirts they wore, and in Didier and Aruna Dindane of Anderlecht – the pair sometimes were called 'Batman' and 'Robin' – they had two strikers of world quality. The squad for the Benin game contained only two players still employed in Africa, the rest travelling from France, Belgium, England, Italy and Ukraine. The Belgium connection was strongest because of a link with the club side Beveren there, a team the best young players from the Ivory Coast soccer academies invariably hoped to join. Those academies were set up during the early 1990s by former French international Jean-Marc Guillou, and he was part of a consortium who bought the then near-bankrupt Beveren and found himself with a ready-made soccer university for his academy pupils. On many occasions three-quarters of the Belgium club side were Ivorians.

The Ivory Coast national side had an experienced coach, too, in former French captain Henri Michel, who had taken France, Cameroon and Morocco to different World Cup finals and he was aware that a heavy price had been paid for failure in the past. After being knocked out early from the 2000 African Cup of Nations, his entire squad were detained in a military barracks for almost a week on orders of the government!

It was unlikely that Didier would suffer the same fate and no doubt it was pleasant for him to escape the Barcelona-Frisk row for a while and concentrate on the job in hand, and he did it so well that he was on the scoresheet twice as Benin were brushed aside 3–0 in front of a joyful 50,000 Abidjan crowd. Auxerre's Bonaventure Kalou opened the scoring and then Didier virtually wrapped the match up with a nineteenth-minute penalty before adding the last goal in the second half. The win put his side on top of the group with fifteen points from six games, four ahead of Cameroon – and Germany was beckoning.

After the excitement of the West African metropolis, next stop for Didier was the much less exotic fixture at Southampton, where he came on after an hour in a fairly routine 3–1 Chelsea victory. The next Chelsea game, however, was to be far less run-of-the-mill: they were at home to Bayern Munich in the first leg of the Champions League quarter-final. Yet again the Blues were faced with a club whose history was festooned with honours and soaked in tradition. One of their greatest sides had won the old European Cup for three consecutive years in the mid 1970s and in 2001 they had triumphed in the Champions League after a penalty shootout against Valencia.

One of the common denominators in all those victories was Franz Beckenbauer, their famed defender and World Cup-winning captain. 'Kaiser Franz' played in the all-conquering team of thirty years earlier and was club president as Chelsea ran out onto the Stamford Bridge pitch to take on the Germans. The visiting side were awash with internationals: Owen Hargreaves the England midfielder, the great World Cup-winning French defender Bixente Lizarazu and Michael Ballack, the tall, aristocratic German international. Probably their most famous player, however, was, somewhat unusually, their goalkeeper, the ferocious Oliver Kahn, the type of formidable keeper who terrified attackers and attracted equal amounts of respect or loathing from fans. He had been voted best goalkeeper in the world on several occasions and, after virtually single-handedly guiding a not particularly impressive German national side to the 2002 World Cup final against Brazil, was officially voted the Player of the Tournament. With such quality, especially in defence, everything pointed to a tight, low-scoring tie. So, of course, football being football, the goals and the excitement flowed again.

José Mourinho's banishment from the touchline didn't seem to have any adverse effect on his side. The game was only three minutes old when a long ball from John Terry was badly dealt with by Robert Kovac and dropped at the feet of Damien Duff. He laid the ball off to Joe Cole, whose twenty-yard shot was deflected off Lúcio's heel into the net. A header from Terry was pushed over the bar and he soon clashed with Kahn, sparking protests from half the German side. Early in the second half, Didier and Gudjohnsen combined to put Duff in, but Kahn managed to take the pace off the shot.

## A NATION'S HERO

Chelsea were soon regretting the lost opportunity as a Ballack free kick bounced off the wall and, as Chelsea failed to clear, Petr Čech pushed the resulting volley to German international Bastian Schweinsteiger, who levelled the score. Chelsea's resilience was there for all to see, however, as Lampard – who had a superb game even by his own high standards – restored the Blues' lead eight minutes later after Didier set him up with a header and then scored again from close range soon afterwards, both with his left foot.

Didier was a constant thorn in the side of the Bayern defence, especially in the air, and it was time for him to get in on the goalscoring act when, with just nine minutes remaining, he was the man on the spot to stab the ball home from close range after Gudjohnsen's shot was blocked in a goalmouth scramble after a corner.

It seemed inevitable, however, this being Chelsea, that there would be a sting in the tail of the match, and it came in the shape of a fairly tame-looking tackle on Michael Ballack in the home penalty area in stoppage time that saw the German hit the deck. To howls of protest from the Chelsea players and supporters alike, a penalty was given, which Ballack himself converted to Čech's left, making the forthcoming trip to Munich a lot less enticing a prospect.

Owen Hargreaves couldn't resist what was becoming an after-match habit from Chelsea's defeated opponents, a moan about their style of play: 'The passes from them were just long balls. They were simply banging them forward and flicking them on, and Didier Drogba caused us problems with his size and his jumping ability. Up until 1–1, I thought we were very much in control of the tempo and the outcome of the game. But they just really hurt us with the long ball.

'Arsenal and Chelsea are two different clubs, exactly the opposite. When you look at Arsenal they were two goals down against us but they were trying to pass it through the middle.

Chelsea reminded me of Celtic. We played them a couple of years ago and they had John Hartson and Chris Sutton upfront, and Henrik Larsson running on to the second ball. It's tough to defend because the ball can go anywhere.'

He wasn't the only one upset, however, as John Terry was still fuming about the late penalty, and he accused Dutch referee René Temmink of making a 'terrible decision'.

'I've seen it seven times on the TV since and it definitely wasn't a penalty,' he said. 'We worked our socks off to get the 4–1 lead and it's disappointing that we conceded that late goal because of a terrible decision from the referee. He wasn't listening all night.'

With all that venom coming from both sides, at least Didier, who had led the Chelsea line superbly in a vintage display, was more sanguine about the match, and his season so far, when he spoke to reporters a few days later before the home match against Birmingham City, which was sandwiched between the Bayern matches.

'I don't get too carried away now because a few years ago I was in the French second division on the bench at Le Mans,' he said. 'It helps me to realise how fast life can change. Life can turn you up and down and for me the pressure was in the second division because I wanted to play in the first division. That was real pressure. I had to change a lot of things in my life. I was young and learning how to be a professional. I have made a lot of mistakes, but when you make them you learn more.

'I learned how I had to prepare mentally to be a top professional because I wasn't being very good. I was playing well one game and the game after I was terrible. It was not the way you should be if you want to be strong in your career. The fee has not put me under pressure. Everything I'm doing is what I have done last year. When you play for a club like Marseilles, you can play anywhere you want without pressure.

'I'm not at 100 per cent and haven't been all season. It has been frustrating because every time I was near to my real top level I had an injury so I had to rebuild everything. I have been more like seventy per cent but I still give my all. The Premiership is very physical and it has not been easy to adapt. I have had a lot of injuries so I am happy to have scored fourteen goals. I hope there is a lot more to come from me because the fans haven't seen the best of me yet. Maybe I felt the contact more this year because my body was tired. Last year I only had one week's holiday because of international games. Next June we have two more international games but I am a professional and I have to adapt. No matter where I go, nobody can tell me to stop playing for my country.'

If Didier was hoping for a rest that weekend, he was to be disappointed. Mourinho decided to rest four of the men from the Bayern match: Didier, Ricardo Carvalho, Claude Makelele and Eidur Gudjohnsen. Unfortunately Birmingham hadn't read the script and for more than an hour they kept the 42,000 crowd strangely subdued, not with any particular threat but simply the manner in which they were stifling the home side. So Didier had been sent on at half-time but he could only watch in the sixty-fifth minute when the Uruguayan Walter Pandiani put Birmingham ahead. Didier had already sent over the bar a header he would normally put on target when, with just eight minutes left, Terry and Lampard combined and, on the edge of the six-yard box, Didier did the rest.

Mourinho, complete with his 'lucky' grey overcoat, was back on the touchline, but it had been a poor performance, certainly by the standards they had set both at home and in Europe that season. Nevertheless in April 2005, Chelsea were favourites to progress into the semi-finals of the Champions League as they prepared for their Tuesday trip to Munich, and Didier said as they headed for the plane, 'When United held us to a 0–0 draw in the first leg of the Carling semi, we had to travel to Old Trafford and pull out a brilliant performance of character and bravery. We won 2–1 and shocked them and that is the attitude we will need in Munich. We put four past Bayern last week but the thing about football is that, who knows, we might concede three here if our attitude is not right. Let's face it, I don't expect that to happen – but we need to go out against Bayern and do what we do best. We can defend, play solidly and show we are flying high with confidence.' As proud of his country of birth as ever, he couldn't resist one final observation: 'The only team in the world which could stop us right now is the Ivory Coast!'

One man who was determined to stop Didier, one way or another, was Bayern's Croatian defender Robert Kovac. He was adamant that his defence wouldn't leak goals as it had done a week earlier and after only eight minutes a wince-producing tackle flattened Didier and meant he needed lengthy treatment to his knee. It would have put lesser men off, but Didier, who missed one chance after just two minutes, refused to be bullied and eventually won his duel with the uncompromising Kovac.

After thirty minutes the 59,000 crowd at the Olympic Stadium were silenced when Joe Cole received the ball from William Gallas and gave Lampard the room to drill it into the net – the shot again coming off Lúcio's outstretched foot. Although there was a full hour left, the Germans knew their chances of winning were slim. To their credit Bayern never gave up and when Čech pushed Ballack's header against a post it rolled along the line for Claudio Pizarro to tap in the equaliser. A desperate Bayern still pressed and Lizarazu's cross took a deflection off Huth to bounce off the bar before Michael Ballack's goal-bound header was hacked off the line by Eidur Gudjohnsen.

If the Germans had any optimistic vision of getting back in the tie, Didier was to end it for them in the eightieth minute. Joe Cole chased a ball that seemed to be going out of play and sent in a cross with which Didier proved his mastery over Kovac by soaring above him to head the ball home for a stunning goal. In a season blighted by injury and in which he had to come to terms not just with new teammates but a new country's way of football, it was his sixteenth goal, a fine achievement. Even

Mourinho, watching the game in his hotel room rather than at the ground, let out a cry of joy.

Many of the Munich fans had left the stadium by the time Guerrero managed to converted Schweinsteiger's right-wing centre from six yards on the ninetieth minute, and five minutes into injury time Scholl forced the ball home after a surge from Ballack, but it was too little and much too late.

Praise from teammates is welcome, but to be flattered by your opponents is, in its way, even more rewarding. Bayern's French international Willy Sagnol, rated as one of the best full-backs in the world, summed it up best when he said, 'Didier Drogba was the difference between the two teams. He is so good in the air, so strong, and so good at holding onto the ball that he kept buying them time and giving them options. He's the sort of player who gives the team confidence.'

Didier said of his header, 'I saw where Joe was, and knew he was going to cross and that, realistically, he was only going to get as far as the near post. So I made a beeline for that area and I'm really happy with the goal. It was great work from Joe and it turned out to be the decisive strike. It's the sort of goal I used to score at Guingamp, so I was overjoyed. The Bayern game was tough. We knew they would push us back, come at us, and they did. But we withstood the storm.'

After such a draining clash it was no surprise really that the strain was showing a week later when Chelsea were hosts to the previous year's champions, Arsenal. The Gunners were without Thierry Henry for the clash, which was good news for Chelsea as the Arsenal striker was the country's leading goalscorer at the time with thirty to his credit, almost twice as many as Didier. But there was no envy in Didier's words when he spoke in high praise of the French international and revealed his own son Isaac was an Henry fan!

'For a long time I studied the way Thierry Henry played and I tried to imitate him, but he always seemed to me to be on another planet compared to my game. I've always believed players who are better than me should be a source of inspiration, not embarrassment. My dream is to copy Thierry's speciality of beating a player for pace, then curling his shot along the ground and past the keeper.

'So far I've never quite managed to get my imitation just right. Now I hope, for my sake and Isaac's, I'm getting closer to being as brilliant as Thierry. In my opinion the perfect striker, if you could build him from different components, would have the right foot of Zinédine Zidane for its finesse, the power of Roberto Carlos' left foot, the intelligence of Ronaldo but the speed and finishing power of Thierry Henry.

'One of the first times we played against each other was back in November 2003, when my side, Marseilles, were playing against the side which won the 1998 World Cup for France. My son Isaac asked for Thierry Henry's shirt to put in his fantastic collection of football jerseys, not mine!'

Whether or not Didier hoped to put on an Henry-like performance against Arsenal, it was not to be, as even he seemed less than 100 per cent and missed several chances that came his way as the two best sides in the Premiership battled it our for a goalless draw. Nevertheless, it meant that Chelsea were still eleven points clear of their rivals from north London and even Arsenal boss Arsène Wenger conceded, 'We knew before we came here that Chelsea would be champions and they are worthy champions because they have been remarkably consistent. That is the most difficult thing in a team sport and we have to respect that. They will win the league unless someone puts a bomb here. It would take a huge accident for them not to be champions. You always congratulate the winners. On the pitch they've done a fantastic job and deserve to be congratulated.'

They were congratulated soon afterwards when, after beating Fulham 3–1 at home on 23 April 2005, the players did a lap of honour at Stamford Bridge to the delight of the fans. It was still mathematically possible that Chelsea wouldn't win the championship, but after the three points earned with the victory over their near neighbours it was a racing certainty that the title would almost certainly be theirs, seven days later if they got a good result at Bolton Wanderers.

In the interim, however, there was the little matter of a match against Didier's old foes Liverpool in the Champions League to be taken care of and he was in a buoyant mood: 'When I played against them for Marseilles last season I scored in both games. I got an important equaliser in Liverpool and then scored the winner at the Stade Vélodrome. That was the best night of my career so far, to beat a team like that. Anfield is one of the best stadiums I've been in and Liverpool are a team who have great and bad memories for me.

'This season I've had very different experiences against Liverpool – both extremes. When we played them at Stamford Bridge early in the season I suffered a bad groin injury and it had an effect on the rest of the season. I was only fit enough to be on the bench at Anfield on New Year's Day. But then there was the Carling Cup Final, when I scored the goal which was so important for us. It seems every time I'm fit enough to play the whole game against Liverpool I score. I want to keep that up.'

Disappointingly, it wasn't to be the case this time. Didier began the game with Gudjohnsen playing in what was now his customary role behind him, but, importantly, neither Robben nor Duff was in the starting line-up. When the high balls that fed Didier in previous rounds and caused Bayern Munich such problems began to arrive, Chelsea found that on the night Jamie Carragher and Sami Hyypia dealt with them with a great deal more ease than the German defence had. Still, Chelsea didn't concede a goal, although the 0–0 final scoreline meant the second leg at Anfield was going to be fraught with problems.

There were far fewer problems on the Saturday, as 30 April 2005 became a historic date in the Chelsea calendar: the day they won only the second league title in the club's history, a full fifty years after their first triumph and a 100 years after the club was first formed. Four thousand or more Chelsea fans had made the journey to Bolton Wanderers' 28,000-capacity Reebok Stadium to mark the day the title came to west London. It needed that rarity, a half-time dressing down from José Mourinho, to give the Blues the impetus they needed, however. After a blank first half he suggested to his array of stars that the side might perform with more energy if he and Steve Clarke donned shirt and shorts, and went out instead of some of them! It worked, and two Frank Lampard goals meant the title was theirs.

Didier and the rest of the squad went wild with delight. Mourinho and Roman Abramovich joined them for public celebrations as the champagne was, briefly, showered everywhere. Unconventional as always, Mourinho declined to give after-match interviews, leaving his players to enjoy the glory, and when he discovered that it would be an hour before the team coach left he decided to go there and then in a local taxi to the team's Preston Marriott hotel and start planning for the second leg of the Champions League match at Anfield in seventy-two hours' time.

It didn't stop Didier celebrating, though, as he and Joe Cole climbed through the open roof of their team coach and enjoyed the moment on the top of the coach with their adoring fans. The players were, understandably, under orders to be careful in their after-match celebrations that evening, given that the Liverpool game was near, but their caution was not rewarded.

Although Liverpool had failed to beat Chelsea on the four occasions they had met that season, the game was the one with which they would break their duck – and it took only four minutes. Urged on by their famed supporters in an almost deafening atmosphere, Liverpool's John Arne Riise surged forward and played the ball in to Steven Gerrard, who moved it into the path of Milan Baroš, who cleverly lobbed the ball over his compatriot Petr Čech. The goalkeeper connected with the striker in what appeared to many to be a penalty, but the Slovakian referee L'uboš Michel' did not allow it and García followed up, and, as his touch forward reached the line, William Gallas rushed across to clear. The linesman, though, signalled the ball was over the line and although countless television replays failed to come up with a conclusive answer, the important thing was that the goal stood, although many complained that since there was doubt, it should not have been allowed.

No matter what Chelsea did to get back in the tie, and they took greater control the longer the match continued, they could not break down the Liverpool defence, even though five minutes into injury time Eidur Gudjohnsen volleyed beyond an open goal and seconds later it was all over. In the dressing room afterwards, some of the heartbroken Chelsea players couldn't stop the tears from flowing. Perhaps Chelsea should have been aware that Liverpool had triumphed in the last four European semi-finals they had reached, and indeed that same year were to go on to a famous penalty victory over AC Milan after being three goals down at half-time.

## CHAPTER 19

# Homesick in the Rain

The 2004–5 Premiership season ended with no more goals for Didier, victories for Chelsea over Manchester United and Charlton and a draw at Newcastle. The Charlton game at Stamford Bridge was won in injury time, when Claude Makelele followed up his own penalty to score the only goal of the match. However, it was memorable mainly for the blue-and-white carnival atmosphere afterwards, when the championship trophy was carried out onto the pitch by survivors from the Chelsea team of fifty years earlier and presented in front of the sell-out crowd, as all the players and backroom staff paraded around the field.

At last Didier could claim some trophies to show for the trials and tribulations of his career: a Carling Cup winners' medal and, more importantly, he had been part of a side who had won – by a massive twelve points – the Premiership title, a league generally reckoned to be the toughest in the world. Yet to say the season had been an unqualified success would be wrong. Of course he had been hampered by injury, but there were murmurings of disquiet. Observers, both fans and the media, questioned whether he had justified that gigantic transfer fee he carried like an albatross around his neck, a fee that, as with all successful players, was decided by others, not him.

There was also a growing feeling that for such a powerful man he 'went to ground' too easily, an accusation that was to resurface several more times in his career. And there were constant reports suggesting that AC Milan's Ukrainian goal poacher Andriy Shevchenko was the man Roman Abramovich wanted to lead his attack and suggestions that, if that didn't come to pass, then the chequebook would be out for Juventus' French international striker David Trezeguet.

As honest as always, Didier felt compelled to admit, 'I am not satisfied with my first season. I should have done better, scoring more goals. At the beginning it was hard because I had to deal with the transfer fee, a new culture and a new way of life. Then I injured my groin in October. I feel homesick. Life in England is not easy. I had to get used to it but I did not, not completely, anyway. This is so different from what I knew. I was down for a while, even though I have experienced fantastic moments here and have won the first trophies of my career, but it is true that I have not always been happy.

'I know that I am not the first offensive option any more, like I was at Marseilles. There are lots of very good players here and everybody scores. But I am going to come back stronger next season. I will never forget where I came from. I do remind myself that a few years ago I was playing in the French second division, even in the non-league for Levallois.'

But he also felt that a lot of the criticism was aimed at both him and the club because of its wealth, because of the 'Abramovich factor'. 'The players have a great admiration for the manager because he is a big leader. And he has lots of respect for us, even lots of love. We are fighting together.'

More disturbingly he also revealed, when talking to the French sports daily newspaper *L'Équipe*, 'I'm feeling a bit homesick. Life in England is not easy. You have to adapt and I'm finding that difficult. It's so different. My morale has suffered from that. On the other hand there have been fantastic moments such as the title celebrations with Chelsea. That was unforgettable and that's what I came for. You have to admit that football in England is something really exceptional.'

Tellingly, he also confided that some of the side's tactics later in the year had not been to his liking, admitting, 'In the second part of the season, I was only getting long balls and I'd rather receive the ball right in my feet.'

But he was not, at that stage, anyway, seriously contemplating leaving Stamford Bridge: 'I will be with Chelsea next season unless they decide to kick me out. I know that the coach fully trusts me and he's shown that throughout this season. When I was not injured, I was a regular first-team member. Mourinho has always backed me up and he knows better than anyone what I brought to the team. He is grateful for that and he knows, like me, that I will be even better next season.'

And that old affection for Marseilles emerged as he added, 'Marseilles is in my heart. I said it when I left and I haven't changed my mind in a few months. Now I'm English champion and one day I want to be French champion, preferably with Marseilles, obviously. But I would return to Marseilles only if they had a team who could fight for the title. It's not the case today, with or without me.'

Didier was one of several Chelsea stars who were allowed to miss the end-of-season trip to South Korea, but it certainly didn't mean that he was allowed to rest. First, he needed treatment for a knee injury that had meant he missed the final moments of the league season, but, importantly, two massive international games in the qualifying stages of The World Cup were looming, which meant flying to Rome on 29 May 2005 with the Ivory Coast squad for preparation for the games, then spending the two weeks in between the matches in his home city, Abidjan. That, however, was no hardship.

'I'm really looking forward to it, as it will be a chance for me to prepare for the match in my home country. It's been ages since I've been able to spend such a long time in the Ivory Coast, and I hope I'll be able to make the most of it to see my friends and family who live over there,' he said before boarding the plane. Unfortunately both he and his fellow Ivorians had all left their shooting boots at home as the match against Libya in Tripoli petered out a goalless draw.

Next came a role in the tribute game for one of his heroes, a former World Player of the Year, the Liberian George Weah, at Didier's old stamping ground of the Vélodrome in Marseilles – his first game there since his transfer – alongside the likes of Zinédine Zidane and the man a lot of Chelsea fans were reading about at the time, Andriy Shevchenko. Like a schoolboy fan, Didier enthused about taking part in the game for 'Mr George', as he called him, who was to leave the football scene for the world of politics.

But there was no hint of an exhibition game about Didier's next match, a key World Cup clash again the Pharaohs of Egypt in Abidjan. Not that his popularity in the Ivory Coast needed to be improved, but the two goals he scored against the Egyptians in his side's 2–0 victory, taking his total so far in the qualifying rounds to seven, made him an even greater icon with the capacity crowd and the rest of the nation. An Aruna Dindane cross saw him open the scoring from close range and his second was more spectacular as his powerful shot proved too strong for the goalkeeper. The result meant the Ivorian Elephants had nineteen points and the Indomitable Lions of Cameroon seventeen, with their vital clash in Abidjan taking place on 4 September. If any proof was needed about his fame in the Ivory Coast it came when the brewers Bock Solibra named their newest beer 'Drogba'. It was promoted as 'the beer a strong man drinks' and was an immediate hit.

## HOMESICK IN THE RAIN

Beer aside, the result against Egypt must have cheered Didier, and a few days later an important interview was published in FIFA's official magazine in which he said, 'Over the last year I think I've played very well. That's why Chelsea were prepared to pay such a high sum for me. As long as I can keep up that level of performance there won't be any pressure on me at all. At the beginning of the season, I thought I was only realising about sixty per cent of my potential. But then it started to go well and it became a dream, winning the Premier League and reaching the semi-finals of the Champions League. Now I feel perfectly at home here.'

He also admitted he was 'blown away' by the celebrations over Chelsea's Premiership triumph. He said, 'I know what the title meant to the fans. We got a taster of what it would be like and what the reaction would be when we won the League Cup. But, really, when it actually happened it was over and above what I had expected.'

But – and it's important to remember that this was a young man whose life had been changed by an urge to be better educated – he also added, 'One of the things I like the most is the language. I have worked very hard at my English, so that I can communicate with my teammates, because that is really important. And I am very happy that it seems to be going so well. My children are also learning English, which will give them new perspectives for their own futures. For me, it's very important that my family are settled here. I can only be happy if they are. If not, then any success I have on the football field would be undermined. But things are going well.'

Didier had been named in a *Sunday Times'* 'Young Rich List' for his weekly earnings, estimated at between £60,000 and £80,000 at the time, and he used the platform of the prestigious newspaper to defend not only his salary, but those of other players, too.

'People have to know that our job is peculiar,' he said. 'We usually get our best contracts for a seven-year period at best.

After that, you leave football. Yes, we do get a lot of money but this is not just down to us. This is the economic situation of football. But people have to remember that a footballer is a man before he is a player; he gives everything he can give. We earn a lot but we give a lot as well.

'For me, it is not just about money. If my family is not happy and not in good health, there is not a lot to celebrate. Football is good, money is good – but health is the most important thing.'

To take his mind off the game, he had a down-to-earth recipe: 'Very simple – I stay with my three children and my family. That is the most important thing for me – nothing else matters. I do not spend a lot of time with them right now but I will give them everything in a few years. They understand the nature of my job and I try to be there for them whenever I can.'

It was turning into a summer of interviews for Didier as he prepared for the start of the 2005–6 season, and one of the most telling was to the *People* newspaper in Britain, where he talked candidly about his first year at Stamford Bridge and what lay ahead. And he revealed that Roman Abramovich had initially wanted the Brazilian striker Ronaldo to lead the goal charge instead of Didier.

'We'll see whether any other great striker will be ready to defend like a maniac for the good of the team like I did last season,' he said defiantly. 'I'll try thinking more about my next season, so that I don't finish fifteen goals behind Thierry Henry again. I did decide to sacrifice myself for the whole team last season while forgetting my own scoring figures. I did think that I would spend less time running after the ball.'

And he emphasised again, 'I do have reservations about our game, especially in the second half of the season. It's true that injuries unbalanced us, but that does not explain everything. I made Lampard and Cole shine. I sacrificed myself in the interests of Chelsea.'

And he obviously wasn't a great fan of the London weather. 'I did not see myself staying. Night falling at 3pm and rain coming down all the time. It was a bit too much for someone who, on top of that, was searching for form and the right touch. I knew such a big change was going to be hard for me, but I never realised just how hard. Let's say I have not always been happy. I do have a bit of homesickness. Life in England is not easy. You have to get used to it and I haven't done so. Not completely. It's so different, it has affected my morale.'

He went on, 'I was always in the starting line-up when I was not injured. Mourinho has always supported me. We can talk frankly and without any problems. So much so I'd even play with a broken leg for him. After all, he was the one who wanted me here when the owner, it seems, preferred Ronaldo.

'The criticism I've had brought us closer together. We need only a glance at each other to say, "We don't care. We know we are right." Mourinho knows better than anyone what I have brought to the team. He knows I have always given everything for Chelsea. He is grateful to me for it. I've gone through fantastic times – like the title celebrations at Stamford Bridge. Unforgettable. I came here for that and I have had my fill on that side of things. You have to be frank – football in England is something quite exceptional. When you see John Terry and Lampard doing ten laps of Stamford Bridge while kissing the trophy, it's magical. When you see the look on the faces of fans who waited fifty years for this title and are close to tears when you give it to them, you think you haven't wasted your time. I am glad to have given such happiness to the kind of supporters you dream about.'

Having coped with the presence of Gudjohnsen the previous year, Didier had another rival for the frontrunner spot as the new season loomed with the return of on-loan Hernán Crespo from AC Milan in Italy. There was no lack of confidence when he said, 'I don't feel pressure. Competition is very good for the squad and for me to improve. I want to play better than last year and it is normal for me to think about last season's games and how I can improve. But for me, I think it was very good for a first season. I played a lot of games and even with the injuries I scored sixteen goals, we won the Championship and I scored in the Champions League. What more can I do? We won the championship, the Carling Cup and I scored important goals. I did my job for the team last season. It is difficult sometimes playing upfront on your own but I did that a lot for Marseilles so it was not a problem. I came here last year after only six days' holiday and I missed a lot of pre-season, which is why maybe I suffered a lot of injuries. But let's hope that you will see the best of me in my second season.'

If the 'best' was about to be seen then the preparation Didier and his teammates put into every game at Mourinho's instigation could be a good reason for it. He explained, 'When I was on the bench, I sometimes heard him predict very precisely what was going to happen next. Sometimes it was a bit disconcerting, as if he had already seen the game. It was as if he could perceive ahead of time things that were going to happen – he was the only one who could guess what would happen next.

'The only time he got it wrong was at Liverpool in the Champions League. We get all the information on our opponents, not only how he plays, but which players face suspension in the next game if they get booked, if players are playing out of position, which players have a weakness on one foot. He has taught us all to look at football in a different manner. All the preparation work helped bring us extra confidence. We always had the impression we knew more than our opponents did. We felt like we were a step ahead.'

When Didier rejoined the Chelsea squad in America for some pre-season games, Crespo was already with them, although he took that in his stride: 'There's no pressure on me and Hernán's arrival is not a problem. It's very good for the team and will help me improve my game. It's a good thing to have more options upfront.' It can't have done any harm, either, when Chelsea met AC

# HOMESICK IN THE RAIN

Milan in the States and Didier cruised past three of their players to score a stunning goal in the team's 1-1 draw.

And he was still in the goal mood when the English season got underway with its traditional curtain raiser, the Community Shield, in front of 58,014 spectators at Cardiff's Millennium Stadium against Arsenal. Chelsea won 2-1 – the first time Mourinho's team had beaten the Gunners – and Didier scored both the goals before being replaced by Crespo. His first came after eight minutes, when he chested down a high ball on the edge of the penalty area and, with Philippe Senderos struggling to keep up, moved into the box and sent his shot across goalkeeper Jens Lehmann. Cesc Fàbregas and Claude Makelele were cautioned for a furious fracas and Didier and Lehmann gave a taste of their feelings for each other when they swapped harsh words after Didier was bundled over by Lauren. After the break Eidur Gudjohnsen flicked on a high ball and Didier stormed through alone and he managed to fend off Senderos, only to stumble as he rounded Lehmann but then somehow regained his balance and swivelled to fire the ball home.

Mourinho was ecstatic after the whistle: 'The first goal was great, the power he showed in the contact. The second one, he was fast and powerful going forward. I think another player would dive for a penalty. He didn't, he kept fighting for the ball and scored.' He went on, 'It's normal that the second season is better than the first. He knows the club. He knows the style of football. He will start this season not like last season when he came late and got a big injury.'

Even Arsène Wenger had to admit, 'It was a very even game and Chelsea were dangerous with the long balls. They would go very direct and we tried to play more our usual game. I'm not here to judge Chelsea. They play their game, we play ours. I just feel that Drogba gave us a hard time.'

Didier decided to relax a few days later with a meal at the Sanderson Hotel in London and afterwards he and some pals decided to sample the champagne at the trendy Chinawhite Club, where he told a fellow clubber, 'I'm having a great night. I'm very hopeful that we will win the Premiership and I hope we do well against Wigan this weekend.'

Indeed, that was where his all-important second season was to begin in earnest, against the side who had come from nowhere and sealed their Premiership place with a victory on the final day of the previous season, Wigan Athletic.

## CHAPTER 20

# Liverpool Destroyed

It may not have been the biggest crowd Didier had ever played in front of, but the 23,575 crammed into Wigan Athletic's JJB Stadium in mid-August was the largest number of spectators the ground had ever seen. Chelsea started the season 2005–6 not only as champions but the favourites with the bookmakers to retain the title, while newly promoted Wigan were the bookies' choice to be relegated.

So there could be no greater tribute to the Northern side than the one paid by José Mourinho at the end of the game. He said that, if you didn't know which team was which, Wigan would be the one neutrals would have selected as being in the running for the title. Indeed, it wasn't until injury time that Hernán Crespo, who came on as a second-half substitute, scored the only goal of the game after he collected a header from Didier twenty-five yards out and unleashed a left-foot drive that flew into the top of the net.

There were eight days before Chelsea's next match – at home to Arsenal – a side they had, surprisingly, not beaten in the league since 1995. It was to be Arsène Wenger's five hundredth match in charge of the Gunners, but there was no time for Didier to relax: he had to travel to France for an Ivory Coast friendly international against a French side, boosted by the return of Zinédine Zidane. Didier played well, but the accomplished home team, who were determined to avoid the embarrassment of the previous World Cup Final, were convincing 3–0 winners.

Mourinho decided to start the Arsenal match with Hernán Crespo upfront, and that meant Didier was on the bench. Still, he was in good – and very expensive – company. Alongside him was Shaun Wright-Phillips, the tiny winger from Manchester City who had joined for £21 million in the summer, and Ghanaian midfield powerhouse Michael Essien, named 'the Bison' by his former teammates for his thunderous midfield performances. He cost a staggering £26 million, which meant Didier no longer had to carry the tag of the most expensive player at Chelsea or the dearest African player of all time. Both mantles fell to the twenty-two-year-old new signing from Lyon. These weren't the only reasons Didier welcomed him to the club, though: he had been a long-time admirer of Essien and played a key role in his coming to the club after a protracted transfer deal that took months to finalise.

Before the friendly midweek international, he had broken off to tell reporters, 'With Michael, we have more chance to go all the way in the Champions League and to retain our national title. It's very good for us. I like him a lot. I've talked a lot with him over the phone and he told me he was desperate to join us. It's going to be a big relief in the midfield. He's one of the best defensive midfielders in the world.' And he couldn't resist mischievously adding, 'And so far Chelsea have not made any mistakes on the transfer market.'

All three of the £70 million trio were to make it onto the pitch against Arsenal, Didier coming on for Crespo at half-time, and he was to win the game for Chelsea in a match that one commentator was to refer to wryly as 'the Battle of Drogba's Knee'.

## LIVERPOOL DESTROYED

In truth, of all the wonderful goals that Didier has scored, this one featured very low down on the scale of merit. To begin with, some people, especially Arsenal supporters, felt there was more than a touch of offside about it as Frank Lampard's seventy-third-minute free kick drifted over the Arsenal defence to reach Didier. The visitors' Swiss centre-half Philippe Senderos, who had a torrid match at the Millennium Stadium and still looked uncomfortable against Didier, allowed the striker space to control the ball, but for once he failed to do so. He *shaped* as though to do it, but it somehow struck his right knee and ran past the wrong-footed Lehmann in goal. An unmemorable goal to win a not very memorable match, although it did enable Chelsea to break a ninety-three-year-old club record: thirty-nine consecutive unbeaten games at home.

At least Didier saw the amusing side of his 'golden knee' goal, saying, 'It was fantastic control from me.' Then he broke into a smile and added, 'I was a bit lucky. It was one of the luckiest goals of my career but at the end of the season it might turn out to be one of the most important.'

The game hadn't been all smiles, though – when a volley of Didier's ended up way off target he had an animated discussion with one fan who expressed his dislike of the effort. When the goal went in, knee or no knee, Didier went straight up to the same man and his pals to ask for his opinion. It was an example of how, despite his goals and unarguable work for Chelsea, there were still those who were only too eager to criticise him.

There weren't too many critics a few days later as he ran off the field at Stamford Bridge to be replaced late in the game against West Bromwich Albion, having scored one goal and made another in a comfortable 4–0 victory. In fact he got a storming ovation from the fans as he left the pitch.

If he was worried about the competition from Crespo – acknowledged as one of the finest strikers in the world – then Didier wasn't showing it. 'I'm not scared of Hernán or anybody else,' he said defiantly. 'I back my own ability and deserve my place in the Chelsea team. He scored a great goal in our game against Wigan but I am also playing well. People forget that there was competition for me last season and I still kept my place and scored goals. I had only just arrived at Chelsea and Mateja Kezman was being talked about by everyone. I had to try to get in the team but he arrived from PSV Eindhoven having broken records all over the place. All the goal statistics were smashed by him in Holland – that is real competition.

'I'm not worried about this season. It's only normal that at a club like Chelsea there are top players competing for each place in the team. I am happy with my game and I think it has showed already this season.'

So he can't have been too unhappy when he was replaced in Chelsea's 2–0 victory at Tottenham Hotspur a few days later. Anyway, he had more pressing matters on his mind, the crucial home game in the World Cup qualifiers against Cameroon in November 2005.

Cameroon had carried the African flag high in recent World Cups, but this was now the golden chance for Didier and the Ivory Coast side to take over as the leading exponent of football on the Continent as the two sides – arguably the best in Africa – met in Abidjan. A quick look at the squads showed the difficulty they and, in fairness, other African countries faced, in that their leading players were scattered around the soccer world. Most of the Ivorians earned their living in France, but in addition to Didier there were Arsenal's Emmanuel Eboué and Kolo Touré, plus players from Tunisia and the lower reaches of Italian football.

The Indomitable Lions of Cameroon were also from around the football globe, and it was their Spain-based striker Achille Webó – who overshadowed the more illustrious Samuel Eto'o throughout the game – who in the thirtieth minute scored the first home goal the Ivory Coast had conceded in the competition when he stretched his left foot to lob the ball over the stranded goalkeeper despite pressure from Kolo Touré. It was a devastating blow for the packed crowd, which included José Mourinho and Roman Abramovich, and Didier was determined to wrest control back.

Didier duly equalised eight minutes later with a snap close-range shot wide of goalkeeper Souleymanou Hamidou after his strike partner Aruna Dindane had floated his way past veteran Cameroon defender Pierre Wome and pulled the ball back.

But Webó struck again three minutes into first-half stoppage time as a far-post cross was nodded back into his path and his header went into the net off the hand of last-minute goalkeeping replacement Gérard Gnanhouan, while several Ivorians stood, still convinced the ball had gone out of play. Didier again sprang into action and after a mere two minutes of the second half his twenty-five-yard free kick was too good for the Cameroon goalkeeper and the crowd went wild.

Ecstatic as they were, the celebrations came to a dreadful halt with moments left on the referee's watch. The Ivory Coast had even hit the post when Alioum Saidou snatched the winner after a thirty-yard Cameroon free kick eluded goalkeeper Gnanhouan, struck the base of a post and rebounded to Saidou, whose brave diving header under pressure from an Ivorian defender flew into the net. It was heartbreaking for all those who supported the Ivorian cause to see such a wonderful match lost in its dying moments.

Across the Continent there were scenes of contrasting emotion as football fever gripped people thousands of miles apart. Some Ivorians left their stadium in tears, others invaded the field in anger, while in the Cameroon capital of Yaoundé there were scenes of delirious joy as traffic jammed the streets and people danced in delight. The victory meant they simply had to beat Egypt at home in a month's time to qualify for the World Cup at the expense of the dejected Ivory Coast side. It can't have been much consolation to Didier that his new teammate Michael Essien scored for Ghana against Uganda in a victory that ensured their place in the finals the next summer at the expense of South Africa.

So strong was the feeling of disappointment in the country that Ivory Coast players were insulted and threatened by some of their supporters after the defeat, causing Didier to think long and hard about whether he wanted to play for the national side again, an astonishing state of affairs given his pride in wearing the orange shirt of the Elephants. He told a football programme on the French Channel TF1, 'If such events should occur again, I would no longer take the risk to come and play for the national team.' Thankfully, he did not carry out his threat.

One of the problems Mourinho faced in having a squad packed with foreign players was that they would virtually all disappear whenever a spate of internationals occurred. He was complaining that he had only one full day to work with Didier and the rest of the international elite before Chelsea's Premiership home game that weekend against Sunderland, who, although they had some players called away, had nowhere near the same pressure on their resources.

So it probably wasn't too surprising that Chelsea laboured somewhat to beat the Black Cats 2–0, aided by a headed goal from Didier, who came on as substitute for Hernán Crespo. There was no doubt that Didier had the lead over the Argentinian when it came to Mourinho's favoured choice of striker, however, and, as if to illustrate the point, he started the match while Crespo was on the bench as the season's Champions League fixtures began. A Lampard free kick was the only goal of the game as the 'mean machine' that was Chelsea ground out a valuable win over Anderlecht of Belgium in front of just 29,575 spectators at Stamford Bridge.

That ninety-minute run-out meant that he was sitting most of the next game out. This was a visit to Charlton, who had won all their four league games played so far and found themselves surprisingly in second place behind Chelsea. No sensible money would have backed them to be there at the end of the season and it turned out to be a comfortable 2–0 win for Chelsea, Didier coming on for the last few minutes.

## LIVERPOOL DESTROYED

The frightening prospect for the rest of the division was that Chelsea hadn't really moved into top gear so far that season and yet they had earned maximum points and set a Premiership record by not conceding a goal in their first six games. No wonder Didier mused, 'It must be frightening for our rivals when we are not playing well but still winning every game. When you play badly our rivals must think, "What are Chelsea going to be like when they *are* playing well?" It's great for us: we're still in front of everybody else and we're not even on top form.

'I think teams are already running scared. It's hard sometimes when teams come to us looking to get everyone behind the ball. They know we're a good side and try to put five in midfield. But we know we can score at any time. Anderlecht in midweek, for example, didn't show any ambition and clearly tried to get a 0–0. But we're strong enough to score no matter what system is played.'

Chelsea needed all that strength at home to Aston Villa as with half-time approaching they conceded their first goal of the season when youngster Luke Moore broke their defensive wall and won the £10,000 prize a national newspaper offered to the first player to score against the Blues. The Villa joy was short-lived as Frank Lampard immediately equalised with a free kick and then won the game with a penalty fifteen minutes from time after substitute Didier burst into the box chasing Lampard's chipped ball, and, with Villa captain Olof Mellberg all over Didier, the referee awarded a penalty. Incredibly, after just a handful of games and before even reaching October, the bookmakers were giving odds of only 4–1 that Chelsea would be champions by the following summer.

Beforehand, though, they had to take on Liverpool twice in a short space of time, the first encounter being at Anfield in the Champions League. Chelsea's 'French' trio of Didier, Claude Makelele and Michael Essien gave a fascinating interview to *France Football* on the eve of the match, in which they assessed both their own roles in English football and Chelsea's outstanding position. Didier's contribution to the discussion was fascinating, especially as he immediately dismissed the media reports that the game was going to turn into a grudge match.

'Everyone is trying their hardest to turn this into a grudge game, a match that'd smell of sulphur,' he said. 'Yes, Chelsea and Liverpool are two big guns, but this will not be a "remake" of what happened last season. It's just the second game of the group phase. But I might say something different if we were playing each other in a quarter- or semi-final. We questioned Luis Garcia's goal at the time, that's all. Looking back, we realised quite quickly that Liverpool deserved to play the final. It all hinged on details, such as this quick goal, a lack of freshness in our team, a few missing players in our squad. Football is not mathematics – and thank God for that! This does not detract from the courage that was shown by Liverpool, who deserved to win the trophy.

'We're playing them twice in a week, but it is impossible to put greater importance on one game or the other. When you play against Liverpool, especially at Anfield, you give everything. There's no other way. And Chelsea want the three championship points as badly as the six Champion League points. To achieve that, we'll have to fight, and then fight some more.

'When a coach tells you clearly that he counts on you, there is no reason to doubt him. Competition for places is fierce at Chelsea, but I personally love it. It keeps me on my toes, it forces everyone to work and work, in order to gain a place on the team sheet. Competition is constructive when it is healthy, and that is the case at Chelsea.'

And he added, 'Maybe we're criticised because we win too much. Yes, please forgive us! Seriously, we've seen so many dominating teams which lost a game on a point of detail, and then lost their rhythm and their confidence. Arsenal had won forty-nine games on the trot when they were stopped at Manchester United, partly because of a dubious penalty. They hurt a lot after that. We're not home and dry yet, far from it. Let's be careful.'

Chelsea certainly had to be careful when they took on Liverpool in their Merseyside fortress. Didier was outstanding as he foraged, mainly alone, upfront, but again English international Jamie Carragher coped better with him than most defenders had in the past two seasons. Indeed, when he was helping back in defence – an element of his game that is often overlooked – Didier had cries for a penalty in the nineteenth minute by the Liverpool fans ignored as he tackled Hyypia in the visitors' penalty area and made contact with the blond Liverpool player but missed the ball.

Liverpool had an even bigger appeal turned down in the second half when William Gallas appeared to handle a Carragher header as Liverpool laid siege to the Chelsea goal. Carragher was convinced it was a penalty and said so afterwards, as did manager Rafael Benítez: 'In this game we did not have the linesman. It could have been a penalty and a red card, sometimes people forget these details. And, as for this occasion, I have seen it on TV – it was clear, unbelievable. The key is that when you play against big teams the small details are crucial. But that was a very big detail.'

He added, 'I felt it was a good game. We played with a high tempo and tried to win. I am pleased with a point against a good team like Chelsea, but we really lost two points because we played better than them. It is good we now have four points, but maybe it should be six. I think we showed the audience we could play well – it was important for us that we showed we could play well in big games like this.'

The result meant both teams had four points from their first two games and, given that it was the first stage of the Champions League, the pressure was not as great as it had been for the knockout match the previous May.

If Liverpool thought they had achieved what other sides in the Premiership had failed to do, they had only a few days to relax in this delusional state. They were woken from it in the rudest possible fashion when they played host to Chelsea again on Sunday, 2 October 2005. The result wasn't just an emphatic win for Chelsea, but also a wonderful performance in the muscular art of leading a forward line from Didier that stunned the Liverpool fans and thrilled the spectators in blue and white.

Even hardened cynics in the press box, many of whom still had to be won over to Didier's cause, were enthralled. A sample of their comments speaks for itself, especially when the fact that Didier didn't even score in the 4–1 victory is taken into account!

The *Daily Mail* said '... Didier Drogba, a striker who arrived yesterday at his devilish, undignified best', while the *Daily Telegraph* called him 'a muscular destroyer of Liverpool's backline', adding,

> Drogba had a field day running at Sami Hyypia and Djimi Traore, the weak links in Liverpool's defence, helping to create goals for Lampard (a penalty), Damien Duff, Joe Cole and Geremi. Chelsea's increasing control, which resembled a slip-knot being tightened as Liverpool slumped to their heaviest home defeat since 1969.

The *Independent* chipped in with, 'Liverpool's defeat was about their failure to contain the awkward, truculent presence of Drogba', as the eighth straight league win turned into Chelsea's biggest at Anfield since 1907 and the first time Liverpool had ever conceded four at home in the Premiership. It also put them an astounding nine points clear of the rest of the pack. No wonder Didier said, 'We said after the match four days ago, "We can do better than this" – and we are happy today. We had the belief we could win today. Four days ago we were frustrated, we felt we could do better. To play like that four days after a very difficult match makes me very happy.'

José Mourinho, loyal as ever to Didier but also aware that the critics might soon have their knives out again, remarked, 'Didier was good against Liverpool in the Champions League and even better in the Premiership. But I know, in the next fifteen days, everyone will forget that and say that he doesn't score enough goals.'

# CHAPTER 21

# The Elephants and the Lions

It was true that Didier still had his critics in England, and the recent disappointment over the Ivory Coast's disastrous loss to Cameroon had practically induced a nationwide heartbreak. Yet he and his compatriots were on the point of entering the nation's folklore.

Paradoxically, it was the events on another pitch that heralded their ascent to superstardom on 8 October 2005. The Elephants seemed to have thrown their chance away with the defeat at home to Cameroon. Nevertheless, they did their duty in a 3–1 victory over Sudan – with a first-half goal from Kanga Akalé and two after the break from Aruna Dindane, the striker who had moved to Lens in France – that seemed to be late to help them qualify.

Meanwhile, Cameroon's home game against Egypt, being played elsewhere on the Continent, was thrilling to watch. Cameroon had the apparently routine task of beating the Pharaohs in order to gain the three points needed to head for Germany and they had gone into the lead after twenty-one minutes. But late in the second half the script was thrown out of the window when Egypt equalised to silence the 50,000 crowd in the Ahmadou Ahidjo stadium in Yaoundé. In the fifth minute of extra time Salomon Olembé went down and the referee pointed to the spot – a reprieve for the men from Cameroon. Barcelona's Samuel Eto'o didn't want to take the kick – although he later said he declined only because a teammate volunteered – so up stepped Inter Milan's Pierre Wome, a defender who had once briefly played for Fulham.

Agony of agony, poor Wome's shot hit the post and rebounded clear. Cameroon were out. Hell for Cameroon, heaven for Didier and the Ivory Coast, since the miss meant the Elephants would be heading for the finals for the first time in their history. They had gathered in the middle of the pitch in Omdurman in Sudan surrounding a cameraman connected on his mobile phone to a friend in Abidjan, who was watching the Cameroon game live. When the penalty was missed, the players of the Ivory Coast were ecstatic and their first act was to be led in a prayer of peace by Didier, who was now national captain. 'Ivorians, we beg your forgiveness. Let us come together and put this war behind us,' he said, in the dressing room after the game.

Even as he was talking, the Ivory Coast nation was going berserk with joy and crowds congaed around the Egyptian Embassy to thank them for their side's performance in Cameroon. The squad returned in triumph to Abidjan airport in the presidential plane and there was mayhem as Didier walked down the plane steps and the team headed for an open-top military-style truck that drove them through the capital. Every player was promptly given a home apiece by the government in recognition of his achievement – a far cry from the recent punishment of a previous national side being confined to barracks and a 'boot camp' regime for failing!

On the streets cars honked their horns nonstop and the population danced the 'Drogbacite', a dance based on Didier's twisting movements on the field, or performed the 'fouka-fouka', a movement mimicking Didier's goal celebrations. All the time bottle after bottle of Drogba beer was being drunk.

Meanwhile, a saddened Eto'o could only pause for reflection and say, 'It is very hard to have had everything in your own hands and throw it all away in the final seconds. I am sad for my country, my colleagues and for myself. There is only one remedy for it all and that is to do well in the African Nations Cup, to give everyone who is suffering with us now a great lift.'

Wome, understandably, had a different story to tell: 'No one wanted to take that penalty, no one. Neither Samuel Eto'o nor our captain Rigobert Song, because they knew what could have happened if they missed,' he told a press conference. 'I have always had the courage and I went to the spot.' He also claimed that some Cameroon fans wanted to kill him because of his miss.

His error meant that the Ivory Coast qualified by means of their one-point advantage and, along with Michael Essien's Ghana, Togo and Angolo would be representing Africa in the finals for the first time together with old stager Tunisia. What it also meant was that all those nations also qualified for the African Nations Cup to be held in Egypt in January and February of the following year, so the stars would be away from their clubs for a long spell at a key time in the season.

The qualification against all odds wasn't all that Didier had to celebrate, as he was in a batch of thirty players named as being in the running for FIFA's World Player of the Year, along with teammates Michael Essien, Frank Lampard and Arjen Robben. He also made a rap record with Parisian artist Doc Gyneco after being persuaded by fellow striker Nicolas Anelka. The 'Doc' had previously worked with the disgraced Marseilles President Bernard Tapie, and Didier said, 'It's just about going to school, trying to be a good person. Dr Gyneco's a friend of mine. This is for children, for charity, so that's why I did it.'

Bolton Wanderers must have wished he'd stayed in the

recording studio as he put them to the sword at Stamford Bridge in the middle of October, almost a year to the day since Manchester City had defeated Chelsea in what had been their only league defeat since Didier joined them. Bolton even had the temerity to take the lead but in the second half Chelsea scored five goals, four of them in ten thunderous minutes, two from Didier. He even had another 'goal' disallowed for offside.

Next for slaughter were Real Betis from Spain, who were hammered 4–0 at Stamford Bridge in the Champions League on 20 October 2005. Didier set the ball rolling with a first half goal after good work by Michael Essien – who had an outstanding match – although he had blasted an earlier chance high and wide. José Mourinho decided to take him off at half-time, not because he wasn't delivering the goods, quite the opposite, but to protect him after a wince-inducing challenge from David Rivas on his left ankle. The knock was so bad that there were big question marks over whether Didier would be fit for the trip to Goodison Park to take on an Everton side who were, surprisingly, bottom of the table at the time. But he did make it and scored a thrilling goal in the sixty-second minute only for it to be controversially disallowed for offside on the part of Eidur Gudjohnsen.

Chelsea had to settle for a 1–1 draw, the first points they had dropped in ten games and a few days later suffered their first defeat of the season at home to Charlton in the Carling Cup. The game ended 1–1 and Chelsea eventually lost 5–4 when Didier – who had come on as substitute – and Robert Huth missed when they had to take part in the penalty shoot-out. The irony was that the match programme for that evening game had picked out Didier as the best penalty taker at the club! Normal service was resumed for both Chelsea and Didier on 29 October when they beat Blackburn at home 4–2, with Didier again scoring. This was Chelsea's fortieth consecutive Premiership game without defeat and it meant they were top of the league table with thirty-one points, followed, surprisingly, by Wigan with twenty-two,

## THE ELEPHANTS AND THE LIONS

Tottenham with twenty and Charlton with nineteen. The other 'big boys', however, were way down the table: Manchester United were sixth with eighteen points, Arsenal were a position and a point further back, while Liverpool were twelfth with thirteen points.

Welcome as the victory and the goal were, the game was tinged with sorrow for Didier. He wore a black armband during the match in memory of a nineteen-year-old cousin in the Ivory Coast who had died from leukaemia. The youngster, whose treatment had been paid for by Didier, had been due to fly to Paris for further treatment but was too ill to travel. Didier kissed the armband and raised his hands to heaven after heading Blues into a 10th-minute lead with his ninth goal of the season. He later told Chelsea TV: 'I was happy to score against Blackburn because I had to do it for my cousin who died last week. It was a difficult week for me but more difficult for his family. It is a drama for all the families who have children or a member of the family who is fighting to stay alive. I tried to do everything for him and to get him to France for the treatment he required. His visa arrived two days after he died. It was difficult for me.'

In the middle of this crisis, Didier somehow had to push it from his mind and to concentrate on yet another big night of European football, this time at Real Betis. For once, however, it wasn't to be the customary Chelsea victory. The result was a 1–0 defeat, the first time they had lost a competitive match – leaving aside the Charlton penalty 'lucky dip' – for six months, since the debatable one-goal loss at Liverpool. Even more importantly, it meant that Liverpool were able to go to the top of their qualifying group and Real Betis moved up to just one point behind Chelsea, thanks to a goal from the Betis striker Dani (Daniel Martín) in the twenty-eighth minute. Michael Essien was unlucky not to put the Blues level when his shot hit one post, rolled across the line, hit the other post and was cleared. Didier came on as substitute and earned himself a yellow card in a very physical battle when he ended up jostling home goalkeeper Pedro Contreras.

211

## DIDIER DROGBA

The bad mood continued after the whistle as Didier argued with both the referee Alain Hamer and his assistants and had to be hauled away by Chelsea officials as his remonstrations became more heated. Mourinho wasn't impressed: 'It was the worst performance since I arrived. I've been here for fifteen months and we have played perhaps eighty games at Chelsea, and this was the worst performance. The first half was too bad to be true. I know everything was bad.

'I cannot find a positive in the game. I don't think it is fair to single out any individual player, the whole team played badly. I think this was a very bad team performance. They had a very bad game.'

Another team who had a bad game were Manchester United, who lost their European clash 1–0 to Lille, not the best warm-up for the Red Devils, who took on Chelsea in front of 67,000 Old Trafford spectators a few days later. Didier tested their Dutch international goalkeeper Edwin van der Sar, but the only man to find the net was Darren Fletcher, who scored for United and ended Chelsea's wonderful forty Premiership games without defeat.

Unlike in Spain, however, there was no verbal onslaught awaiting Didier and the rest from their coach. 'I am not happy because we have lost, but I am proud of the team because they deserved to win. Manchester United defended with great spirit and a lot of effort and their future is only looking better for them now. But they are not good enough to be champions, only to finish closer to us and not drop quite so many points. There is still more pressure on them than there is us and, if you asked them if they wanted to change positions with us, they would do so in a moment.'

If any more proof was needed of the pressure on international footballers, it came the next week when Chelsea were not playing, due to international fixtures. That didn't mean a break for Didier, though: he was off to Le Mans, where he had once played, and he starred for the Ivory Coast in a 2–1 friendly international against Romania.

## THE ELEPHANTS AND THE LIONS

Didier's verdict: 'It was a good game between two good teams and it was very important for us to win.' Hard on the heels of that came another friendly in Geneva, this time against one of the traditional powerhouse teams of world football, both in tradition and ability: Italy. The Ivory Coast squad were experiencing at international level the type of side they would find waiting for them in Germany, and they almost became the first side to beat Italy – who had outplayed and beaten Holland at the weekend – in fifteen games. Didier scored the first goal of the match after sixty-nine minutes, bringing down Arthur Boka's long ball and lashing it into the roof of the net and the Italians, one of the favourites for Germany, had to wait until four minutes from time before equalising.

The Italian coach Marcello Lippi, one of the most respected in world football, enthused, 'Drogba is an outstanding player.' Former Everton defender Marco Materazzi, who was destined for World Cup infamy after his clash in the final with Zinédine Zidane, marked Didier during the match and he said, 'When you find yourself facing players like him, it means you are playing at the highest level and that is good.'

The two internationals seemed to have given Didier a boost of confidence, for he was very bullish about Chelsea's prospects, given that they had lost three of their last five games: 'This year, we at Chelsea have everything to prove. The only difference between Milan, Real Madrid and Chelsea is the trophy cabinet. Give us a bit more time. We will get there this season and I think we'll face Lyon in the final or semi-final.

'Chelsea is different from any club I have played at before. Here, it is really the highest level of football. Chelsea are rigorous, meticulous, but I wouldn't say we have a star system. All the players around me are humble, really simple. We play as one, a team, for one of the great clubs in the world. We know deep down that we will lose games. The most important thing is to perform consistently and carry on bagging the points. Even when we were not at our best last season, we still picked up the points.'

## DIDIER DROGBA

Suggestions that Mourinho might be in the market for another striker soon were met with defiance and confidence: 'I am not afraid. I see it as a way of strengthening the team. There is one thing of paramount importance. Whoever is playing should make the difference on the pitch. The others should be as supportive as possible. Both Hernán Crespo and I understand we have to give our best for the good of the club.'

Speaking in *Champions League*, the official UEFA magazine, he also showed that no matter how much money and fame he had at his feet now, they were still planted very firmly on the ground: 'I'm not complaining. How could I? I don't forget that it is only four years since I was playing in the lower divisions of French football. I am now at Chelsea but I like sitting down from time to time and looking back at the good times I have had over the last few years. I had some exceptional moments at clubs like Le Mans, as well as at Chelsea, of course.'

Didier had plenty of opportunity to be supportive during the next three games. While on international duty he had picked up a knee injury and missed the home 3–0 victory over Newcastle, anyway, due to a suspension for the yellow cards he had totted up during the season. He was among the substitutes for the entire ninety minutes of a comfortable 2–0 win at Brussels against Anderlecht that ensured Chelsea a place in the last sixteen of the competition, and he wasn't even on the bench for the victory by two goals at Portsmouth, Mourinho saying he was still injured. But he did make it back onto the pitch for the 1–0 home victory over Middlesbrough, although the Blues had to rely on a John Terry goal, as they missed several good chances, the worst, it must be said, coming from Didier, who blasted high over the bar from just 10 yards when completely unmarked.

As December 2005 arrived Chelsea were faced with the prospect of losing three key players for the forthcoming African Nations Trophy: Didier Drogba, Michael Essien and Ndjitap Geremi. So great was the excitement back home that records such as 'Thank you Elephants' and 'Drogba Champion' were being bought by Ivorians. Reports in the Ivory Coast suggested that Mourinho would somehow stop Didier from playing, so the striker took the remarkable step on 5 December of explaining why he hadn't been in the team recently, and stating in the clearest possible terms that he would be off to the finals, by putting the following statement on his website:

> I wanted to give you an update to explain why I haven't been playing over the last few weeks. Since the match against Romania, I've been having knee pains which didn't prevent me from playing against Italy but which got worse after that. So that's why I didn't play in the Champions League match against Anderlecht. Considering the score, my coach was wise enough to rest me so my injury didn't get worse and to give young Carlton Cole a chance to play. Since then, I've been receiving treatment but Hernán Crespo's recent injury has brought me back into the team sooner than I thought, and with only one training session in me. Fortunately, the match went well and I didn't have any pain. It's a good sign for the upcoming home game against Liverpool even though I won't be 100%.
>
> I'll be playing in the African Cup. The month of December will be key for Chelsea because last year, it was the month when we won the matches which gave us the title. I hope I'll be back on form over the Christmas period and score and win some matches again before going to the African Cup. Yes, it's time to put an end to all of the rumours and criticisms against my coach and club, Chelsea Football Club. I'll be playing in the African Cup with my coach's approval!

The African Cup was, of course, a precursor to the World Cup in the summer, and when the draw was made for Germany it meant that Didier and his compatriots were in what was generally felt to be the toughest of all the qualifying groups. Not only did they face one seeded side, Argentina, but they were also against one of the aristocrats of world football, the multitalented – if somewhat unpredictable – Holland with Arjen Robben and a host of other gifted Dutchmen. To complete Group C, the 'Group of Death', there was also the dangerous Serbia and Montenegro national side. The Ivory Coast were unlucky in that the classifications meant that Holland were the unseeded side everyone had hoped to avoid, but the Ivorians had certainly drawn the short straw.

All that lay ahead, however, as Didier played on through discomfort in the goalless Champions League match at home to Liverpool, which meant the Merseyside club would top the group. The game itself was memorable mainly for a horrendous tackle by Michael Essien on German Didi Hamann, for which he wasn't even booked.

Afterwards Didier admitted, 'I have a big problem with my knee. I was out for two and a half weeks but it is still not right. Normally, I would not have played against Liverpool or Middlesbrough. I am still in a lot of pain and it was difficult because I was not confident. Physically, I am not 100 per cent and I think you could see that in the matches.'

By this time he hadn't scored since the 4–2 win against Blackburn on 29 October, which prompted him to emphasise again, 'I've had this injury since November 12. I'm not supposed to play but I have to because Hernán Crespo is injured. I was not confident against Liverpool, I'm in a lot of pain. But I need to help my team, as I will be absent for the African Nations Cup in the New Year.'

And he played through the pain barrier yet again for forty-five minutes as, for the second week running, Chelsea won by a solitary John Terry goal, with visiting Wigan this time the victims.

Media attention, for once, wasn't concentrated on Didier: Michael Essien had stepped into the spotlight. His tackle on Hamann, for which he had apologised, landed him a two-match

## THE ELEPHANTS AND THE LIONS

European ban and then, on 18 December 2005 in an invaluable 2–0 win at Highbury, the Ghanaian clashed with Arsenal's Lauren, sparking a mini-riot. Didier too was involved in a row during the match when he was hauled back by yet again a troubled Senderos as he caused the sorely tested centre-back more problems.

Another man with problems was FIFA president Sepp Blatter, who decided to highlight Chelsea when he criticised the number of overseas players some leading clubs had on the payroll. 'If a club can only have five foreigners among their starting eleven, then they will have to build on their own youth system,' he said in an interview with FIFA's official 2006 World Cup countdown magazine. 'If Chelsea were forced to have five foreigners, then Roman Abramovich could not go on buying the best players across the world for exorbitant fees. Chelsea is the example of what should not happen.'

He also told reporters, 'The solution is that there should be a minimum. FIFA's idea is we should have at least six players eligible for the national team of the country in which they play. The national identity of clubs is very important,' he said. '[But] the regulations of club competitions are not made by FIFA but by the national associations. It's up to them and their leagues to limit the entry of foreign players.'

Didier immediately hit back when he told a press conference: 'Our English players are still the spine of our team. Frank Lampard is one of the best players in the world and John Terry is one of the best defenders.' And Didier showed that, as the time neared for him to fly to Africa, he was determined to give 100 per cent in the short time that remained.

'It is a frustration because I like to play big games. Maybe I will miss big games for Chelsea, but at the same time I will play big games for the national team. When I am in Chelsea I am 120 per cent for my club, and when I go to the national team it is the same, so while I am here I am going to give everything. I think I will learn a lot of things from going. It will be my first one, so I want to come back with the trophy to give me more and more confidence.

'I think I have played some games not far from my best level, like Liverpool away, and for me against Arsenal, after a few weeks with a difficult injury, it was a very good game. I am quite happy. I had one difficult year because of the injuries and the changing of country. Some people take two years, four years, or some people just take one year and go.

'I'm very proud because I'm in one of the best teams in Europe. I'm a very lucky player. In the last three years my life has changed. I was on the bench in the French second division but slowly, step by step and year by year, I keep working. I've always had big ambitions and did everything I could to get here today. I enjoy myself and these have been the best three years of my life. I'm fresh because I've only played at the high level for two years. I hope there's a lot more to come.'

And, on the eve of what was potentially a very difficult local derby against Fulham, Didier also sprang to the defence of the much-criticised Essien, saying, 'Michael has been given a hard time but is not a naughty guy. He is trying to give his best for Chelsea. What happened is because he wants to win – not to hurt people. That's why he apologised to Hamann. I don't have to give him advice, he knows what he can and can't do here. My first season was difficult. It is not easy. Some people take two or four years – some stay for one year and go.'

That local derby did indeed cause Chelsea and Didier some difficulties as Fulham pulled back from a two-goal deficit only to lose out to a late, volleyed winner from Hernán Crespo. Didier was in the thick of it, too, in another Christmas programme match, when a Joe Cole goal was enough to bring victory at Manchester City. Didier's major involvement came in a dull first half when a penalty appeal was turned down after City goalkeeper David James appeared to bring him down. City captain Sylvain Distin had misjudged a hopeful ball from Asier del Horno to allow Didier in goal in the twenty-third minute. Initially, he appeared to lose his footing as he looked to control the ball, but then he was caught by both Distin and James as he attempted to round the goalkeeper.

To many it seemed to be a penalty, but the referee decided not to give it. But neither was Didier booked. The incident sparked a brief bout of pushing between several players and the game became ill-tempered until half-time.

At least 2005 ended on a more humorous note as 40,000-plus watched Crespo – who was replaced by Didier with twenty minutes remaining – and Arjen Robben score the goals that defeated Birmingham City at Stamford Bridge. The visiting manager, Steve Bruce, put into words what many in football were thinking.

'I was fortunate to play in a team in '94, which I thought was a bit invincible,' said the former Manchester United centre-half, 'and this Chelsea team have the same about them today. You can see they're pretty formidable. They've got such strength and depth – top, top players everywhere you look and a manager who knows how to handle them and get the best out of them. When you've got all those things that's a pretty formidable outfit you're playing against. Back-to-back titles is always the most difficult. You've been there, done it and worn the T-shirt, then you've got to go again. With Man United and Arsenal rebuilding, they're going to take some catching, that's for sure.'

And he added, with a wry smile, 'I did ask him not to bring Drogba on at the end! It seemed a bit unfair.'

## CHAPTER 22

# Out of Africa

Didier wouldn't have had too much time for fun and laughter as the year 2006 began: he was too busy playing football. He was named in the Ivory Coast squad, of course, for the African Nations Cup in Egypt; he also scored the best goal of the match as Chelsea triumphed 3–1 in front of a 34,000 crowd at West Ham. It came ten minutes from the end after Eidur Gudjohnsen sent him clear for Didier to let loose a thunderbolt of a shot past the helpless Hammers goalkeeper Roy Carroll for his tenth goal of the season. It was Chelsea's ninth successive victory in the premiership, and their fourth over the holiday period. Didier had at least said goodbye, for the time being, to Chelsea in style for a few days later he was off to join up with the Ivory Coast squad.

José Mourinho was ecstatic about his performance against West Ham. 'It was a fantastic performance. He fought a lot and gave us everything. He played upfront on his own, with Hernán Crespo and wide on the right. He helped us defensively, he chased Paul Konchesky and he won balls in the air. He was fantastic!'

## DIDIER DROGBA

The row over Didier's leaving the Premiership struggle for the Ivorian get-together and then the lengthy tournament in Egypt rumbled on, especially as Michael Essien had to pull out of the Ghana squad, albeit for the very valid reason of injury. Didier himself summed it up: 'I have been well aware for some time that this was coming up and with the competition for places at Chelsea really hotting up obviously I have taken a risk. However, not only do we have the African Nations but also our debut in the World Cup finals in June.

'It is really important that we use this as a dress rehearsal for the World Cup finals but that is not to say we are going to take it lightly. I realise it's not good to miss games for Chelsea and I was worried I'd have to go without the blessing of the manager. But I owe José for allowing me to leave. I realise it is an important time for Chelsea but I know how to repay the boss. He badly wants to win the Champions League this season – and I am going to do my best to make that happen. It will be my personal mission to get Chelsea to Paris and win it for the boss.'

Didier was certain to miss four important Premiership games in January 2006, starting with a clash at Sunderland and including the Blues' FA Cup fourth-round tie against Everton or Millwall. There was also a strong chance he would miss a fifth league match at Middlesbrough, depending on his country's progress in the tournament. José Mourinho was to criticise the Ivory Coast publicly, but not Didier personally, for not allowing their star striker to miss the first day of his country's training sessions so that he could fit in one more game for Chelsea. He added that he would never buy more than one player from any African nation because he did not know how each individual African FA would react to his requests.

Didier simply wanted a fair deal for all players saying, 'Africa will be truly respected the day European clubs accept with good grace to free their players as easily as for a European Championship. All this blackmail in recent times by certain European clubs to retain a maximum of selected players was scandalous. And things have not moved too much on that level.' He went on to say, 'We obviously want to do as well as we can in Egypt and to win it would be a magical moment for me after all the success I've had with my club. I hope people can see that it is important for me to represent my country. I will come back determined to improve on last season, no matter how we do out there. I want to win the Premiership again, as well as the FA Cup and Champions League.'

He also let slip, somewhat strangely, that at times he had bigger laughs at meal times or on the team bus with his fellow Ivorians than he did with the Chelsea squad: 'There are laughs from start to finish. Not like at your club, where, as soon as there is a burst of laughter, everyone falls silent and looks at what is happening. In Europe, each man is on his mobile and occasionally complaining about not being in the team. We all sing like kids, even the ones who will be on the bench a few moments later.'

Even as Didier was jetting out of Britain to link up with his national side at Nogent-sur-Marne near Paris, one of his potential rivals, Egypt's Mido, his old partner from Marseilles days, was making a remarkable prediction about the forthcoming tournament. 'I think Egypt will play Côte d'Ivoire in the final,' said the twenty-two-year old Spurs striker, adding that the Ivorians were 'the best-prepared team on the continent'.

The preparation took a bit of a hammering, however, when the Ivory Coast beat Jordan 2–0 in a warm-up friendly in Dubai that saw Didier score and then get sent off and his side end the game with nine men! But the problems in Dubai were nothing compared with the worsening situation back home in the Ivory Coast, where there were four days of riots against UN and French peacekeeping troops. While the players no doubt wanted to concentrate solely on the football that lay ahead, Didier, now captain of his national side, had to make a public statement that flashed around the world on the Reuters news service: 'I am an Ivorian footballer and I ask for just one thing – that's peace in my country,' he told reporters as he prepared for their opening African Nations Cup game against Morocco.

'I'm not here to take up a position and say who's right and who's wrong. I'm like all the Ivorian citizens who dream only of one thing – for calm to return. We are playing our role as kind of "ambassadors". But everyone has to assume their responsibilities. We are asked to do our duty on the pitch and when we're not doing well we get criticised. But I think everyone in their job has to accept their responsibilities as well.

'It would do a lot of good if we could achieve something here. Once again, we have enormous responsibilities and we will do everything we can to meet them. It won't be easy. Of course, it has an effect on the players. We have to be professional, but also at times we have to be able to go beyond professionalism and show our patriotic spirit. With that, we can reach a new level in matches. It's a shame what is happening in our country but we have to use that to reach new heights.'

One reporter asked him how long he felt the Ivory Coast had been a truly 'national' side and he replied, 'For a long time, since the start of World Cup qualifying [in 2004] and since the start of this crisis.'

It must almost have been a release to get on with the job of actually playing football, and Didier certainly did that with style. He scored his eighteenth goal in his twenty-fifth international from a first-half penalty against Morocco in the opening round of the tournament in front of a disappointing crowd of just 8,000 in front of a stadium holding 74,000. He had already had a header cleared off the line when in the thirty-ninth minute Didier was tugged back by Hoalid Regragui trying to run onto Emerse Faé's through ball and from the resulting penalty Didier made no mistake. With over twenty-five minutes remaining, Ivory Coast coach Henri Michel then took Didier off and replaced him with the inexperienced Arouna Koné, leaving the side without both their leading marksmen: because Aruna Dindane had to return home because of his baby daughter's death shortly before the game had begun.

For Didier the 1–0 victory came at a price, as coach Michel explained: 'He has been carrying this knee injury for a while now. He has three days to recover before the next game and we'll have to see what we're going to do.' Fortunately he recovered in time for the 2–1 victory over Libya in the next game and scored the first goal after a dreadful error by goalkeeper Muftah Ghazala. Didier tapped the ball in before performing a colourful, if bizarre team celebration by the corner flag. Libya managed to level just before half-time to the delight of the Egyptians in the crowd, but they weren't so happy when, soon into the second half, Didier was booked for a two-footed challenge on his Libyan goalscorer Khames. It was a thrilling match and it was decided by the goalkeeper's error when Ghazala's poor punch under no pressure at all dropped onto Gnegneri Touré's head and the ball rebounded off the underside of the bar and over the line.

With the Ivory Coast already through to the next round, Didier and others were rested for the game against Egypt, which was lost by the 'scratch' side 3–1. Reasons for his being left out varied, however, as coach Henri Michel said Didier and midfielders Gilles Yapi Yapo and Didier Zokora were rested because another yellow card would have triggered a suspension for the forthcoming quarter-final. Arsenal defender Kolo Touré was also among the five players rested as the Frenchman rotated his squad.

'I wanted to find out what some of the others could do in a competition and that was the match to do it in,' he said. Some unconfirmed reports gave a different view of events, saying that Michel was unhappy when Didier kept the squad waiting on the bus for fifteen minutes at their hotel and when they got to the training ground the Frenchman ordered him back to the hotel. Although the Ivory Coast were already through to the next round, the defeat meant they would be facing the much-fancied Cameroon side and Didier's long-time foe Samuel Eto'o.

## DIDIER DROGBA

Cameroon captain Rigobert Song, formerly of Liverpool and West Ham, and a man with a vast knowledge of the game, sensibly picked out Didier before the kick-off as the man his side would have to watch. 'Didier is one of the best strikers in the world and he's someone that not just me, but all our players, have got to keep an eye on,' Song told reporters. 'He's not the only one, it will be a collective effort, but Didier is a special player – he's got all the goalscorer's qualities and he's already shown that,' he added himself (a player with the 'distinction' of being sent off in the final stages of two World Cups, the 1994 and 1998 tournaments). 'With players like him in the team, you have to be careful.'

Cameroon midfielder Geremi, Didier's Chelsea teammate, had even better knowledge of his capabilities. 'He's a key part of the Ivorian team. But at the same time we must not just focus on him. If we do everything just to stop him, we risk being caught by surprise by another one of their players. We really do have the motivation after missing out on the World Cup. It has been a challenge for us to get back quickly to our usual level, and the Nations Cup is an opportunity to show those who doubted us that Cameroon are still one of Africa's big teams.'

No one could have predicted the astonishing game that was about to take place. The first ninety minutes were, if truth be told, pretty drab and spoiled by continual fouling, and it wasn't until extra time that the game came to life with more excitement in its first two minutes than the whole match so far, as Emmanuel Eboué's power drive came back off the bar and Koné was on hand on the edge of the area to rifle the ball home for the Ivory Coast. Then Geremi rattled the bar to shake the Ivorians, and a minute later the Indomitable Lions were back on level terms as Jean Makoun's header found Eto'o. Although he lost control, it fell into the path of Meyong and he made no mistake.

With extra time ending at 1–1, that led to the penalty shootout that was to go down in the record books as the longest in international football history. Every player, including both goalkeepers, took his turn with the spot kicks so they all then had to start again. With the scores tied at an almost unbelievable 11–11, Samuel Eto'o stepped up to the spot and promptly ballooned the ball over the bar.

Didier, who had had a much better game than his illustrious rival, calmly stepped forward and brought the nail biting to an end with a scoreline of 12–11. No wonder Ivory Coast coach Michel said, 'This victory is as good a day as I have had in one match since I coached France to the 1986 World Cup semi-finals. I am proud of my players, who I never doubted, especially as before we came here people said that we did not merit our place at the World Cup finals. We disproved that here tonight.'

As if one shoot-out wasn't enough, in another quarter-final being played at the same time, Nigeria beat Tunisia 6–5 on penalties. In all, including the missed shots, forty-one penalties were taken in the two games.

Back home in West Africa the Ivorians were overjoyed and Didier took the opportunity to say on the country's television station, 'It is difficult to concentrate on Chelsea when the future of my country depends on the national side's results.

'That's never a good thing. I'm not too happy about it but that's the way things are. We have pulled off something great in qualifying for the World Cup and the squad wants the whole country to pull in the same direction for once.' He added that the players had promised to 'bring back peace to our country saying, "Excuse me, but put down the guns! Let's reconcile!"'

Coach Michel, who had to base himself in Beirut to avoid anti-French feeling in the Ivory Coast, said, 'Right now, we're heroes back in the Ivory Coast but if we had lost to Cameroon, all hell would have broken loose. There's no sense of proportion in football anywhere, but in Africa it's much worse ... Everything's great now, everyone's having a party and I'm glad because people have suffered too much in recent years ... the only moments of happiness they have had have been from football.'

## DIDIER DROGBA

Victory over Cameroon meant that Didier and his pals had another tough game ahead against Nigeria and another one of the large England-based African contingent, Everton defender Joseph Yobo. 'That's going to be exciting and a real challenge,' Yobo told Reuters on the eve of the match. 'A tough one. He's a top player, no doubt about that. I've played against him a few times already. It will be very, very exciting. He is obviously a very special player but I'm not worried about him specifically. My first concern is the match itself and helping my team to make it to the final.' But that was Didier's main focus too and, if it was possible to increase his status back home, it came when he scored the only goal of the game against the Nigerian Super Eagles. He proved the big difference between the two West African countries when, a minute into the second half, he pounced on a loose ball after a long cross by Koffi Ndri, to ensure a place in the final against hosts Egypt.

Nigeria's coach Augustine Eguavoen admitted his team were outplayed by the Ivory Coast but questioned the winning goal. 'We did not play well. This was our worst game at this tournament and we were clearly outplayed in all departments by our opponents. However, the goal that finally beat us was scored from an offside goal. Drogba was at least seven metres offside before he scored but the referee gave the goal.'

The captaincy certainly didn't seem to have had an adverse effect on Didier's game, as he reflected shortly before the final: 'Quite simply, I'd be really proud to win this Cup, whether that's as a player or a captain, because a continental title means a great deal,' he told a news conference.

'It's enormous. It's a degree of recognition that comes just below that of the World Cup. But today, simply the fact of being in the final is just happiness. I try to stay as I was before, to keep talking. You might notice the armband but it's just a piece of material and you don't need that to be able to speak your mind in a team.'

# OUT OF AFRICA

Even as they were getting ready for the press conference, back in the Ivory Coast, President Laurent Gbagbo was emphasising the importance of their performance to the war-torn country. He said the national team 'must know that the country is mobilised behind them, that the whole country awaits their victory, that the entire country is waiting for their return to have a little bit of happiness. All Ivorians must stay mobilised behind the Elephants. There's nothing more discouraging than to know that you're fighting for your country but that no one supports you.'

On the streets youths were chanting an Ivorian saying to illustrate how the animal that gave the country its name always managed to overcome obstacles and to show that the people too would triumph. 'The elephant is stronger than the forest,' they cried.

Sadly the Elephants weren't stronger than the Pharaohs of Egypt in front of 75,000 spectators in Cairo's International Stadium. And, to make matters worse, Didier, who had been one of the outstanding players of the tournament and whose performances had taken his team so far, was the 'villain' of the piece. The game went to another penalty shoot-out, although it shouldn't have done so, as Didier fired a golden chance over the bar with just eleven minutes of what proved to be a goalless game left. It was the kind of chance he normally buried. Then, when it came to penalties, his hard, low effort was superbly saved by goalkeeper Essam El-Hadary springing to his right, who also then stopped the Ivory Coast's third spot kick by Bakary Koné, making the home side 4–2 winners on the day. Didier was practically tearful at the end of the game.

If anyone thought defeat would mean the Ivorians would be returning home in disgrace, they would be wrong, as thousands turned out to give them a rapturous reception when they returned home that weekend. Several thousand fans were at the airport to greet the Elephants with banners proclaiming, 'You have lost but we remain proud of you,' waved in their honour. The fans fought to catch a glimpse of the squad with excited men and women climbing onto the roofs of cars as well as friends' shoulders. The Ivory Coast's goalkeeper Jean-Jacques Tizié was overcome by their reception. 'We weren't expecting such an extraordinary welcome', he said. 'That only goes to prove the unique bond between the people and the team.'

As for Didier, he was embraced by the famed Ivorian singer Aïcha Koné at the airport, who cried, 'Oh! Look at him, he is so sad.' Didier simply thanked her before heading off with the rest of the squad for the motorcade trip to meet the President. Police desperately tried to clear a way for the motorcade as it threatened to be swamped by the crowds, and it took four hours for it to edge its way through to the main football stadium – several supporters tried to climb onto the truck and shake hands with the players, who were smiling and some were bare-chested – where hundreds more fans awaited them.

If they had won the tournament, the celebrations would probably never have ended!

## CHAPTER 23

# The Knives Are Out

It's true to say that, while Didier had been away in North Africa, he was badly missed back home at Stamford Bridge. Chelsea were still rampant, but on 11 Febraury a 3–0 defeat at Middlesbrough took the wind out of their sails temporarily, and the situation wasn't helped by Didier's fitness problems as he headed back to England.

'For three months I have had lingering pain in my knee,' he admitted. 'I am fine in my mind but I can't play as I would want to. When I kick, and change direction, I am not at my best. Even for my goal against Nigeria, I didn't kick the ball as I wanted. I am only at sixty per cent of my abilities.' And he spelled out what everyone knew: that his club boss would have preferred to keep his £24 million player alongside him. 'At first, Mourinho said, "You are on holidays, you have to come back perfectly fresh,"' Didier revealed. 'It was a way of letting me understand he would have preferred me to stay.'

So it came as no surprise when José Mourinho said, 'We miss his presence. That's no reflection on Hernán Crespo or Carlton Cole, who have both done well. I just think Drogba gives us something different and you can't get away from that.' But it was slightly more surprising that the sentiments were echoed by Didier's rival for the striker role, Hernán Crespo. 'I am waiting for Didier to be back because I know I cannot play all the games. In the Premier League you need to fight every game against two centre-halves who are usually very tall and very strong. It's like a war and I am struggling now. I am doing the job, but I hope Didier is back soon so we can share our duties.'

Four days after his rapturous reception in Abidjan, Didier was back in training for the not-so-exotic FA Cup fifth-round clash with Colchester. Not that Chelsea could afford to ignore the prospect of any successful cup run. They had just recorded a pretax loss for the last accounting year of £140 million, a British football club record. It dwarfed even the previous record, Chelsea's £87.8 million loss the previous year! The main expenditure was, of course, the massive transfer fees that the club had been paying out, plus the hefty salaries that went with them, a scarcely believable £108 million in one year!

But chief executive Peter Kenyon said the business was much healthier than it looked: 'These figures reflect the continuing restructuring which we began in 2003,' he explained. 'The overall loss increase is, in the main, down to some exceptional items that were necessary in order to help us achieve our strategic business aim of break-even by 2009–10. In simple terms we have taken some pain now for long-term gain.'

The accounts covered the year to the end of June 2005 and included the £25.5 million cost of terminating the club's sponsorship contract with Umbro early and the £13.8 million write-off of striker Adrian Mutu's potential transfer value after he was sacked for drug taking, which also inflated the losses. Other one-off costs were £5 million on recruiting Frank Arnesen from Tottenham to run youth development and wiping £9 million off the paper value of midfielder Juan Verón after he decided to complete his contract on loan at Inter Milan.

*Above*: Back in his home town of Abidjan, Drogba gets to grips with excited fans.

*Below*: Making sacrifices as young parents, Clotilde and Albert Drogba have seen their son reach the stratosphere of international football. Here they gather in France before the World Cup while Didier endorses 'Chocolat du Planteur'.

*Above*: A brave performance as captain and a goal from Didier could not stave off a 2-1 defeat to the Netherlands in June at World Cup 2006.

*Below*: In action against Argentina in the 'Group of Death' at World Cup 2006, Drogba shows off his silky skills to stick one past the sprawling Argentine defence to score in a 2-1 defeat. But with defeat came acclaim for player and team alike.

*Above*: The hero returns to his homeland. Drogba received a rapturous reception along with the other Elephants upon their return from the World Cup, at which they performed with great credit.

*Below*: Reflecting his growing goalscoring record and popularity at Stamford Bridge, Didier signs an extension to his Chelsea contract with Peter Kenyon and David Barnard in November 2006.

*Above*: On form for Chelsea, and Didier celebrates another strike against Liverpool in the FA Cup semi-final in April 2006.

*Below*: Didier shapes up to unleash a fearsome left foot drive to score against arch-rivals Barcelona in the Champions League, October 2006.

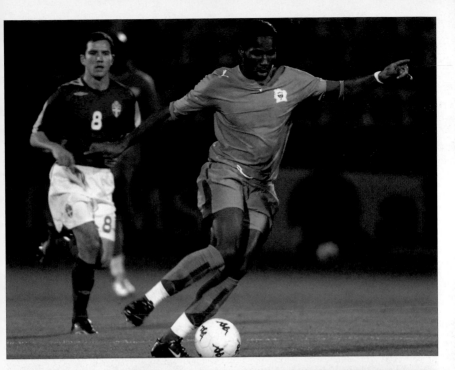

The classic Didier pose – composed and quick on the ball, and in his familiar celebratory pose after netting for the Elephants against Sweden in November 2006. The game was played at his old stomping ground at Le Mans.

*Above*: Living it up in the capital, Drogba has become a firm favourite on and off the pitch at Stamford Bridge.

*Below*: Didier with his sometime Chelsea strike partner, and at £30m one of the most expensive players in the world, Ukrainian Andriy Shevchenko.

Didier cradles the 2006 Barclays Premiership trophy with his children.

*Above left*: A high profile multi-millionaire, Didier is keen to give his time to helping those less fortunate than he. In January 2007 he was appointed as a United Nations Goodwill Ambassador to fight poverty, with a symbolic salary of US$1 a year.

*Above right*: His deadly eye for scoring in cup finals continues, as Drogba picked up the FA Cup in May 2007 after netting the only goal of the game in extra time.

*Below*: Drogba celebrates after scoring in the Champions League semi-final against Liverpool in 2008.

So, with bills to be paid, it can't have been all that pleasing for the Chelsea directors to see their side go behind to a Carvalho own goal at Stamford Bridge on 19 Febraury against Colchester. With the Blues, frankly, not firing, it became necessary for Joe Cole, Frank Lampard and Hernán Crespo to come on as substitutes before order was restored and they ended up winning 3–1. Didier didn't score, but he did manage to last the full ninety minutes.

The home game against Colchester may have been a bit of a struggle, but Chelsea had opponents of a different stature to take on three days later at their ground – Barcelona. For the second year running they had been drawn against the Catalans, and given the storm over their previous meeting – with Didier's sending-off, the criticism of referee Anders Frisk, who then quit the game, and Samuel Eto'o saying he was racially abused in London – it promised to be a night to remember. Mind you, there was no need to wait for the whistle to sound before the fun and games kicked in.

Samuel Eto'o – fresh from the African Nations defeat – set the ball rolling when he claimed Chelsea were running scared of him, saying José Mourinho had put special plans in place to try to stop him from scoring. 'My friend Geremi told me Chelsea are preparing a special system for me. I want revenge on Chelsea and my desire is to score a goal in London. I know I am better than all of the Chelsea team. The proof in that is Chelsea wanted to buy me. Didier Drogba is a good striker but I am better. His Ivory Coast team knocked Cameroon out on penalties in the African Nations Cup, so I have another reason for revenge. Ever since we were knocked out by Chelsea last year I have dreamed of playing them again. Our elimination was unjust. The way we will beat them will be spectacular – there will be many goals.'

It didn't take Didier long to hit back when he said, 'I outdid Eto'o in the African Nations Cup and now I want to do it again against Barça – my dream is Champions League glory. It's not just about me and Eto'o because there are so many good players on both sides. But every time I play against Samuel I just seem to come out on top.

'It could be that he is starting to feel afraid every time he sees me opposite him on a football pitch. At this moment I feel I am the king of African football.'

And he added, 'I am not worried about losing my place in the Chelsea team to Hernán Crespo, despite the fact that he has been scoring goals since I have been away. It shouldn't be a surprise to anybody – he is just doing his job. I think Crespo and I could play together successfully.

'There is no team better than us in England at the moment. We have been proving that for the last two seasons. The game against Barcelona will be filled with passion. There is not much between us – we are two of the best clubs in the world, and we are both capable of winning away from home, so it is not that important that we are playing the first leg at Stamford Bridge.'

What *was* important, though, was that Chelsea should have eleven men on the pitch for all ninety minutes, and again it was something they could not achieve. Just thirty-seven minutes into the game, referee Terje Hauge sent off Spanish defender Asier Del Horno after he lunged at Barcelona's brilliant Argentinian Lionel Messi. There was no score at the time, and it left Chelsea yet again with a mountain to climb against one of the top sides in the world.

Paradoxically when Del Horno left the field, Barcelona were on top but they hadn't created a clear-cut chance. As often happens in football, ten-man Chelsea then started to play their best football of the match. Didier was among the substitutes but he came on at half-time and with almost an hour gone, Brazilian Tiago Motta turned in Frank Lampard's free kick under pressure from John Terry and the reduced Chelsea side had gone into the lead. Unfortunately, this own goal was then cancelled out by another as Terry touched Ronaldinho's seventy-first-minute free kick past Petr Čech. As the excitement mounted, late substitute Shaun Wright-Phillips missed a good chance to restore Chelsea's lead, only to regret it moments later as the dreaded Samuel Eto'o – who had just narrowly beaten Didier to the African Player of the Year award – rose to head in an eightieth-minute winner for the Catalan side. Those two precious away goals meant that Chelsea would have to win and score at least two themselves to stand a chance of progressing into the final eight of the contest.

Afterwards, Mourinho said Chelsea should think about asking UEFA to punish Messi for 'play-acting' and to revoke the red card. He also said, presumably in jest, that he would consider taking a B team to the Nou Camp and instead concentrate on the Premiership and FA Cup. It was Chelsea's first home defeat against Spanish opposition and, leaving aside the Carling Cup penalty shoot-out defeat by Charlton, remarkably it was Mourinho's first at Stamford Bridge in fifty matches in all competitions.

'What changed everything was the fact we were playing ten versus eleven when we should not have been', he said. 'To play with ten men is always difficult, even against a small team. Against a good team it is, of course, *more* difficult.'

Referring to the previous encounter between the teams – at the same stage of the same competition, a year ago to the day, when Didier was sent off in the first half of the first leg – he couldn't resist adding, 'Again, we had to play them with ten players, and not for a small period of time. When you play ten to fifteen minutes with ten men you have the energy to fight such a situation. When you play with ten for an hour it is difficult to close the door all the time. Sometimes the door has to open, that is the reality.

'When it was eleven versus eleven, we beat them last season. When it was eleven versus eleven last night the game was open. When it was eleven versus eleven in Barcelona we were winning 1–0. But ten versus eleven is very difficult. When you play ten versus eleven you can't press in the centre and you can't double up on the wings – you are struggling.'

Confused? Well, he certainly made his point on that but, unlike twelve months earlier, he was reluctant to let rip in his criticism of the referee.

'If I say what I thought about the sending-off I can be suspended. Can we take back the suspension for Del Horno? Can we suspend Messi for play-acting? It is a cultural city, Barcelona, you know all about theatre. Would it be right to send a B team to the Nou Camp and concentrate on the Cup and the League? We can discuss all these issues but the final result is 2–1. But I do not want to talk about the game like that. I want to talk about how proud I am of my players and the fans. I prefer to lose like this than like Middlesbrough. I prefer to go to Barcelona in a positive mood. We have to go there and compete and do our best.'

It was a good job Chelsea didn't have to take the Stamford Bridge pitch with them. The surface was coming under growing criticism and, after a routine and, it must be admitted, fairly uninspiring 2–0 win over a Portsmouth side, who seemed at that stage of the season to be heading for relegation, it was announced that the surface was to be relaid. The three games in six days it had been forced to endure were final proof that it wasn't of the standard necessary for such a top-flight club.

But the playing surface can't have been the most worrying concern for Didier in the victory over Harry Redknapp's side. During the match he was the victim of the Chelsea boo-boys, unhappy at his performance. It is always a worrying time for any player when a home crowd decide he is to be the victim of their pent-up anguish and a section of the Stamford Bridge crowd had decided to ignore his injuries and enforced absence on international duty, and to select him as the target for their vitriol. It was a mood that had been simmering for some time, and it was to get worse.

Even an away game didn't bring any respite from controversy when a visit to West Bromwich Albion brought a 2–1 victory – and a furious pitch and touchline row. Didier, who had opened the scoring, and William Gallas both came out late for the start of the second half. And the striker was then accused by the opposing supporters of diving after Arjen Robben had been sent off for lunging at Jonathan Greening.

West Brom manager Bryan Robson – who was involved in a series of arguments with Mourinho during the game – could not contain his anger afterwards. 'The bell had gone ages ago and our players had gone out to get on with the game. For whatever reason Chelsea came out late. Whether they believe it takes the sting out of the game or drops the tempo, I don't know, but it annoyed me as my players wanted to get on with the second half. For me if the bell's gone, why wait for the players who were late? If they're not there, get on with the game! I'm happy to play Chelsea with nine men.'

Robben got a straight red card by referee Mark Halsey for a touchline tackle on Greening before Didier went to ground after a challenge by the same West Brom midfielder. Robson, a former Manchester United and England captain, said, 'I thought Robben was a bit unfortunate to get sent off but Drogba tried to even it up. Jonathan Greening didn't touch him – he dived. José Mourinho had a different opinion to me but at least the referee didn't buy it.

'I thought Robben was a little unlucky to be sent off. If I'd been playing in the game I wouldn't have been happy with a decision like that. Jonathan Greening didn't touch him and the way he reacted was not good. José didn't see it that way and that's why we had a difference of opinion.' Mourinho had to be restrained by police and stewards in the technical area as he reacted to Greening's challenge on Didier.

John Hollins, one of Chelsea's most loyal and popular former players, went on Radio 5 Live and commented 'The strangest thing is, you've got two players in that side – John Terry and Frank Lampard – who play every single game committed, get into people, tackle people, score goals, stop goals, and they play every week. They're very rarely booked for anything, and yet the guys around them let them down because they give you a bad name.'

Even the newspaper of record, *The Times*, thought that Drogba had gone down too easily while the tabloid *Daily Star* joined in to say 'Didier Drogba has to be the biggest baby in football. The Chelsea and Ivory Coast striker is built like a tank and is one of the strongest forwards in the Premiership. How come, then, he goes down like a big girl? Instead of concentrating on scoring goals he spends too much time writhing about in agony.'

When it comes to England footballing legends they don't come much bigger than Sir Bobby Charlton, who said, 'The British always used to be called the gentlemen of sport. They would play the game correctly, with a stiff upper lip – but we did it right. We seem to have drifted into some of the bad habits others have brought with them. We didn't used to have any of this in our country until players from abroad came in.'

The criticism was practically universal, but, row or not, one thing was certain: Chelsea were poised to retain their title and it was only the first week in March. They led the league table with seventy-two points with Liverpool in second position on fifty-five, an amazing seventeen-point gap. Not that this comfortable position meant Chelsea were in any mood to take their foot off the gas, or that the pressure on them would ease off. Just two days after the row at the Hawthorns, Mourinho was jeered, jostled and spat on at Barcelona airport by home fans angry over his criticism of Lionel Messi's 'play-acting' in the first leg. Messi hadn't been too impressed either, saying, 'I want to produce the biggest match of my life against Chelsea to silence the mouth of Mourinho and his players. They claim I am an actor; they are wrong. I am a professional footballer and I have received many kicks this season. The actors are for the cinema and not for sport. I do not want contact with Mourinho because he was deceptive with me through his behaviour. He should look at the bruises on my legs.'

It didn't look as though there were any prisoners going to be taken during Chelsea's stay in northern Spain. One newspaper front page had a picture of José Mourinho with the headline HERE COMES THE MONSTER. Didier sprang to his boss's defence. 'Not everyone in the world likes Mourinho but he deserves respect. He is the greatest. There is no other coach that I would want in this situation. He leaves nothing to chance and knows how to react to any situation.' And he added, 'With all due respect to Barça, I'm convinced we will come back.'

Sadly he was very wrong. For once Chelsea could not provide the magic needed to beat Barcelona in front of their 90,000 fans and, although Frank Lampard scored a ninetieth-minute penalty, it was not enough. A superb Ronaldinho goal after seventy-eight minutes meant the game had gone away from Chelsea and there was nothing Didier, who was replaced by Crespo in the fifty-eighth minute, or the rest could do about it.

It didn't take long for the knives to come out. One commentator, the avid Chelsea fan, former Tory MP and former Heritage Secretary David Mellor wrote, 'Watching Didier Drogba trying to head the ball with all the skill of a dying duck was not only depressing, but predictable. That's how he is. So why did Mourinho play him?' The *Guardian* pointed out that the majority of Chelsea's chances had fallen to 'Drogba, a tree of a man with the finesse of a lumberjack'.

It was Didier's twenty-eighth birthday that weekend, so he could have done without such a barrage of criticism, much of it misplaced and unwarranted. No wonder he had doubts about whether his long-term career was with Chelsea or whether he should look elsewhere given his high standing in the football world. He did break off from birthday celebrations long enough to defend Mourinho again, much in the way the coach rebutted any criticism of Didier.

'Anybody who cannot see the genius of Mourinho must be blind. His intelligence is beyond anybody I've ever met. He's always three steps ahead and his mind works in ways other managers can only dream of. Of course, the results aren't always perfect for us –

but José has changed us beyond anything anyone outside the club could have imagined. His only interest is winning. He prepares us in minute detail and studies our opponents until his brain hurts. He has also instilled a spirit which makes us strong and able to come back from any disappointment.'

It must have been a relief to get back to the comparatively simple task of playing football that weekend. In March 2006 Didier came on as substitute against Tottenham Hotspur at Stamford Bridge in the second half with the score 1–1 and watched as William Gallas scored a last-minute winner. At least the game passed without any more controversy for Didier, but it was only the calm before yet another storm as far as he was concerned.

As newspapers reported on more negotiations to bring Andriy Shevchenko to Chelsea and that the club was interested in German playmaker Michael Ballack, Chelsea suffered a rare defeat, 1–0 at Fulham, their first loss at Craven Cottage for thirty-nine years. But it wasn't the result alone that captured the ensuing headlines: they focused more on William Gallas' late dismissal for stamping on the ankle of Heidar Helguson as Fulham tried to run the clock down.

Amid Chelsea protests over the red card, Gallas ripped off his gloves and threw them to the ground in a clear sign of dissent, and then he goaded the Fulham supporters as he left the pitch and fighting broke out between rival fans.

Didier too was involved in a storm. He appeared to have equalised midway through the second half and neither referee Mike Dean nor his assistant on the line, Paul Norman, seemed to be about to disallow it. The Fulham players were outraged, however, protesting that Didier had handled and after consultation the officials decided not to allow the goal.

Mourinho was philosophical. 'Because it was handball, the decision is correct, but I can promise you the linesman didn't see it. He was where I was. I couldn't see, he couldn't see.

'His flag was down, the goal was allowed, my players went back to their half to wait for the game to carry on, the Fulham players put pressure on the ref and on the linesman. When Chelsea does this and surrounds the referee, it's the end of the world and we are punished. The FA runs after us. When opponents do it, nothing happens.'

Mike Dean later said that he had been buzzed by his linesman through the electronic tagging devices by which Premiership officials are linked up. 'I went to speak to him voluntarily. It was not pressure of the Fulham players. Paul was convinced it was handball.'

At least Chelsea got back on the right track as far as the results were concerned, thanks to a John Terry goal at home to Newcastle on 16 March 2006 in the quarter-final of the Cup, although the team's display was not one of their best.

Didier was booked for his part in a fifty-ninth minute mêlée after Newcastle's Robbie Elliott piled into Joe Cole. Still, his yellow card went relatively unnoticed compared with the next storm he was about to be involved in, the famous 'Sometimes I dive...' sensation.

## CHAPTER 24

# 'Sometimes I Dive...'

The record books show that on 25 March 2006 Chelsea beat Manchester City 2–0 with both goals coming from Didier. Not only that, he was chosen as Man of the Match. It should, therefore, have been a day of happiness for the twenty-eight-year-old. Instead it was one of the darkest moments of his career, a day that made him and his family think long and hard about whether he should stay with Chelsea, or even remain in England itself.

Didier had gone down in the twenty-fourth minute under a tackle from England full-back Danny Mills, although TV replays later showed that contact, if as any at all, was minimal. But things seemed to be going smoothly when he put his side ahead with a left-foot shot in the thirtieth minute after a good piece of link-up play with Eidur Gudjohnsen, and three minutes later Asier del Horno deflected Joe Cole's drive towards Didier in the six-yard box. The striker seemed to use his arm to control the dropping ball before driving in a low shot past David James in the City goal for number two. Like Fulham a week earlier, the City players were furious, but this time there was no reprieve from the officials.

## DIDIER DROGBA

City's Sylvain Distin and Kiki Musampa earned themselves yellow cards for their protests and there was worse to come for skipper Distin. As the half ended he carried on expressing his feelings to referee Rob Styles and even refused to hand him the match ball. That earned him a second booking and meant that City were condemned to spend the rest of the match with just ten men.

Just after half-time Didier dramatically jack-knifed under a tackle from Richard Dunne and with ninety minutes almost up the two clashed again. Didier surged into the box, Richard Dunne's hand came into contact with his face and Didier crashed to the deck. He was led to the touchline, and at the same time a core of Chelsea supporters began singing the name of Peter Osgood, one of the all-time greats of Stamford Bridge, who had just died at the age of fifty-nine. The implication was clear: Ossie, a tough competitor as well as a supremely gifted player, would never have gone down in such a manner.

At the same time it was announced over the Tannoy that Didier had been made Man of the Match – and a very vocal minority of the fans made their feelings clear by booing the choice. Didier had walked back around the touchline to the dugout and, when he got there he heard the full-time whistle blow and quickly disappeared down the tunnel. It didn't seem as though it could get much worse, but it did.

First, the handball. Didier was honest when he said after the game, 'Yes, it was handball but sometimes this is the game. I don't know how to explain. The ball comes to me and I can't do nothing but this.' When asked whether he felt it was unfair to score in such a way he replied, 'OK, so take off the goal I scored.'

Then came the famous diving questions. He was asked on BBC's *Match of the Day* about his 'diving' and he replied, 'Sometimes I dive, sometimes I step over, you know. I don't care about this. In football you can't stay up every time. The people who are criticising me maybe should come on the pitch and we will see if they dive or not.' But then he was quickly, and rather confusingly, to backtrack when he was asked if this was a diver's confession. 'No, no, no, I don't dive,' he added.

It is important to remember at this stage that Didier was far from fluent in English, and the nuances of language involved in the never-ending 'what is a dive, what isn't a dive?' debate were probably more than his fledging knowledge of his new language could cope with after such an emotional, and some reports suggested tearful, afternoon. Either way, he quickly added late on that Saturday night in a statement, 'Unfortunately, in the emotion of winning the game, my comments have come across partly in the wrong way. I want to make clear that I don't dive. This was the intention of my answer.'

No matter what he said, the debate became a roar. City boss Stuart Pearce said, 'When I first saw it I thought it was handball and I've watched it again and it was handball. Simple as that. These things happen. It was a quick game out there and if they miss the odd decision it's not for me to criticise. One or two of my players were aggrieved and the captain has got sent off for questioning the decision. The referees have a difficult job and hopefully next week we will get one. Drogba's a good player. He scores goals, he costs a lot of money, he's good in the air and a handful to play against. I haven't thought about anything else.'

But he couldn't resist saying later, when asked if Didier should stay on his feet more easily, 'I've no idea. Maybe his studs are not the best. Maybe his boots aren't the greatest any more.'

Gordon Taylor, chief executive of the Professional Footballers' Association (PFA), weighed in, saying, 'The spotlight is on him. Referees are going to be looking out for him and if anything it might be counterproductive. He's a big lad and, if he's not careful, he's going to get done even when he doesn't mean to do anything wrong ... We're an entertainment industry, and there's a difference between what lengths you go to win a game and playing it in the right spirit. Certain players are in danger of getting a reputation that will go before them and, as a result, they're going to leave themselves open to be done when they're maybe not guilty.'

Taylor stressed he was talking about players diving and pretending to be injured rather than incidents where a goal follows a handball offence. 'I have looked at the second goal Drogba scored and it wasn't exactly a Maradona Hand of God. It was really one for the match officials. This is not quite in the same category as players who roll over and feign injury outside the box to try to get opponents sent off. That's the thing we're trying to prioritise.'

At least there was one person who could be relied on to defend Didier: José Mourinho, and he was adamant that the last-minute incident with Dunne had not been diving. 'It was a big thing. It was a finger very strong in his eye and it was completely full of blood. Of course, he is not blind but it was something serious. The referee saw it as an accident and I accept that.

'Sometimes he is a player who does not get what he deserves. Didier is a fighter. I am happy with him and we are happy to have a professional like him. Players are not just about the skilful, beautiful ones who play for the stands. It is very important to have players who fight for the team, work for the team, attack and defend. He is the kind of player [to whom] I would say, "With you I could go to every war." He is a very important player for us.'

Didier later said that his eye was 'OK' but felt the criticism of him resulted from his playing for the team at the top of the Premiership, and – amid some newspaper claims that he went down in an over-theatrical manner – he said again that he was confused during the interview. He added that was devastated by the fans' reaction, saying, 'In every game I always give everything for my team. And I always have a lot of respect for my shirt, for my club. So I don't know why they do this.' He told Chelsea TV, 'Yes, I handled it but, as I said, this is a part of the game. If the referee saw it he has to whistle, but he didn't.'

That didn't stop some Chelsea 'supporters' from carrying on the criticism, though. The message board on the club's website was flooded with complaints about his 'play-acting', one fan writing, 'He is bringing shame on our club by acting this way.'

While Mourinho's defence of his star striker was to be expected, the support of another leading coach came as a surprise. None other than Arsenal's Arsène Wenger said, 'Drogba is a bit in the spotlight at the moment, but overall I like his attitude. He is not an unfair player, basically. He makes sometimes more of it, like many strikers do, but sometimes he is maybe pushed or pulled when nobody sees it – defenders cheat on the strikers as well. What he got wrong maybe was on the handball when he scored the goal. But, overall, I do not think that you have to single out Drogba.'

Sensible words from Wenger, but Didier was already telling friends he was thinking of leaving Chelsea. The latest storm was making him more convinced than ever that it might be the right thing to do. His uncle, Michel Goba, who had spent the Saturday night after the match with Didier, confirmed it. 'I believe Didier could leave if he keeps hearing whistling from Chelsea fans. It wouldn't surprise me if he looked elsewhere,' he said. It was only much later, when his talent and goals had won over the doubters, that he was able to reflect on this difficult period in his life in an interview in the *Sunday Times*. He said,

'The adjustment was difficult. Leaving Marseilles was not like leaving France, the city is like a separate country, and London is very different – especially the weather. The football was different too. I wasn't used to the English style, and running the channels, when I was used to having the ball played to my feet, was very hard. People think I'm big and strong, so I shouldn't fall over, but I wasn't used to the English style and at first I didn't use my arms to protect myself. I played exactly as I had in France. In England you can use your body more. I had to learn to fight for the ball, to be more physical, and while I was doing that, people misunderstood me. Part of the problem is that challenges that are penalised as fouls in France are seen as OK here.'

And he tried to clear up any lingering misunderstanding over his diving 'admission', explaining, 'I said something in English and when it appeared in the newspapers it did not have the meaning I intended. It was reported as, "Yes, I dive", but that isn't what I meant. What I intended to say was, "It is difficult to stay on your feet when opponents come to fight you for the ball and you are not used to the physicality of it."

'While we're on that subject, it seems to me that in English football people don't like it sometimes when you tell the truth,' he continued, referring to the Manchester City handball. 'I was asked, "Did you handle the ball?" and I said, "Yes, I did."

'After all the fuss, it would have been better if I hadn't admitted it. In France, if the same thing had happened, the reaction would have been, "OK, he's admitted he was in the wrong, end of story."

'When your own fans are having a go at you, of course you think about it,' he said. 'I didn't like that because since I've been at Chelsea I've always given everything for the club. I thought, "Maybe it's time to think about moving, maybe the fans are right. If they don't want me here, I'll go." As a player, you have to consider these things, and that's what I did.'

Whether it was the controversy of that Manchester City match or simply tiredness as the season drew to its close, both Didier and Chelsea were somewhat lacklustre in a goalless draw at Birmingham City the next week, a game where Didier's cousin Olivier Tébily – with whom he had stayed briefly during his youth in France – was undoubtedly the best player on the field in an otherwise forgettable game.

Despite his personal problems on the pitch, Didier still found time to discuss a far greater issue, that of racism in football, and he told Chelsea's official magazine, 'I would think about leaving the field if I was being abused. The great thing about football is that it is a game for everyone, no matter where you come from or what you look like.

'It brings people from around the world together, but some people don't realise this and they want to make chants about players' colour. I have had some problems with this in the past and it is wrong. We have to think about what we can do to let these people know we do not want this. It is not right.'

Manchester United's Rio Ferdinand had recently called on the game's governing bodies to stop paying 'lip service to the widespread problem of racism' after high-profile incidents involving Shaun Wright-Phillips for England and Barcelona's Samuel Eto'o and FIFA had reacted by launching a new crackdown in which clubs could be docked points or even relegated for persistent problems.

'It seems that the money they take as punishment is not enough. It is not working. It is not just a problem in Spain or in football but something everyone needs to put right', said Ferdinand

While all the off-pitch publicity surrounding Chelsea continued, Manchester United had started to snap at the Blues' championship heels, so on 9 April 2006 both Didier and the team decided to settle matters in the best possible way, on the field with a thrilling victory over West Ham United. The Stamford Bridge game started disastrously with James Collins heading the Hammers into a tenth-minute lead, and then matters got worse six minutes later when Maniche was sent off for a foul. Cocky West Ham fans even started to sing whenever Didier got the ball, 'Dive in a minute, he's going to dive in a minute ...' Things looked grim, but Didier ignored the crowd and started to take control, playing upfront alongside Hernán Crespo in the 4–4–2 formation he preferred.

Didier collected Frank Lampard's pass and, although his first shot was blocked, he smashed in the rebound. The Stamford Bridge fans sprang to life and a mere ninety seconds later they practically lifted the roof when Didier's cross shot was deflected towards

Crespo, who finished off the move. The fact that they were down to ten men in no way seemed to restrict Chelsea, and in the second half, after Essien hit the crossbar, John Terry put them further ahead. Now there seemed no chance that the East End side would force their way back into the match and Didier headed a free kick into Gallas' path for goal number four. It was a wonderful victory after weeks of controversy and it meant that the gap over Manchester United in second place had increased to ten points. Didier was replaced in injury time as a precaution, and this time he left the field to a standing ovation from all corners of the ground. Mourinho put his fingers to his lips as if to tell his star striker, 'Don't say anything – you've said enough on the field.' For the second home game running, Didier was voted Man of the Match, and this time there were no jeers. In fact the fans who had chanted Peter Osgood's name at the last home game were now singing 'That's Why We're the Champions'.

Mourinho was ecstatic: 'We played with 10 men and it looked like we had twelve on the pitch. When you're losing 1-0 and with a direct red card it's very, very hard. Only a team with great character could do what the players did. It was fantastic. We had a week together, a long week to experiment to focus on the game. we were together, we talked,' he said.

'Didier closed a few mouths today, not mine, because I always support him. I think he was amazing. The team performance was unbelievable. But the way he worked for the team and the effort he put in was unbelievable too. The best way for players is to speak on the pitch. I think Drogba should go home, switch on TV and listen to the pundits. He should buy every single paper to see if the same people who wanted to kill him now have the common sense to give him the credit he deserves.'

As always, the remarks of an opponent were revealing too. Hammers' boss Alan Pardew said of Didier's performance, both in defence and attack, 'He was world-class. I think we knew that Chelsea were gearing up for this game after they'd been some criticism at their door. The ten players they had showed world-class performances today.'

The *Guardian* newspaper, not known for exaggeration on its sports pages, contained this telling line about Didier's performance: 'He gave a demonstration of the centre-forward's art that is unlikely to be bettered on an English pitch this season.'

The *Daily Telegraph* went even further, saying,

It was an extraordinary performance, bristling with pace, power, potency and above all, perhaps, a deep-seated desire to prove people wrong. Having single-handedly terrorised West Ham's dishevelled defence, Didier Drogba reminded an enraptured Stamford Bridge exactly what he is capable of. And it is a pretty frightening sight when everything clicks. The standing ovation that greeted Drogba's late substitution was wholly justified.

And the same newspaper also referred to the growing number of stories linking Andriy Shevchenko and other players with the Blues, adding, 'If that means Drogba being sacrificed, at least he can go safe in the knowledge that he put in a performance one Spring afternoon that will be remembered in these parts long after his exit. Not everyone can say that.'

The next week Chelsea were at the Reebok, where they had claimed the Championship a year earlier, and found little difficulty in beating Bolton 2–0 with goals from the ever-reliable pair of John Terry and Frank Lampard. As he preferred, Didier started upfront alongside Hernán Crespo, but neither made it onto the scoresheet or even lasted the full ninety minutes. Didier still managed to get booked, though, ironically for handball. This year the victory didn't give Didier's side the title, but it meant they were virtually home and dry.

And they took another step towards retaining it on 17 April with an efficient 3–0 home victory over Everton. Didier was again in sparkling form, scoring one goal, making another and being innocently responsible for Everton's being reduced to ten men when Lee Carsley was dismissed, for a rash challenge in the forty-seventh minute. His mood was, understandably, far more buoyant than during the Manchester City débâcle, so much so that he kissed two female fans in the Matthew Harding Stand, saying afterwards, 'They had the Ivory Coast flag. I wanted to kiss them.'

By now it was nearing the end of April 2006, the time of year when many clubs were winding down and players were checking out their holiday brochures. There was no way that would be the case at Chelsea. They had one hand on the League title and a precious League and Cup double was theirs for the taking. First, however, they had the little hurdle of a team called Liverpool to overcome. Neutral Old Trafford was packed with 64,475 spectators on 22 April as the two teams, who had fought out a series of epic matches in recent years, ran out onto the pitch.

But it was one game too many for the Blues after their exhausting season. Liverpool went ahead midway through the first half when John Arne Riise scored from a free kick, curling a low shot between Paulo Ferreira and Frank Lampard at the near end of the wall and past unsighted Carlo Cudicini. Worse was to follow after fifty-three minutes when a clearance fell to Luis García and he raced away from three defenders to hit a dipping shot high into the far top corner. Didier, who was booked for dissent, had missed two good first-half chances but he pulled his side back into the match with a brave header after seventy minutes. Chelsea pressed forward relentlessly, pinning Liverpool in their own half, but they ran out of time. Although in head-to-head matches Chelsea's Mourinho had a better record than the Merseyside club, the Liverpool semi-final 'jinx' had struck again.

As always with semi-final defeats, there was an air of inconsolable despair about the Chelsea players as they left the pitch. But after such a fine season, they at least had the chance to experience wild elation a week later when they took on

Manchester United at Stamford Bridge knowing that one point would confirm what everyone in football had suspected for a long time: that the Premiership title was theirs. And given the nature of the side they didn't just settle for one point – instead they collected all three, comfortable 3–0 winners in front of an excited 42,219 crowd. Goals from Gallas, Cole and Carvalho made the difference; Didier clashed with Wayne Rooney, and at the end of the match José Mourinho threw his winner's medal into the crowd and said afterwards he didn't need it, as he'd already got one! By that evening it was for sale on eBay.

One of the paradoxes of top-flight football, where winning is all, is that other events can at times overshadow the actual result. So, even though the match clinched the title, many of the ensuing headlines were devoted to the incident twelve minutes from time when Paulo Ferreira perfectly fairly tackled Wayne Rooney – one of England's main hopes for the forthcoming World Cup – and the young striker fell badly and lay in agony. Even the die-hard Chelsea fans fell silent, fearing the worst, as six men carried him off on a stretcher. They were right too: he had broken a metatarsal in his right foot.

Chelsea's hopes of beating their record total of ninety-five points gathered the previous year were dashed, however, with a couple of anticlimactic defeats at Blackburn Rovers and Newcastle United to end another memorable season. Didier didn't play in either game but that didn't mean he had a summer's rest ahead of him: the World Cup beckoned.

## CHAPTER 25

# World Cup Heartache

Marketing forms a massive part of modern football, and with such a charismatic figure as Didier Drogba, one who is an icon and hero in his homeland, the advertising opportunities are endless. So, in the run-up to the World Cup in Germany he was spotted in, of all places, a park in Richmond, Surrey, kicking a ball about with some young boys. One of them even asked him to autograph the ball only to wipe it clean in disgust when he saw the name he'd written on it. But it wasn't an insult: it was a tongue-in-cheek advert for a McDonald's television advertisement. And the promotional work didn't stop there.

In another filmed clip he stood bare-chested and glistening with cocoa butter, tapping the ball between his feet as a bead of chocolate 'sweat' rolled down his face. Booting the ball away, he looks at the camera and declares proudly: 'Ivory Coast – my land of cocoa.' The film clip was to be beamed across Europe during the run-up to the World Cup as part of a public-relations drive by his war-divided country to coincide with the tournament.

## DIDIER DROGBA

Le Chocolat du Planteur – Planter's Chocolate – was targeting chocolate connoisseurs around Europe, and who better to spread the word than Didier?

'The Elephants have become the vehicle for promoting Ivory Coast's cocoa. At the farmers' request, they have agreed to be ambassadors for Ivorian cocoa and in particular Le Chocolat du Planteur everywhere they play their football,' said Tano Kassi Kadio, director of Ivory Coast's Coffee and Cocoa Bourse marketing body. He added that the project would boost farmers' income by paying a premium for the high-quality cocoa used.

The country and its economy needed all the good publicity it could get. At one stage the British Foreign Office rated it even more dangerous to visit than either Afghanistan or Iraq on the basis that at least some small parts of those war-torn countries were comparatively safe, but *all* of the Ivory Coast was a no-go area.

'I don't believe that soccer is going to reunify the country,' said Bonaventure Kalou, the Ivorian squad member playing for Paris Saint-Germain. 'But it will allow the people a moment of *rapprochement* and help create the climate where we can resolve the conflict.'

The interest in Africa was immense, and Didier and his wife Lalla spent three days in her home country of Mali, just north of the Ivory Coast, meeting President Amadou Toumani Touré in his palace. Didier said afterwards, 'My heart is in Mali and I have always loved the country as if I had been born there. Following the meeting with the President of the Republic, I feel even more reassured. He always gives me wise advice about my marriage and my career. It is an honour for me to be able to serve the country.'

Lalla's father had been a footballer and her uncle, Aguibou Diakite, based in Mali, said that before every big match Didier telephoned to ask for 'blessings' and good fortune in the game ahead. The success of Didier, given that he was married to a woman from Mali, also helped promote good political links between the two countries, he added. And, when the Ivorians qualified for the finals after Cameroon missed their vital penalty, crowds of excited Mali folk besieged Diakite playing balafons – a local type of xylophone – and tom-toms and carrying posters of Didier Drogba with such fervour that his wife was terrified until he explained what all the fuss was about.

Didier's father Albert was, understandably, also talking about his son. Drogba Sr was busy planning the official opening of his 'marquis' – literally 'scrubland' but in reality an open-air restaurant – in Abidjan as soon as the World Cup ended, but it was already in business, with seating for 500 and no fewer than nine giant screens on which to watch the football matches.

'The idea came from the fact that Ivorians need to entertain themselves, so they can share something among one another during the World Cup matches,' said Drogba Sr.

Proud Albert recalled the days he would take tiny Didier to and from the local nursery and even collect him during his lunch hour at the bank until he was five and had, sadly, to be sent to France. Many years later Didier said he wanted to be a professional footballer. 'Like all parents, I wanted him to be a lawyer or a doctor. I wanted him to earn a good living. I know what a hard job it is to be a footballer. The question I asked myself was, "Could my son put up with criticism from others?" Luckily I realised nothing could shake him up that badly.

'For me, he had to go to school first and reach a certain level before becoming a footballer. Because of this he refused an approach from Paris Saint-Germain. Didier signed a youth contract with the club but I was against it. Like all parents, I thought school should come first. Didier was in Le Mans and wasn't playing regularly and it was then that the Ivory Coast's national coach approached him to play for his country's side. Even before all that, Didier loved the Ivory Coast. When he came here on holiday he became close to his cousins. He has a very strong sense of duty to his family.'

## DIDIER DROGBA

Albert also said he didn't realise just how bad the drug problems were among certain sections of French youth until the time Didier came home when he was about eleven. 'I didn't want him to go back to France. I kept him here for a while.' Fortunately for Didier, and world soccer, the worried father then changed his mind.

And Didier's mother Clotilde couldn't be kept out of the picture either at their headquarters at the Robinson country club in Fleesensee. She was doing the cooking so the team would have some 'home cooking' during their stay in Germany, meals such as the national dish foutou, a carbohydrate-rich woody shrub on a bed of bananas, often drenched in aubergine sauce. It tasted even better with free-range chicken, or 'bike-riding' chicken, as it is often called in the Ivory Coast. Didier said, 'Our parents have come together, my mother is in charge of them, and they organise everything for us off the pitch. They cook for us and make sure we are looked after.'

It was ironic that Didier could have played for one of the more fancied countries in the tournament, France, but had opted to compete for the land of his birth, saying, 'It was a natural decision for me. It was not difficult to choose. I feel Ivorian in my heart.' And he made it clear that he had immediately felt at ease when selected for his national side, saying, 'It was very easy. It was as if I had never gone to France. The older players in the team welcomed me and helped me feel confident.'

If Didier wanted to focus totally on the 66–1 chances of his national side it must have been hard, because the end of the season was prompting a hectic spell of coming and going at Chelsea. The main signing was the much-discussed £30 million transfer of Andriy Shevchenko, a move many said would mean the end of Didier's reign as the main striker at the club, and Michael Ballack in midfield. Just to add intrigue to the situation, in France Lyon president Jean-Michel Aulas – no doubt concerned that in spite of winning five consecutive French titles they had been eliminated from the Champions League quarter-finals three years in a row – said his club were 'ready to break the bank' to sign Didier.

Aulas said, 'Didier is one of the best players in Europe. It would be a dream to sign him. We have the ambition to win a sixth title and to do much better in the Champions League. We want to give ourselves the means to match our ambitions.'

With the talk of the new arrivals, José Mourinho was publicly at any rate playing hardball with Didier after his comments about being unhappy at the club. Didier had said, 'It's not a joke. I want to move on and get away from all the pressures here. Those things hurt my feelings and I want a place where I can play without any drawbacks.' Mourinho told a press conference, 'The situation is that he has two more years of a contract with Chelsea and he is one of the players we consider not negotiable, so he has no chance to leave. He has to play for Chelsea and, if he plays with happiness, then fantastic because we get the best of him. If he doesn't play with happiness, he doesn't play. It's his problem.'

Wherever the truth lay, the message seemed to have worked. Just days before the World Cup kicked off, Bernard Lacombe, adviser to Jean-Michel Aulas, said, 'Didier will not be coming to Lyon.' Lacombe had spoken with Didier the night after the Ivory Coast had drawn a 'friendly' with Chile, 1–1 in France.

'He said he was a little tired, that he was suffering from a pollen allergy and he said that Mourinho wanted to build the team around him and Andriy Shevchenko.'

Whether all the transfer deals had upset Didier or not, he looked slightly listless during the Chile match and Elephants coach Henri Michel admitted, 'He is trying to get back to his best level, after a few weeks' break. It would not be normal if he was already at 100 per cent.' Didier played only the first half of a fairly bruising game that saw five Ivorians booked and Didier Zokora sent off.

He was a conspicuous absentee from the Ivory Coast French training camp for two days, although it later emerged that he had been busy on a sponsor's film shoot in the Ivory Coast and had travelled with a federation official, although his absence was wrongly interpreted by some as indicating a troubled state of mind. This didn't seem to be a problem a few days later when he scored twice in the first half in a 3–0 win over Slovenia in a friendly match, taking his goal tally to a remarkable twenty-three goals in just thirty-four internationals.

Some 15,000 Ivorian fans, many of them from France, descended on Germany in their bright orange clothes, carrying tom-toms and waving flags in preparation for the first match in the Group of Death, against Argentina. They were all hoping to do *le coupé-décalé* – a frantic pogoing with bonus scissors kicks to celebrate a goal – that Didier was an expert in. Or, of course, there was always 'the Drogbacite', the hip-shaking dance in honour of their hero. The squad itself probably came from more nations than the supporters: the twenty-three players earned their living in nine different countries.

As seemed to be almost compulsory with Didier, there had to be a battle of words before the battle on the pitch commenced. He made his feelings clear ahead of the meeting with teammate Hernán Crespo and compatriots: 'Crespo is scared of me and scared of playing us at the World Cup. I'm not worried if we beat them and it causes any bad blood. I want to score the goals that put Argentina out of the tournament.

'This is not a time for club teammates to worry about each other – and I certainly won't be, whoever I play against. Hernán told me before we came out to Germany that he is afraid of playing me and my country. He said Argentinians don't like playing African sides, as they have had bad experiences. They lost to Cameroon at the 1990 World Cup and Nigeria in the Olympics in 1996.

'My goal is to win the World Cup. That's why I am here. It is only seven games to the final, which does not seem a lot. It is going to be hard but you can dream. Everything is possible here. Myself and Hernán have spoken about facing each other and we both know that it will be tough. Argentina are talented but it does not mean that they are better. We are here because we deserve to be here and we all want to do something.

'With the situation of our country, it can help a lot of people to focus on us. We have to give a signal to everybody to show unity. It is important that we can show the strength of our nation. We are here to make people happy, to make the whole of Africa happy. It is not easy for us but this is the pressure we are under.'

Manchester United's Argentinian Gabriel Heinze replied, 'He is a dangerous forward. He usually plays on the shoulders of defenders and uses his diagonal runs. I faced him once in England and I lost. But in France, we clashed three times and I won all of them.' Sadly for Didier, he was to win again.

Argentina, loved for their football flair but loathed by some for the inner darkness they sometimes allowed to come to the surface, were one of the great names in the history of world football, and among the crowd at Hamburg to see the new boys from Africa take them on was the greatest of all their players: Diego Maradona. And he was roaring along with the rest of the South Americans when Hernán Crespo put them ahead after twenty-four minutes when a free kick from Riquelme on the left caused havoc in the Ivorian defence and Didier and Heinze rose for the ball and touched it on, only for it to reach Crespo, who was on hand to tuck in the loose ball from close range.

In the thirty-fifth minute Didier headed down across the goalmouth and Kader Keïta's diving header from a couple of metres out was smothered superbly by goalkeeper Roberto Abbondanzieri. It was a telling save, because just three minutes later Argentina grabbed a crucial second after a spell of intense Ivorian pressure, when Riquelme's slide-rule pass reached Saviola, who beat the offside trap and he slipped his shot home. Gabriel Heinze's verbal assault on Didier turned into a physical one soon after the restart when he was booked for a two-footed tackle on the striker, the culmination of a running battle between the two.

## DIDIER DROGBA

Didier continued to be his side's main hope for a goal and, with just eight minutes left, he latched onto a low cross from the left by Aruna Dindane and magnificently fired in on the turn. The Ivory Coast pressed desperately for an equaliser as the drumbeat from their supporters urged them on, but a minute into injury time Didier was booked for throwing the ball at the Argentinian goalkeeper. His understandable frustration could not be contained any longer. Although he had scored, Didier had led by example, but he was devastated by the loss.

'How can I be happy with defeat?' he asked. And he added that his goal was not a consolation because, 'Soccer is not an individual sport, so I'm not happy. We missed a lot of chances to score and that's the difference between a real big team and us. Our team is young. We have to learn and we have two more games. We started well, we were not timid. We put pressure on Argentina at times, but we must do that for ninety minutes.'

The next ninety minutes that faced the Ivorians were against the Dutch. For three decades Holland had produced some of the best footballers in the world but had rarely turned their skills into trophies. Nevertheless, it was a daunting task facing Didier and his team on 16 June just six days after the disappointment of Hamburg. It wasn't a help that he had to miss out on some training, sitting on the sideline with an icepack on his knee, in the run-up to the match. It gave him time, however, to digest the news from Stamford Bridge that with all the new arrivals there was also a key departure: Eidur Gudjohnsen was being transferred to Barcelona.

Victory for the Dutch would mean they progressed into the next round while condemning the Ivorians to an early exit. Didier was the main threat to the Holland side but their coach Marco van Basten insisted he would not change his team's tactics to cope with any one player. 'We have no special anti-Drogba plan,' he said. 'We know he is very good. We know he can score a lot of goals and we know he can create a lot, too, because he is so strong. But we have to look after him as a team. Even though he has a lot of qualities, we cannot change everything just for one player. They are strong individually and collectively and we know it is going to be a very tough game for us.'

Didier knew that too. 'We missed a big chance against Argentina, which shows we still have much to learn. But the defeat only makes us more determined to do well against Holland. It is not going to be easy for us, we always knew that. But we have good players and we will give it a go.'

They certainly did, in a classic World Cup game. For all the criticism of the tournament and the number of forgettable games it can produce, there is still always the possibility of football being played that will stay in the memory long after the game has ended. This was such a match.

Although the two sides were in the grouping dubbed the Group of Death, this match in Stuttgart was described as being part of the Group of Life, due to the exuberance of the football on show. Ruthless strikes by Robin van Persie and Ruud Van Nistelrooy seemed to have sewn up the game for the men from the Netherlands to the delight of their fans, who had travelled across the border. But a stunning goal from the five-foot-four Bakary Koné pulled his side into the game when he sprinted past two defenders and planted his right-foot shot into the top corner of Edwin van der Sar's net. They also had what appeared to be a valid claim for a penalty turned down when Emmanuel Eboué fell under Giovanni van Bronckhorst's untidy challenge.

Robben was then booked for a theatrical dive in the area after falling under a trailing leg before he was joined in the book by Didier, after his boot had caught Van der Sar and referee Ruiz thought it merited a yellow card. It was a stifling hot day and the Ivorians found it hard to maintain the pace of their revival, even though Didier had a header chested off the line by Van Persie. It was the end of the dream for the Ivory Coast nation.

Robben took time out from the celebrations to commiserate

with his disconsolate Chelsea teammate. He said, 'I feel sorry for Didier because the Ivory Coast have played two excellent games – but at least he can go on holiday and come back fresh for the new season with Chelsea.'

A drained Didier commented, 'My goal against Argentina was an historic one so I suppose there is some comfort in that – it's important to leave your mark. Yet the cold hard truth is that it was what I would call a meaningless goal because it didn't change the outcome. I will always look back and feel that we got it tough, landing in a group like this. To have Argentina, the Netherlands and Serbia and Montenegro – those are top-drawer teams. All through the section I was telling myself that the reason we are here is to take on the big teams, but looking back I wouldn't have minded meeting them a bit later. The Dutch are a team who have everything: they are strong in the challenge and they are young and ambitious.'

The two yellow cards he had collected meant that Didier couldn't play in the last, history-making group match against Serbia and Montenegro. On 21 June for the first time since England let a 2–0 advantage become a 3–2 defeat in Mexico in 1970, a side came back from two goals behind to win a match in the finals.

The Europeans' striker Nikola Žigić calmly rounded the keeper to slot home in the tenth minute, while Saša Ilić got the second ten minutes later after sloppy goalkeeping by Boubacar Barry. But the Ivorians quickly recovered, even without the suspended Didier, and Aruna Dindane smoothly converted a twice-taken penalty in the thirty-sixth minute.

With coach Henri Michel urging them to attack after Serbia's Albert Nadj was shown a red card before the break, the Ivorians stormed forward and Man of the Match Dindane popped up to head home his second goal, glancing past Dragoslav Jevrić after a perfect cross from Abelkader Keita in the sixty-seventh. An eighty-sixth-minute penalty by Bonaventure Kalou gave the Ivory Coast the victory an entire nation wanted, and, indeed, deserved.

## WORLD CUP HEARTACHE

Stoppage time saw Cyrille Domoraud sent off for a crunching tackle in a game that featured nine yellow cards, but it did nothing to dampen the celebrations, which ended at the final whistle with a standing ovation from the 66,000 crowd. Didier joined in the rainy after-match celebrations as though he had scored the winning goal. 'We played well, we showed our quality, and that is what mattered. We showed that we belonged at the World Cup.'

# CHAPTER 26

# 'Sheva' Arrives

Although the Ivory Coast's first-round exit from the World Cup must have been a blow to Didier Drogba, it did at least provide a blessing in disguise. For the first time in four years he was able to take a proper holiday. José Mourinho gave him permission for a full month away from football, a much-needed break after the continual pressure of playing at the top level or spending time on the treatment table.

Part of the time was spent in Abidjan meeting up with friends and relatives he had not seen for what seemed an eternity, as indeed did several others from the Ivorian squad. And there was no danger of any backlash, even though the side had not progressed, with Didier pointing out, 'Everyone was generally very positive about the way we'd played, so it was good to be there with the people, to enjoy it all with them. As usual I was treated as a king and everyone gave us an extremely warm welcome.'

He didn't spend all his time in West Africa, however. Didier also visited Morocco and Paris as well as stopping off in Marseilles – he had, after all, kept his name tag from the Vélodrome Stadium locker in case he ever needed to use it again! When he returned for training in London at the end of July 2006 he must have felt refreshed – and he needed to be. The talking point of football was the arrival of the Ukrainian captain Andriy Shevchenko, a man with an unrivalled goal record and a stunning finisher at the highest international level, both with his country and at AC Milan. It had been one of the most protracted transfers in recent history. The first stories linking 'Chelski' with him had appeared as long ago as 2003 and they were continually being given credence by the fact that the striker's model wife Kristen Pazik was a close friend of Roman Abramovich's wife Irina.

When the deal was done for a British record sum of £30 million, one of the first questions raised was whether this would mean the end of Didier Drogba's Chelsea career. Given the barracking he had received at times and the open hostility of some Chelsea fans, Didier – wanted by many leading clubs around the world such as his beloved Marseilles and Inter Milan – could not have been blamed if his thoughts had wandered elsewhere, especially as French champions Lyon were in continual contact with him.

Instead he was remarkably positive when he sat down after the club's pre-season games in America and told the official *Chelsea magazine*, 'I know I can do better this season than I've done so far at Chelsea, especially because I know we'll be playing with two strikers ... Sheva [Andriy Shevchenko] has been brought in to play with me, but we'll do it in our way.'

He elaborated on the fact that the side had twin strikers, saying, 'Even when I played with Hernán Crespo it was fantastic. The most important thing with strikers is the relationship between the two players. But with Sheva I think everything is going to be OK. We've only played together for a short amount of time so far but already I know, I just know ... Sheva and me need to develop a good understanding very quickly because I think there will be a lot of pressure on us. But we'll do our job, I'm not worried.'

# 'SHEVA' ARRIVES

He was slightly more circumspect when he admitted elsewhere that during the summer he had seriously considered moving on. 'It's true, I wanted to leave at one time. The club sent an official to me in Paris and I agreed to remain in the team.

'I was satisfied with the boss's explanation on what his priorities are for the upcoming season. He assured me that the changes in the attack were not made to neglect my role in the team but to complement it.'

One thing was sure: there wouldn't be any competition for the front places from Hernán Crespo, who was allowed to return to Italy, the country he preferred to live and where he had taken out citizenship. But he was quick to praise Chelsea, saying, 'They behaved really well. They understood me as a man. I would like to thank them from the heart. I had a wonderful time at Chelsea with the support of the greatest fans, which, for an Argentine playing in England, is not easy.'

A victory over Feyenoord and a draw with Celtic in friendly games heralded the new season, which got under way with a clash against Liverpool at Cardiff's Millennium Stadium in the FA Community Shield game. Andriy Shevchenko's stunning finish was one the brighter moments in a 2–1 defeat with goals from John Arne Riise and Peter Crouch, and some of the Blues' side, rest or no rest, seemed to be suffering from a World Cup hangover.

It was Didier's turn to get on the scoresheet next when he came on as substitute and scored a late goal, a spectacular diving header late in the game to clinch a 3–0 victory over ten-man Manchester City at Stamford Bridge on 20 August. One observer with a record book to hand pointed out the remarkable fact that the last time a side coached by José Mourinho had lost in a competitive home league game was when his Porto side were beaten by SC Beira-Mar – on 23 February 2002!

There was no such illustrious away record, however, as in midweek Middlesbrough scored two goals in the final ten minutes to rain on Chelsea's parade after Shevchenko opened his league account with a sixteenth-minute goal. Didier had a valid appeal for a penalty turned down when he was bundled over in the area, but the two late goals meant the Riverside Stadium side had beaten the Blues two years running at home. Despite the defeat he was still buoyant. He mentioned again that he had considered leaving when some of the fans turned against him, but added, 'I just salute the fans for believing in me. They were amazing and now I just want to concentrate on helping Chelsea win the title again.

'Our team is compact and we play for each other. It is not a stars' workshop but a bunch of good guys just having fun on the field and entertaining the audience. Football is all about entertainment.' And he dismissed the midweek defeat saying, 'People think Chelsea will fall like a pack of cards but that won't happen.'

Despite the upbeat words it was Didier who was sitting on the substitutes' bench when Chelsea started against Blackburn Rovers, but he came on and scored the second, decisive goal with just nine minutes left, saying afterwards, 'We are a big team with a lot of players, so you have to deal with it when you are not playing. It was a good chance for me to score. The team had been finding it difficult to score before that, so I knew what I had to do.'

He knew what he had to do again as Chelsea, complete with their much-publicised new signing – Ashley Cole from Arsenal – used Charlton Athletic as shooting practice in the first half of their clash at Stamford Bridge. Despite all the pressure they scored only once, when Didier put them ahead after just six minutes following a Frank Lampard corner. The goal feast didn't materialise and matters got worse when ex-favourite Jimmy Floyd Hasselbaink levelled for Charlton, only for Ricardo Carvalho to score the Chelsea winner.

Didier was starting a run of success in front of goal that was only temporarily halted by Werder Bremen, when the Germans came to Stamford Bridge for the first Champions League game of the season. But after Michael Essien's opener it was Didier's presence in the box that led to the vital second goal when he was fouled and Michael Ballack, taking over penalty duties from Frank Lampard, duly scored his first Chelsea goal. Ballack quickly went from hero to zero when he stamped on Momo Sissoko as Chelsea took on long-time sparring partners Liverpool a few days later. It was a dreadful tackle and the German can't have had too many complaints as he was shown the red card, although he did at least have the grace to apologise after the match. It was hardly the best advert for the game that watching golf legend Tiger Woods had ever seen, but at least his afternoon was saved by a goal from Didier. And what a goal it was!

With his back to the goal, he took a lofted cross from Frank Lampard on his chest while England international Jamie Carragher stood guard like a muscular shadow just inches away. Didier let the ball bounce and, in an astonishing show of athleticism and control, swivelled and volleyed the ball with his left foot past goalkeeper José Reina, who stood and watched the ball go past. It was the only goal of the game and Didier said, 'It was my best goal since I came to the club. It was the kind I used to get when I played for Marseilles.'

Goalkeeper Petr Čech echoed those views: 'Against Liverpool, he was the man of the game. He did everything. He was fighting and he kept fighting to the end of the game when everyone could see he was tired. He was on his limits, working hard, and he scored a spectacular goal. He's scored goals like this before, in his first season, but he's a great striker. He can do everything.'

Andriy Shevchenko must have wished he was being asked questions about 'super-goals'. He was replaced again and, although Mourinho and his teammates all went out of their way to stress that he would 'come good', there was a growing feeling of disappointment with the way he had not yet reproduced the form of previous years. The *Daily Express* headline on its match report summed up what a lot of people were feeling: SHEVA PUT TO SHAME BY DROGBA.

Those sentiments were about to be repeated on a much larger

scale when Chelsea, having beaten Fulham 2-0 in the Premiership, flew to Bulgaria for their Champions League game against Levski Sofia. Didier took the exceptional step of describing in detail the preparations he and his colleagues were to go through before the match when he wrote on the 'diary' page of his website,

We'll be leaving on Tuesday morning [26 September]. We should arrive around midday. As usual, a training session is planned for the afternoon at the stadium where we'll play the match. In the evening, at the hotel, we'll have a video session just before dinner. It's important, so that we know who we'll be playing. José Mourinho believes it to be really essential and two years ago we even picked apart the game-play of a team in Division 4 for a Cup match. After our meal, we go to our individual rooms. I don't go to bed before 1am, even before Champions League games, because we can sleep in until 11am. It's quite relaxed in the changing rooms just before the game. Like in any English changing rooms, we listen to music, some read the newspaper. At home, we sometimes even watch TV.

After the match, we go home directly in the club's private jet. The next day, our timetable varies between a winding-down session at 11am or a free day. If we work out, the players who played at least seventy minutes do a half-lap of the pitch, play a bit of basketball in a fun atmosphere. We get treatment for the rest of the time. It's often a busy morning for the club's physiotherapists. As for the others, the substitutes or those who didn't play, they have a normal training session.

Didier also revealed that this was the first time he had even been to Bulgaria. He must have wished he could go there every week as he came off the pitch that night with a hat trick to his name!

The Bulgarians should have been forewarned about his danger as both Didier and Michael Ballack had hit the woodwork before

# 'SHEVA' ARRIVES

Didier's opening goal in the thirty-nineth minute. Levski had surprised many observers with the quality of the football, but they had no menace in the penalty area, and when goalkeeper Georgi Petkov saved well, Didier illustrated how it should be done by being on hand to volley his side ahead.

He again showed the Sofia defence how lethal he could be in the fifty-second minute when he latched on to Bridge's long ball and took just one touch to beat his marker. Although Petkov managed partially to stop the shot, there was enough force on it to see the ball slowly trickle over the line. Fortune favours the brave and his third gaol came when his heel deflected a long-range shot from Lampard. The Bulgarians managed a late consolation goal, but at the final whistle Chelsea found themselves 4–1 second favourites to win the Champions League behind their group rivals Barcelona at 7–2.

Didier's odds on being the Champions League top scorer had also been slashed from 40–1 to 10–1.

'I scored three goals and I'm very happy but the most important thing in the Champions League is to win away', he said. 'It means a lot because I was looking for it since I came here so I am very happy'. And he insisted that, despite growing criticism of his Ukrainian strike partner, Andriy Shevchenko would come good: 'With Sheva I think everything's going to be OK. We've only played together for a short amount of time but already I know ... So far I have been the one who has scored the goals but I'm sure that Shevchenko will start scoring very soon as well.'

The pressure on Shevchenko was growing as Didier went from strength to strength, scoring Chelsea's goal in a 1–1 draw at home to Aston Villa on 30 September, the first point they had dropped in the Premiership at Stamford Bridge since January. To make matters worse, Manchester United's home victory over Newcastle the next day took the Old Trafford side to top place in the division. Even at this early stage of the season, all the talk was of Didier's astonishing form and his goal streak. The only place where it seemed to have run out of steam– albeit temporarily – was in Abidjan, when he played his part in the Ivory Coast's 5–0 victory over humble Gabon but had to take a goalscoring back seat for once as Arouna Koné took the honours with a hat trick.

And Didier was also out of the headlines again for a much more dramatic and serious reason on 14 October, after Chelsea's 1–0 win at newly promoted Reading. The newspapers, radio and television all concentrated on the two horrific injuries to men who were in goal for Chelsea that day. First, Petr Čech was taken to hospital after suffering a head injury during a match of extraordinary drama at the Madejski Stadium. The game was only twenty seconds old when Reading's Stephen Hunt on his Premiership debut caught Čech on the head with his knee as the goalkeeper slid out to collect a through ball. Then his replacement Carlo Cudicini was carried off after a collision with Ibrahima Sonko forcing John Terry to go in goal for the closing moments of the match. That meant Didier had to come back in defence, and he managed to contribute with one goal-line clearance.

Afterwards he joined a chorus of Chelsea complaints against Reading, especially the Hunt challenge, and was quoted in the French newspaper *L'Équipe* as saying,

'Don't tell me tall stories, this was not an accident. He saw that he was going to collide with Petr and he didn't try to avoid it. We went there to play a match, but we soon realised that the guys facing us were out for the game of the season.'

Hunt, meanwhile, was saying that he had written to Čech wishing him a quick recovery and insisted the collision was an accident.

Such was the intensity of the level of football that Chelsea were playing at that time that there was hardly a moment to pause before the prospect of yet another nerve-racking game loomed: for the third successive year they were facing mighty Barcelona in the Champions League.

## CHAPTER 27

# Barcelona Revisited

In three short seasons the Chelsea-Barcelona Champions League clashes had grown to epic proportions. The games had all the ingredients needed for great football: superb skills, memorable goals, red cards and – it must be admitted that this was the vital ingredient of the cocktail – a genuine dislike of the opposition running through both teams. Pre-match vitriol between the sides was reminiscent of boxers at a weigh-in trying to goad each other in an attempt to boost ticket sales. There was certainly no need for either side to do that, but it didn't stop Barcelona's precociously talented nineteen-year-old Lionel Messi from throwing the first punch before the sides met at Stamford Bridge, claiming none of the Chelsea big names were good enough to break into the Catalan team.

'There will be no excuse if we lose. We have come up against José Mourinho's mind games before. Chelsea have put together a super team but I think we are better.

'I wouldn't take Didier Drogba, Andriy Shevchenko or Michael Ballack for any of our players. When I hear the name of Chelsea it brings back bad memories. I got injured there last season and couldn't make it back in time for the Champions League Final. That day Asier Del Horno wore himself out kicking me. I'm sure if I'm playing they will try to stop me playing my natural game. There will be millions of people watching us on TV. The champions of Europe have to show that they can repeat the achievement this year. We are not going to London as tourists.'

Didier was a little more restrained, although equally determined, on his website, saying,

Barcelona. Episode III, Act I. It's the third time in three years that Chelsea have come up against Barça in the Champions League. Of course, I have good and bad memories of these encounters. For instance, I got my first red card in this competition two years ago in the first leg at Camp Nou. There was a big controversy around the Swedish referee, Mr Frisk, who claimed to have received death threats from Chelsea fans. This rumour gave us bad publicity. Since then, it's been quite difficult for us, especially with regard to referees, who don't let us get away with anything.

Now, besides this match, which is worthy of a final, the most important thing for us is to remain unbeaten at Stamford Bridge. We've been saying that to ourselves for the last three years, every time we walk onto the pitch. We'll say it to ourselves even stronger this time against Barcelona because the Catalans were the last to win ...

What else about FC Barcelona? I don't think they have many weaknesses. They're a good all-round team. From a defensive viewpoint, they're a lot more aggressive and they're no longer just a playmaking team. Besides scoring a lot of goals, they're now very good at retrieving the ball. They make practically no mistakes! But they're still human and we'll find a way to get past them. Trust me, I've got my idea of how to do it, but I'm keeping it a secret.

But it didn't stay 'a secret' for long: on 18 October the packed crowd and millions around the world watching on television saw one of the greatest goals in the competition's history, and it was enough to give Chelsea victory. Even the most hardened, and neutral, of journalists were lost in praise of Didier's strike just after half-time. Agence France-Presse, who had chronicled Didier throughout the years, called it 'a moment of brilliance'. The *Daily Mail* said he 'produced the one piece of magic that separated these sides', and *The Times* reported, 'Didier Drogba has never looked better, poor Andriy Shevchenko has never looked worse.'

The goal came when he received a pass from Joe Cole with his back to goal on the edge of the penalty area. He intelligently dragged the ball across his body to fool curly-haired defender Carles Puyol, turned in a flash and whipped a shot beyond the diving Valdez in goal that redefined the word 'unstoppable'.

Didier raced towards the corner flag to celebrate and soon vanished beneath his delirious colleagues, including third-choice goalkeeper thirty-year-old Henrique Hilário playing that night, who ran virtually the length of the field to join in. The old cliché 'a goal worthy of winning any match' was never more appropriate as Barcelona trooped off, beaten again at Stamford Bridge, thanks to Didier's fourth goal in the Champions League that season and his ninth in total.

Yet even in this moment of triumph, Didier was touched by sadness as he dedicated the victory not only to his injured colleagues but to Victoria Buchanan, who worked for the Chelsea Pitch Owners' Association but was killed shortly before the game when her bicycle collided with a lorry on her way to work. Buchanan was just twenty-eight and had been due to get married the following year. 'It's a difficult moment and difficult to say. But Chelsea is a big family and we dedicate the victory to Petr, Carlo and to the girl.'

Towards the end of the match Shevchenko's frustration at being unable to add to the goal tally was becoming clear, but he did at last find the net in a 2–1 victory over Portsmouth a few days after the Barcelona triumph. Michael Ballack was the other scorer, after a cross from Didier, and both superstars ended up being booked for their celebrations.

There was no doubt that Didier was in the best form of his life and it was no surprise that there was constant talk about his future at Chelsea. After the will-he-stay-or-will-he-go? question only a few months earlier, it seemed just a matter of time before he either left the club or his contract was improved and extended. He let slip as the return leg with Barcelona neared, 'The fact that Lyon chairman Jean-Michel Aulas keeps on making it clear that he wants me is flattering. I'm often on the telephone with his right-hand man Bernard Lacombe, who asks me how it's going at Chelsea and whether I'd be interested in returning to play in France one day. But I have become an undroppable player for Chelsea.

'When I arrived from Marseilles it was as if I was a complete unknown but I have contributed to the two Premiership titles and I have imposed my personality and my game on the Chelsea team.'

On the face of it fairly confident remarks, slightly bordering on arrogance, but they were also very truthful and realistic.

Didier was busy too in the penalty area again at Sheffield United 28 October, but giving away only a spot kick in his own box, a call he strongly disagreed with. Fortunately, the kick was saved by Hilário and Chelsea went on to win with goals from Frank Lampard and Michael Ballack, but worryingly as the return leg of the Barcelona game approached, Didier failed to come out for the second half because of a foot injury. Ironically, the man who was ruled out by injury was Andriy Shevchenko, and Didier was fit to take his place in the starting line-up against Barcelona.

As had become almost obligatory, there was a war of words before the referee's whistle even sounded the start of the game. José Mourinho criticised Barcelona's recent recruit from Chelsea, Eidur Gudjohnsen, for picking up bad footballing habits during his short time in Spain. Samuel Eto'o replied in kind, saying that Shevchenko had made a mistake in going to Chelsea and wasn't liked by his teammates. The game itself could easily have been an anticlimax. Instead, it turned into a classic of skill, pace, retribution and revenge, with a fair amount of theatrics on display from many of the players. One observer was to reflect that it had been a night of 'magic and mayhem' – and that was probably an understatement.

If anarchy didn't exactly rule, it certainly was the controlling force on that unusually hot late-October evening in 2006. The players frequently squared up between an Olympic-style selection of dives and Hollywood-worthy displays of play-acting. Stefano Farina, the Italian referee, deserved his share of blame for losing control, but in fairness it was virtually a 'mission impossible' he had chosen to accept. He ended up giving out yellow cards to six Chelsea players and four to the home side, so bitter was the feeling between the teams. And, in the midst of all this madness, there was also some fabulous football being played.

The first dazzling display of skill came from the argumentative Deco, who had played for Mourinho at Porto. After just two minutes, he raced in from the left, proving too fast and skilful for Khalid Boulahrouz and, too late, Ricardo Carvalho threw himself at the shot coming in from Deco that accelerated past both him and goalkeeper Hilário.

Chelsea seemed to be on the point of being reduced to ten men when referee Farina waved yellow cards at Ashley Cole in the twenty-seventh and thirty-seventh minute but failed to produce a red card for the second offence. It later emerged, during furious Barcelona protests, that one of the bookings had been for Lampard, not Cole.

Cole and the teenaged Messi seemed to be having their own private running battle, but they were not alone. Michael Essien went down and the Barcelona players said he was faking. Rafael Márquez did the same with a similar reaction from Chelsea. Didier too went to ground on several occasions and soon afterwards accidentally ran into Thiago Motta.

An angry Márquez pushed Didier to the ground and appeared to kick him for good measure. Either way, he was fortunate to stay on the field. Tempers were soaring on the pitch, and off it the two sets of benches were also squaring up. In between, Messi, Deco and, of course, Ronaldinho were playing divine football. But Chelsea wasn't to be outdone: John Terry was massive, Frank Lampard seemed to be working harder than anyone else on the pitch and Didier was a constant menace.

Ashley Cole tackled Messi superbly and fed Didier, only for him to shoot disappointingly wide. A subdued Michael Ballack shot over and Hilário saved well from Xavi before, at the other end, Victor Valdes denied Essien and Arjen Robben.

As well as Chelsea had played, there was no denying who had won the first round on points, so the Blues must have been relieved when the half-time whistle went. They certainly started the second period with more menace and Robben could have scored twice; once he was thwarted by a save from Valdes and then he wastefully shot over the bar after a marvellous pass from Lampard. The England midfielder decided to take matters into his own hands after he initially failed to control Essien's pass in the area. There is an old saying in soccer writing about players who can 'turn on a sixpence', but it was a *half*-a-sixpence pirouette from Lampard before he chipped the excellent Valdes from the most acute of angles and saw the ball go in off the far post, a truly marvellous goal.

Any side with the quality of players Barcelona possessed would not take such an equaliser lying down, and brilliant Brazilian superstar Ronaldinho produced a defence-destroying cross with the outside of his foot to allow Gudjohnsen to slide in behind Terry. The blond striker didn't have the perfect night he hoped for, however, as after seventy-six minutes he was carried off on a stretcher after landing badly following a tackle from Carvalho. The

Portuguese defender showed no sympathy for his recent teammate as he lay on the ground waiting for treatment, visibly urging him to get up and continue.

In years gone by this would have been a typical 'plucky' display from an English side before they were beaten, but Chelsea were scant respecters of the history books. With 180 seconds of extra time already played, John Terry thundered into the penalty area to head down for Didier. He burst past his formidable marker Márquez as though he were a man of no consequence and ignored the intimidating rush by Valdes to slide home a goal that many others would have excitedly blasted high and wide. José Mourinho slid along the touchline grass in ecstasy, destroying the knees of his expensive suit in the process, as the Barcelona fans started to throw water bottles in his direction; Frank Rijkaard imploded and minutes later, when the whistle went, was demanding to know from the referee why he had played six minutes of injury time. It made no difference: Chelsea had managed a marvellous draw in a memorable game, even though possession was 61–39 per cent in the home side's favour. True, Chelsea were under pressure for much of the night and yet outplayed Barça for periods of the game and had more shots on and off target than the Catalans.

Mourinho had said before the game that, thanks to satellite television, 'half the world will be watching'. If so, they had seen a game in a thousand. The world's media that night and in days to follow were fairly unanimous in their condemnation of much that occurred, but also enthralled by the spectacle they had witnessed. A few lines in the next day's *Daily Express* summed it all up:

Half the world was eager to watch this match, according to José Mourinho. It can only have been because soap operas are so popular all over the planet. And because Chelsea and Barcelona continue to bicker, connive, kick and fight like the best of the day-time TV hams. Ladies and gentlemen, the award for the best performance of swooning before a live audience of multi-millions goes to our old friend, Didier Drogba. But to the hissing, seething anger of the Nou Camp, he also pinched the prize for most dramatic ending.

The *Guardian* had a similar view: 'It would take an archaeologist to get to the very bottom of all the grubby layers of misconduct that made up too much of this match. Bewilderingly, there were treasures in the midst of the debris.' And so on and so forth, not just in the British media, but around the world.

Mourinho was furious about the attitude of some of the Barcelona players, saying, 'There were players rolling around the pitch and a lot of yellow cards – and only one team contributed to that. It was not an aggressive game but at times there were seven or eight players around the referee urging him to give cards.' And he added, 'Drogba made a magnificent contribution with that crucial goal.' John Terry labelled the Spanish side 'cynical'.

Barcelona skipper Carles Puyol showed he was as eager to put the boot in off the field as on it when he said that Chelsea players 'threw themselves to the floor first. I don't care what Mourinho says. Chelsea are an aggressive team.' Midfielder Edmilson chipped in, 'The worst thing about playing Chelsea is having to listen to Mourinho afterwards.'

Didier had truly become a superstar on the world stage, admired by most, loathed by some. But even those who criticised him had to admit in the next breath that he had become a player of prodigious ability, an attacker of power and menace equal to any on the global football stage and (a part of his game often unfairly overlooked) an energetic worker in both attack and, surprisingly, defence.

The same news wires and television stations who reported on his heroics at the Nou Camp that night were soon filled with more detail on his extraordinary life and the turn it was taking. There had been numerous stories linking Didier with other clubs, especially Lyon, and pointing out that although his £60,000-a-week salary was hardly peanuts, it left him trailing others at

## BARCELONA REVISITED

Chelsea, especially newcomers Michael Ballack and Andriy Shevchenko, both of whom he had outshone since their arrival. So the talk was all of his negotiating a new deal, at figures ranging from £100,000 to £120,000 a week.

It came as no surprise, therefore, when, in the wake of the Barcelona game, it was officially announced that he had signed a new four-year contract, taking his stay at Stamford Bridge to six years in total. He said, 'I am not playing well just because I wanted to sign a new contract. I am playing well because I feel good and I am happy to train with my friends. I want to say thank you to José for believing in me since the beginning and now we will be together for a long time – the best period of my career, I think.' On his website he said,

I'm pleased and proud to announce that I've extended my contract with the Blues for another two years. My dream is to win more titles with Chelsea, especially the Champions League this season. I've chosen stability because I feel good here in London and I want to go down in this club's history. Since I arrived in 2004, I've made progress alongside some of the best players. Under the orders of my manager, José Mourinho, I've learnt a lot from a human and professional viewpoint. I'd like to thank the Blues' fans who have always encouraged me, as well as my own personal fans. I'd also like to thank my previous trainers who helped me get to where I am today. I won my first titles as a professional player with Chelsea and I'm sure that the Blues will enable me to lift even more trophies.

He was later to add that he wanted to see his career out with Chelsea.

José Mourinho summed up his views, and those of thousands of Chelsea supporters worldwide: 'This is good news for Chelsea. Didier deserves a big new contract. Now he can go to Milan to shop and no one can say he goes to sign a contract. His friend from Lyon can call and people won't say he is calling to sign him. It's fantastic.'

# CHAPTER 28

# Ambassador Didier

Margaret Thatcher was still Prime Minister and Nelson Mandela was behind bars the last time Tottenham Hotspur had beaten Chelsea in a game of any significance way back in February 1990 at Stamford Bridge in the old First Division, when Gary Lineker scored the winner. All that history meant little, however, since, days after the return from Barcelona, Spurs beat Chelsea 2–1 at White Hart Lane.

Both sides may have been exhausted by their midweek games. Spurs had defeated Bruges, but Chelsea seemed to have made the better recovery when Claude Makelele put them ahead after seventeen minutes – only his second goal in 149 games. Chelsea thought they had gone two goals ahead through Didier Drogba's header, but referee Graham Poll cancelled out the goal for a foul that he, and not many others, had seen John Terry commit. Worse was to follow when he sent Terry off for fouling Ledley King. Goals from Dawson and Lennon were enough to give Spurs their first win over Chelsea in an astonishing thirty-three league encounters, and to severely dent the Blues' chance of retaining the title for a third year.

## DIDIER DROGBA

There were no such problems in midweek, when they cruised to a 4–0 victory over Aston Villa at home in the Carling Cup with goals from Frank Lampard, Andriy Shevchenko, Michael Essien and finally from Didier. Many of the Premiership teams decided to leave key men out of their line-ups for the competition, but Chelsea's first-choice side were on display for the game.

Such victories almost always seem to come along in pairs, as that weekend poor Watford were rolled over at Stamford Bridge. The main difference this time was that Didier provided the final blow. His goals in the twenty-seventh, thirty-sixth and sixty-ninth minutes – interrupted only by a rare goal from Shevchenko – were a masterclass in finishing.

His first came when Geremi's low cross from the right was scuffed by Shevchenko into Didier's path. And his second, from an acute angle, came after an excellent passing movement, and it was obvious even then that Chelsea were on their way to their fiftieth consecutive home match in the league without defeat. His hat trick came in the sixty-ninth minute, volleying home a cross from Geremi to the delight of the crowd. Afterwards Mourinho enthused about his striker – and who could disagree?

'He is unstoppable at the moment. Right now I don't see a better striker playing anywhere in the world. He has improved his game all round: he has so much power on the ground; he is so strong in the air and he makes a contribution in defence, too. Drogba is just playing amazing stuff and I have never seen him better. The challenge for him is to keep at this level consistently for a long time.'

Didier just couldn't stop scoring. Even a fairly low-key Ivory Coast friendly against Sweden at the ground of one of his earliest clubs, Le Mans, saw him on the mark again when he headed a Bakary Koné cross past Swedish goalkeeper Rami Shaaban thirty-seven minutes into a match that never rose above the ordinary. The greatest event of note from the proceedings was the fact that Didier's goal was the twenty-fifth for his country in just thirty-seven outings – a phenomenal ratio of goals to games.

At least he had a rest from goalscoring in the 1–0 home win over West Ham soon afterwards, although Geremi's thunderous free-kick winner came after Didier was fouled on the edge of the area by Danny Gabbidon. Even more fruitless was the slightly surprising 1–0 defeat by Werder Bremen. Although Chelsea were through to the next stage of the trophy, it was nevertheless a disappointment and one made worse by Didier's having to come off the field due to injury in the sixty-ninth minute.

If there was one game that the Chelsea faithful didn't want him to miss, it was the upcoming away game against Premiership leaders Manchester United at Old Trafford, so they must have been relieved to read days before the kick-off, 'I am over the knee injury I suffered at Werder Bremen but the decision rests with the doctors and José Mourinho. The match is vital. I am convinced Chelsea will win because we play better than United at key moments. Shevchenko's arrival means my game has changed and I'm much better for it.'

There were a fraction under 76,000 in the Theatre of Dreams for the Chelsea visit, and they weren't to be disappointed by the game they saw. Louis Saha gave United the lead, but towards the end of the match, as Chelsea surged forward for an equaliser, he seemed to get in the way of goalkeeper Edwin van der Sar as he tried to stop Ricardo Carvalho's strong sixty-ninth-minute header. Afterwards Sir Alex Ferguson reckoned his side deserved to win and had coped well with Chelsea. His main comments, however, were directed at Didier and the booking he collected after his arm made with Serbian centre half Nemanja Vidić's head, saying Didier was lucky not to have been sent off.

'We could have lost a player for six weeks with a fractured jaw. Fortunately, it wasn't, but it could have been. When I watched it again on video, I could see him [Drogba] looking round to see where he [Vidić] was. He could have done a lot of damage.'

## DIDIER DROGBA

If Didier felt intimidated by the United boss's comments he wasn't allowing it to show, saying, 'Defenders fear me because they know that just to give me a minimum advantage will finish in a goal. All my rivals respect me and that can only be good for Chelsea. I am in the best form of my life but still want to do even better for Chelsea.'

Mourinho agreed, again labelling him the best striker in the world at the time, and Didier added, as if to console his Ukrainian strike partner, 'Andriy is the key to my success. Without him defenders search for me all over the field, but with him in the side I have more freedom.'

Perhaps those words encouraged Shevchenko as he was on target in the 2–0 home win over Champions League rival Levski Sofia soon after – his fifty-seventh goal in European club football – and even second-half substitute Shaun Wright-Phillips scored his first goal for the club after eighty-three minutes.

For once, Didier didn't score, but at least he and the rest of the team managed to celebrate Christmas as they polished off between them £15,000-worth of Cristal champagne later on at the Funky Buddha nightclub for their pre-Christmas party.

The drinking was well and truly over by the time the next match came around, a home fixture against Arsenal. Didier had given centre back Philippe Senderos a torrid time in earlier meetings, but the young defender rewarded Arsène Wenger's faith in him by keeping Didier comparatively quiet.

For once the Blues had to manage without a goal from Didier, an unheard-of event in recent times, instead relying on a late thunderbolt from nowhere by Michael Essien to counteract Mathieu Flamini's goal. While he may not have scored, but it was impossible to keep Didier out of the headlines. He actually dominated them the next day after clashing with Arsenal's giant goalkeeper Jens Lehmann in what could only be described as comical circumstances. First, Lehmann gave him a half-hearted push that sent Didier plunging dramatically to the ground. When he sprang up he ever so gently bumped the German, who in turn went down as though shot.

The referee booked both men and the general consensus was that the yellow cards were fully merited – for bad acting if not violent conduct! The duo's ridiculous behaviour was mercilessly examined in the aftermath of the game by both television companies and newspapers.

At least the German had the grace to kiss and make up, saying, 'Nothing happened with Drogba. I like him. I think the handshake between us says it all. You can have passion in the game, but as long as you get on with people nicely it's OK. Drogba didn't insult me in comparison to his teammates – I never insult anybody – and I can't complain with him.'

That was more than Newcastle United could say soon afterwards, as Didier caused them problems big time when he stepped off the bench to score the only goal of the game after good work by fellow sub Shevchenko in the sixty-eighth minute. As he celebrated, the crowd began chanting the chorus of the pop hit 'Who Let the Dogs Out?', specially customised into 'Who Let the Drog Out?' for his benefit with its infectious 'woof, woof, woof, woof' chanted in his honour. To think that only a few months earlier he had been the subject of their ridicule and now he was their hero. That goal may not have been a classic, although it earned his side three points, but the one that followed certainly was.

Chelsea were trailing 2–1 at Everton in a ferocious game until, with less than ten minutes left, Frank Lampard brilliantly levelled the score. Then Didier, who had just struck the post, spun on the ball and without even glancing at the goal unleashed a first-time drive from a distance that baffled goalkeeper Tim Howard as it swerved at speed into the net. Didier disappeared under his adulatory teammates and Mourinho did his famous 'dance' along the edge of the pitch punching both fists in front of his body as he moved along.

# DIDIER DROGBA

Didier said afterwards, 'It was probably the best goal I've ever scored – but for sure it was the most important goal I've ever scored. The goals we got were special, not just mine, but Frank Lampard's as well, because it was as good as mine. Maybe, given how far out we both were, we could count ourselves lucky they went in. But the way we won that match, when everything was against us, showed we believe in our destiny. But we showed Chelsea are more than money. We showed everybody we have the best team spirit in the world.'

Throughout his career Didier has shown remarkable strength and concentration throughout games. Physically or mentally, he never wavers in a game's dying stages. The goals he has scored near the final whistle are evidence of that, so it shouldn't have come as a surprise to poor Newcastle when on 20 December he proved too good for them for the second time in a week. This clash was in the Carling Cup at St James's Park and Didier, who had replaced Shevchenko with seventeen minutes remaining, blasted home a superb free kick to break the deadlock and Geordie hearts. The goals just kept coming.

For once Didier wasn't on the scoresheet, but he jumped over Robben's shot in the ninetieth minute of the league clash at Wigan to fool the defence and give Chelsea the narrowest of victories, 3–2, a few days later.

But Boxing Day disappointment was to follow at home to Reading when, even though Didier scored twice with headers, the visitors managed to leave with a 2–2 draw and the Blues had lost the chance to go briefly to the top of the table. As Christmas presents go, the loss of a possible two points at home was just what Chelsea didn't want in their chasing of Manchester United.

But at least they had Didier. On BBC's *Football Focus* over the holidays he explained how low he had felt in the summer and how close he had been to leaving: 'Every end of the season you have to think about what you have done. I had some teams who wanted to sign me, so I had to think, as I had won the league here for two consecutive years. I was thinking, but not too much, because Chelsea showed how they respect me and how they wanted me to stay. It was not about Shevchenko, but was just about Chelsea and me.'

Didier was carrying a thigh injury but by now he was so hot that nothing seemed capable of stopping him from scoring. Sure enough, he got another goal in the 2–2 draw with Fulham, although two more points were 'lost' by Chelsea's failure to beat a team they should have triumphed over, certainly at home. Didier was one of the few exempt from criticism by Mourinho when he said, 'Maybe we are not so good as we think. Maybe I am not such a good manager, maybe the players are not such good players. We cannot defend, we concede incredible goals and in attack we have one player.'

On a more upbeat note Didier was, to no one's surprise, one of three nominees for the 2006 African Player of the Year Award alongside Michael Essien and Samuel Eto'o and it came as no surprise when he was also voted the Ivory Coast Player of the Year ahead of Lille's striker Kader Keita, Lens' striker Aruna Dindane, Tottenham's Didier Zokora and Arsenal's Kolo Touré.

Award or no award, on 2 January he still managed uncharacteristically to fluff an easy chance in the seventh minute and then headed over the bar in injury time at Aston Villa in a goalless draw against the struggling side from Birmingham. He also picked up his fifth booking of the season in the process. At least that meant a rest for Didier, as he would be ruled out of the Carling Cup clash with Wycombe, and he was also rested, along with Claude Makelele and Michael Essien, for the 6–1 thrashing of Macclesfield in the FA Cup. It was probably a good time to take a well-deserved break given the enormous role he had been playing in Chelsea's season. One wag even suggested calling him 'Taxi', since so many of the other players were taking a ride from him.

In fact stories of unrest in both the Chelsea dressing room and between Mourinho and the club owner Abramovich and the board were growing with every passing day to such an extent that in a routine 4-0 destruction of Wigan on 13 January, in which Didier scored, the fans chanted 'Stand up for the special one' to show support for the coach. Mourinho was, according to the reports, not happy with his lack of control of transfers at the club and the thorny old question of having Shevchenko 'foisted' on him reared its head again. It was being strongly suggested that Mourinho would soon be leaving the club and the players, with Didier prominent, were horrified at the suggestion. Any Mourinho exit would be 'painful' and akin to 'losing a good friend', he said, adding, 'José has built a culture that has become Chelsea's. We're in love with his style of coaching and the confidence he has infused into the team. I just hope people give us and the boss a break about this talk because it's not good for the team.'

Captain John Terry put it even more strongly: 'We all agree that we don't want José to go and, if it takes five or six of the top players to tell them, then that's what we are prepared to do. We are all loyal to José and not just the ones in the team, but also the ones trying to break through. He's the best in the business, there's no doubt about that, and he will be for the next twenty years. That's what we want at Chelsea – the best coach and the best players.'

A 2-0 defeat at Liverpool on 20 January, their first Premiership defeat in thirteen games, was hardly the best result in such trying times, and one disastrous moment when Didier gently rolled a free kick towards Michael Ballack, only for it to catch him unawares, seemed to sum up the malaise temporarily affecting the players. The Merseyside fans chanted 'Bye-bye, Mourinho' in anticipation of his departure. At least Didier had missed through suspension the embarrassing 1-1 draw at Wycombe in the Carling Cup, but he was back for the 4-0 second-leg triumph.

In the midst of all this mayhem, Didier flew to Geneva, where he was made a UN Goodwill Ambassador, an honour he richly deserved and for which he would be paid the princely sum of $1 a year. He was to be a figurehead in the battle against poverty, AIDS and discrimination. While there he spoke openly about the situation at Stamford Bridge with a candour and insight that impressed everyone.

'We have lacked aggression and determination in the last few games and against Liverpool looked nothing like a team challenging for our Premiership title,' he admitted. 'Perhaps this is the end of the Mourinho era. Over the last few months it is true this Chelsea side has been unrecognisable. I only wish I knew where our team spirit has gone. I just cannot understand why Mourinho is being attacked – particularly from within his own club. It's now obvious to all of us this club is no longer a compact unit.

'I know people are just going to turn around and say I am Mourinho's pet but I simply don't care. José truly is the Special One and it would be a shame for him not to continue here. The truth is that not everyone at this club is pulling in the same direction – and that is immensely dangerous. It is clear to the players that our bad results have only one explanation: the poor atmosphere around the club. It's not rocket science or a big secret.

'A team is always pictured in what is happening at director level. As soon as directors and manager are not pulling in the same direction, it has repercussions on the performances of the players. This is not a situation that is easy to live with. As long as everybody is not on the same wavelength, the team will keep on struggling. But the players are united. We can't stop tensions being there. I simply cannot understand why we have put ourselves in such a difficult situation. If people dismiss what I'm saying as keeping in with Mourinho then they are wrong. I know what I owe him and so do men like John Terry and Frank Lampard.'

And, as if to show his English had improved during his two and a half years in the country, he added: 'The gaffer improved us as players and we have to support him now. If he was to leave, it's not the case that I would just follow him blindly. But this is a man who made me come here, improved me as a player, helped me win trophies and who also extended my contract. I wouldn't simply follow him anywhere, but if he left and wanted me then I'd only have to ask myself a few questions.'

He added, 'I know we don't look or feel sure of ourselves at the moment. But we have to hang on to our belief and our dreams. It's clear some people in England don't like him, but without Mourinho Chelsea simply wouldn't be where they are now.

'The players all know that everything he does is for them. In fact the Premiership also owes him. The boss's provocative edge has also given a new lease of life to this league. Sir Alex Ferguson and Arsène Wenger are fine coaches but they will never be as "box office" as José Mourinho. If you are around him everyone has fun – he's been fresh, new but, above all, talented.

'How can I not be totally behind someone who has always supported me, who has helped me win things and who has put the name of Chelsea back at the top of English football? There were very good players at Chelsea before his arrival but he brought his winning culture. He has already won four trophies in two years at Chelsea. What more can be asked of him?'

In all this talk of football, it would have been easy to overlook the purpose of Didier's visit, the battle against poverty. He had recently lent his support to the Homeless World Cup, along with the likes of Ringo Starr and Ian Botham – a football tournament that raised the awareness of the plight of those without homes. He said at the time, 'Around me I have friends who have been through very difficult times and poverty, difficulty finding food. That's what it was like for us. To get one meal a day, it was, it's really very difficult indeed, so we try to help them. When we've been lucky enough, as I have, to succeed, then we try to help them to overcome their hunger.

'I have a number of friends who have experienced poverty, real poverty, but who managed to pull through. It's true that it is really unpleasant to experience it, but I think that when you have the support of lots of people that enables everyone to have a chance to pull through. That's very important too.'

So perhaps it should have come as no surprise that this intelligent young man whose astonishing life had shown him the best and worst the world had to offer had not lost his sense of perspective. In his jet-set life at Chelsea he could be seen driving around the fashionable haunts of London in his black, French-registered Mercedes playing his favourite Beyoncé CDs and dining at Santini's restaurant, a haunt of such stars as Tom Cruise and Mariah Carey, and where Princess Diana and Frank Sinatra had regularly dined. Yet there was no sense of hypocrisy when the man from the poor part of town in a deprived African country said, 'My being named by the UN, alongside great players like Zinédine Zidane and Ronaldo, will hopefully help me show the real Didier Drogba.

'It is a great honour for me to be named Ambassador. I am only the third footballer to be given this title. Don't forget that only five years ago I was a substitute for a second-division club in France. Today, I'm a UN Ambassador.'

And in words that summed up his remarkable life and battle to succeed – and his care for others less fortunate – he added, 'Before I became a rich footballer, I was on the other side of the fence for a very long time. I lived with my family in a tiny flat, but that didn't stop me from learning about hard work and respect. Those are the values I want to pass on to others. I believe you have to battle hard to get to the top. It's only through adversity that you improve.'

## CHAPTER 29

# Wembley – and History is Made

If Didier's well-earned UN honour indicated a stability in his place in football's roll of honour, the same could not be said at the time of events at Stamford Bridge. There were continual reports of differences between coach Mourinho and owner Abramovich over the signing of players – especially Shevchenko – and the power base within the club. Story after story said that Mourinho would be leaving unless the matter was resolved to his satisfaction.

Didier was among several of the players with strong views on the situation when he was widely reported as saying, 'Clearly there are tensions at the club now, but let's get one thing clear: when Mourinho says we need new players to help us achieve our ambitions, he is talking on behalf of the whole group. All the players here feel the same way as José. It doesn't take a genius to see that not only are there arguments between the different management branches but also that those arguments are having a negative effect on the team. When the bosses and the manager are not rowing in the same direction, there are bound to be repercussions. I just cannot understand why Mourinho is being attacked – particularly from within his own club.' He added later, 'Perhaps this is the end of the Mourinho era. Over the last few months it is true this Chelsea side has been unrecognisable. I only wish I knew where our team spirit has gone.

'It's now obvious to all of us this club is no longer a compact unit... I know people are just going to turn around and say I am Mourinho's pet but I simply don't care.'

He amplified his views further, adding an ominous footnote for Blues' fans: 'It is clear to the players that our bad results have only one explanation: the poor atmosphere around the club. It's not rocket science or a big secret. If he was to leave, it's not the case that I would just follow him blindly... I wouldn't simply follow him anywhere but if he left and wanted me then I'd only have to ask myself a few questions.'

Didier was also asking questions about Andriy Shevchenko's place in the squad, telling the highly-respected *France Football* magazine: 'I like to share. But when I give, I like to have something in return. That is what happened last year with Hernán Crespo. This season, let us say it is a bit different.' But he added, 'We know we are not rivals as there is room for two up front, which was not the case in past years.'

At this stage of the season, the very end of January, the millionaire from Ukraine had scored just three goals in his twenty-one Premiership games, causing Didier to ponder, 'Maybe he thinks he must justify his transfer by scoring no matter what it takes. It is really hard to deal with for him. But I was also in that position when I arrived in Chelsea. At Chelsea more than anywhere else you have to think of the squad before thinking to yourself.'

None of this seemed to be causing Didier too much of a problem on the field, however. He scored in a 3–0 defeat of Nottingham Forest in the FA Cup – as did Shevchenko – and again in a similar home league victory over Blackburn, his twenty-third goal in all competitions so far, although Chelsea remained six points behind leaders Manchester United.

Didier reckoned one of the reasons for his phenomenal form was simple: he was at last allowed to wear the lucky 11 shirt he had worn at Marseille and Guingamp but had been unable to until Damien Duff's transfer to Newcastle United. He also revealed, more realistically, 'I went to see the manager last summer to tell him I wouldn't do another season like the one before. I was fed up working like a dog upfront without too much resulting for me in return. For my teammates I was like some sort of removals lorry, freeing up space in the crowd and knocking the ball off for the others.'

With his success came some drawbacks, though: 'I have noticed teams now try to unsettle me before a match by declaring, "Drogba will do nothing." I never used to get that kind of special treatment. On the pitch I also find the tackles and collisions are even heavier, as if they needed to intimidate me even more. But that sort of thing doesn't bother me. I'm used to this way of defenders saying "Hello". As long as it is fair I love this kind of combat.'

Didier wasn't in too competitive a mood during, by his standards, a quiet game in the 1–0 victory at Charlton. The winning goal came from Frank Lampard, but the best sight for Blues fans was seeing John Terry return from his long back injury with a brief substitute appearance. But the goals returned when Drogba was the only scorer in an Ivory Coast 1–0 victory over Guinea, making him the biggest international goalscorer in Chelsea's history, overtaking the sixteen scored by the legendary Jimmy Greaves, a man who had criticised Didier in the past.

Two more goals followed in the clinical 3–0 home defeat of Middlesbrough and – while sporting a new, 'weaved' hairstyle – Drogba scored another in the FA Cup 4–0 rout of Norwich. But the next game, away to Porto in the Champions League, was far more taxing. Didier managed to hit the post during the match, but

## DIDIER DROGBA

Chelsea's saviour was Shevchenko, who seemed far more at ease in these European games than back in England. The Ukrainian's equaliser meant his team headed back to Stamford Bridge with a satisfying 1–1 draw.

It seems strange that such a vital Champions League game would be overshadowed by a domestic clash, but that is exactly what happened the next weekend at the Millennium Stadium in Cardiff in a game that was later labelled 'Mayhem at the Millennium'.

The game in question was the Carling Cup Final – or 'snarling cup', as one wag put it – and Didier wrote his name into the record books by scoring the two goals that gave his side victory after Arsenal's teenage Theo Walcott had given the Gunners an early lead. That simple fact hides a game of massive endeavour and passion and one that will live in the memory for years to come.

With the scores level at 1–1, John Terry suffered a sickening injury and went blue in the face after being accidentally kicked in the head by Abou Diaby in the fifty-seventh minute as he bravely tried to score. There was such force in the kick that Diaby even hurt his ankle in the collision.

Terry had to be taken off on a stretcher in a neck brace and given oxygen as players on both sides feared the blow could be fatal, but he was astonishingly back at the ground to join in the celebrations within two hours, after being given the all clear at University Hospital, Wales.

But, as he had lain on the turf, a terrifying image leaped into Didier's mind: 'The second goal was for John because I was scared when I saw him lying down. I thought the signs were not good,' he said after the game. 'It is difficult when you see these kind of things. There were ten minutes when I didn't find my game and my legs were shaking. When I saw John lying there it was very emotional for me because it was the second time I have gone through that. I remembered what happened when Mama Ouattara, our assistant manager with the Ivory Coast, died on the training pitch in Paris three years ago. Mama just collapsed and never regained consciousness and when I saw John lying there I felt my heart beating so much faster than normal. I had been there before and I feared the worst. I was scared, very, very scared.

'Already this season I've seen Petr Čech and Carlo Cudicini both carried off with head injuries in the same match at Reading. JT is a hard man but when you see him laid out like that without moving it sends a shiver down your spine. We really feared the worst.'

The celebrations Terry made it to that evening were thanks to Didier's eighty-fourth-minute winning header, but even that late in the game there was plenty of drama in store.

Well into injury time, Chelsea substitute John Obi Mikel pulled Kolo Touré's shirt as he went on a surging run. Referee Howard Webb blew for a free kick but an angry Touré ran up to Mikel, and, as the young Nigerian got up, Touré grabbed him and tried to push him down again. The referee tried to separate the two, rapidly followed by Lampard and Cesc Fàbregas, who soon become entangled with one another. Didier, Justin Hoyte, Ricardo Carvalho and Emmanuel Adebayor joined the mêlée, which developed into the sort of rolling maul normally seen on a rugby field, although it must be said no lethal punches were thrown. Even Arsenal's goalkeeper, Manuel Almunia, ran sixty yards to join in, as both managers and other coaching staff became involved, coming onto the pitch to restore order.

Just as tempers seemed to be calming down a second fracas started on the fringe of the main group, involving Wayne Bridge and Emmanuel Eboué. Bridge fell down clutching his head as Eboué fell on him. Referee Webb spoke to his assistants and showed red cards to Mikel, Touré and Adebayor – who took a lot of persuading to leave the field – and yellows to Fàbregas and Lampard. The clash resulted in an FA fine of £100,000 for each club and a reprimand.

## DIDIER DROGBA

Nevertheless, many of the Chelsea players, including Didier, still managed to make it to the Aura nightclub in Mayfair, where a bar bill of around £30,000 was clocked up as the Cristal champagne, Grey Goose vodka and Brahma beer were downed.

Everyone had recovered by the time the Blues won 2–0 at Portsmouth in their next game, with Didier opening the scoring, but unsurprisingly they found visitors Porto a much more difficult task in the second leg of the Champions League match. A lacklustre first half meant they trailed at half-time to a fifteenth-minute lead from striker Ricardo Quaresma. Chelsea equalised through Arjen Robben three minutes into the second half and Michael Ballack eventually smashed in a seventy-ninth-minute winner to secure a 3–2 aggregate victory.

Every game now seemed to border on the irresistible, and on 11 March, the day after Didier's twenty-ninth birthday, he laid on the chance for Salomon Kalou to smash a spectacular late equaliser in a thrilling 'old-fashioned' 3–3 draw at Stamford Bridge with Tottenham Hotspur in the FA Cup quarter-final. Chelsea had been favourites before the start, but in the end had to fight back from a 3–1 deficit in a game neither side deserved to lose.

A 1–0 victory through a Frank Lampard penalty at Manchester City was hardly in the same excitement zone a few days later and that was quickly followed by a 4–0 home win over struggling Sheffield United before Spurs' replay, where stunning goals from Shevchenko and a Didier-assisted Wright-Phillips special gave the Blues a 2–1 entry to the semi-finals. The game was marred at the end by a Tottenham fan who decided to tangle with Lampard and Didier at the final whistle, but was hauled off for his troubles.

Didier then had to make the long journey to Madagascar in the Indian Ocean to captain the Ivory Coast team in their 3–0 win in an African Nations Cup Qualifier over the national side, 'the Oxen', before returning home to see his new international teammate Salomon Kalou score Chelsea's late winner at Watford.

## WEMBLEY – AND HISTORY IS MADE

There was hardly time to pause for breath before the next 'must-win' game came along, the Champions League quarter-final home leg against Valencia, where Didier's header was his thirtieth goal of the season – and his first for seven games – and it levelled David Silva's early stunning strike into the top corner from long distance. Many viewed it as a poor result and it seemed that Chelsea faced an exit from the competition in the return leg. Mourinho, however, prophetically said, 'We go to the Mestalla [Valencia's ground] and if we win we go to the semi-finals. If we lose I will go to Earl's Court for the twenty-four-hour wrestling with my kids... but it is 1–1. There is no reason to panic. We can make it a very difficult game for them there. Everyone now thinks Valencia are one step ahead; everybody is enjoying this result. But if I was in their place I would be very, very cautious. I hope we have a good referee there who is not influenced by the atmosphere. We can win there. Why not?'

The sentiments were echoed by Didier – whose Valencia goal meant he was the first Chelsea player since Kerry Dixon over twenty years earlier to hit thirty in a season – who said, 'There will be no pressure on us in the second leg. The pressure was here when they scored. It is not the best result but we can still do something there.'

A rare goal from Portuguese centre-back Ricardo Carvalho was enough to earn three points in the 1–0 home victory over Tottenham before the Blues were off for the thunderous second leg against Valencia, with many critics predicting the task ahead was too great for them.

Those critics seemed right when Fernando Morientes put Valencia ahead and the Spanish took charge in front of 50,000 spectators at the stadium where no English side had ever won. Didier's header produced a world-class save from Santiago Cañizares, but the omens were looking bad for Chelsea at half-time. After the break, however, a close-range goal from Shevchenko, his fifty-ninth in Europe, put the Blues level and their small but vocal group of supporters in a corner of the ground were in seventh heaven in the dying moments when Michael Essien stormed into the edge of the penalty area in front of them and scored a true last-gasp winner.

If the odds had been against Chelsea to triumph in Spain, then they had swung in their favour by the time the Blues met Blackburn Rovers in the FA Cup semi-final at Old Trafford. Football being what it is, though, it didn't work out as predicted, and, even though Lampard opened the scoring, Jason Roberts equalised in the second half and Blackburn had enough chances to claim a famous victory. As it was it took a 109th-minute goal from Michael Ballack to ensure the place in the first final to be held at the new-look Wembley.

A convincing 4–1 Premiership victory at West Ham, with Didier scoring again, was a great deal less trouble but Chelsea were unable to capitalise on Manchester United's failure to beat Middlesbrough when they got only a point in a goalless draw at Newcastle. Didier also came second best to United winger Cristiano Ronaldo, who won the Professional Footballers' Association Player of the Year award that weekend with United's Paul Scholes in third place.

José Mourinho reckoned that one bunch of players who would be voting with their boots for Didier would be the Liverpool side, who were next to visit Stamford Bridge for the first leg of their Champions League clash. Didier was one of a group of Chelsea players with two yellow cards and another one would rule him out of the return leg. 'It would not surprise me if they chased Didier Drogba around the pitch tonight for ninety minutes to try to get him suspended for the second leg,' said Mourinho.

They didn't 'chase' him hard enough, however, as Didier had a stunning game, leading the Chelsea attack with all the power and control he had shown all season, and laying on the twenty-ninth minute only goal of the match, scored by Joe Cole. Even the comparatively restrained *Daily Telegraph* called Didier 'this magnificent beast of a striker' and *The Times* said, 'If Drogba is on song, so are Chelsea.'

Mourinho hoped to rest Didier for the home game against Bolton that followed, but he had to bring him on at half-time as the northern side held on for a 2–2 draw, and gave Chelsea's title hopes a massive jolt in the process.

Worse was to come at Anfield. A twenty-second-minute goal from Danish defender Daniel Agger gave Liverpool a 1–0 lead in the Champions League second leg and Chelsea were to lose on penalties by a 4–1 margin – heartache again over failure in the trophy Didier was desperate to hold aloft.

Even supermen get tired, and the hunt for four trophies was now taking its toll on the squad. Didier was ruled out for the difficult game at Arsenal that Chelsea had to win to retain even a mathematical chance of winning the title, and, although the result was 1–1, a brave ten-man Chelsea, hampered by the early sending-off of Khalid Boulahrouz, went down fighting with a wonderful second-half display that simply oozed pride.

Even at the moment of his managerial triumph, United boss Sir Alex Ferguson said, 'I kept saying to people, "Will somebody please shoot Drogba?" because his performances were unbelievable. He carried their team, I thought, and he kept getting these incredible goals. Like the one at Everton with the last kick of the ball. That was incredible. I thought he may win the title on his own at one point, but the drawback for them was that he had to play all the games because they couldn't leave him out.'

He didn't have to worry about Didier, who was rested when the top two teams, both fielding weakened sides, fought out a goalless draw at Stamford Bridge, but Didier returned in style for the final league game of the season, the 1–1 home draw with Everton. It saw Didier score his twentieth Premiership goal of the campaign – and thirty-second in total – to earn him the Golden Boot award as the league's top goalscorer, taking Chelsea to an incredible sixty-three consecutive home games without defeat. It wasn't enough to earn him the Chelsea Player of the Year award, however, which went, somewhat surprisingly, to Michael Essien a few days later.

Anticipation grew as the final game of the season loomed, the first Cup Final to be played at the 'new' £800 million Wembley Stadium. It was only fitting that Chelsea and Manchester United, by far the best two teams in the Premiership, should play each other in front of 89,826 spectators on 19 May in a game that had all the ingredients necessary for a classic. Didier gathered the Chelsea team around him in the dressing room as they prepared to go out onto the pitch and looked them all straight in the eye. 'I'm nervous,' he said. 'Everybody's nervous We're all feeling the same. But one thing's for sure: we're going to fight and give everything for every player.' John Terry, who usually gave the 'team talk' before kick-off, said later, 'I didn't know he was going to do that. It touched a lot of people.'

Sadly, and almost predictably, the game was something of an anticlimax. Didier – who used to watch the English showpiece match as a small boy in Africa – hit the outside of the post with a free kick and Ryan Giggs claimed that a close-range shot blocked by Petr Čech had crossed the line, but these were rare moments of excitement in what seemed to be a game too many for some of the tired players toiling on the heavy turf.

So it was only fitting that the man who never seemed to tire, whose powerful legs – not to mention inexhaustible heart and lungs – would make the day his own. The game was in its 116th minute and penalties seemed a certainty when Didier took a pass from John Obi Mikel, and cleverly flicked the ball towards Frank Lampard on his right. The England player immediately returned it towards Didier, who somehow had the energy to accelerate away from the Manchester United defenders who had guarded him closely all afternoon.

The ability to stay as strong at the end of a match as he was at the beginning has been one of the hallmarks of his career, and the other has been the gift of remaining calm when lesser players might lose control at crucial moments. So it was that, as goalkeeper Edwin van der Sar realised the danger and raced out to meet him, there was going to be only one winner in the duel. With calculated delicacy and a deftness of touch, Didier guided it past the Dutchman with just enough power to make it unstoppable. The 'Blue' section of the crowd on that historic day went wild with joy; the 'Red' half had seen Didier score his first ever goal against United – and they knew they were beaten. Four minutes later, the whistle went and Didier raced off to fetch Mourinho, who had disappeared down the tunnel to telephone his family in Portugal.

Post-match critics were unanimous in their praise for Didier. Lampard said, 'If anyone was going to score the goal, then it had to be Didier. He is the real player of the year in my eyes. The whole team were heroes, but if anyone deserved to score the winner it was him.'

That wise old judge Sir Bobby Robson agreed: 'Nobody deserved to be Wembley's first match winner more than Didier Drogba. It's almost poetic justice that he's ended an outstanding campaign by making a piece of history. He is the first FA Cup Final goalscorer at the new Wembley and nobody can ever take that away from him.'

Didier said, after his thirty-third goal of a tumultuous season, 'There were so many emotions when I scored. I am just happy ... When you win you have to enjoy yourself because tomorrow maybe you will lose.'

One person who wasn't coming forward to share the limelight with him was his beautiful wife and mother of their three children, Lalla Diakite, whom he first met in January 2000. By her own admission, 'I am a person who is naturally reserved ... I do not like to show myself. I prefer to remain behind. Frankly, I hide. Didier reproaches me sometimes for the fact that I am never seen. He would like me to be seen more.' His Muslim bride, who originally planned to be a nurse, added, in a rare interview, that her family did not object to her marrying a Christian, saying, 'I will not force him to convert to Islam. I practise my religion, he practises his. Balance was found... I am not an "extremist". I do fast but I also wear trousers at times.'

She confirmed Didier's view that it was hard to settle in England at first: 'Frankly, at the beginning, that was very hard. But I did not have a choice: where Didier goes I am obliged to follow.' And a typical day for Lalla, when she was not taking English lessons, would see her husband drive off to work and then, like millions of other working husbands, just lie on the sofa and watch TV when he returned – sometimes dropping off to sleep. Mind you, not many London-based millionaires tuck into one of Didier's favourite meals: *tchep*, a rice dish from Senegal.

Lalla, a frequent visitor to the Ivory Coast, where the Drogbas are building a house, says she and her husband – whom she calls a devoted family man, with a special soft spot for their young daughter – plan to have a permanent home there for when he retires. Not that that will be for a while, she reckons. 'One will request that God will let Didier play until he is thirty-seven at least!'

Amid the mayhem of the end of the season, Didier had even found time to record a Snoop Dogg-style CD under the name *Drogbacite* – and, more importantly, pick up the African Player of the Year award in Ghana, ahead of Barcelona's Samuel Eto'o and teammate Michael Essien. His mother helped him dress in full Ashanti tribal clothing for the emotional ceremony.

His words at the ceremony and soon afterwards are a fitting end to the Didier Drogba story – so far. For they capture the essence of the man in that he places his success in the context of greater events elsewhere: 'I always want to put my country forward and that is why I hope that soon peace will return there.' He said, before remarkably taking his Golden Ball award to the separatist north of his homeland in an effort to bring unity and peace to the country, that his African origins remain all important to him: 'It's true that I haven't spent all that many years in the Ivory Coast, but bizarrely I have more memories of Abidjan than Angoulême or Brest, where I spent more time. Even though I went to France young, I don't feel like I left my African roots behind. They are anchored deep inside me and it all comes out as soon as I'm back in the country. If I spend too long away I get nostalgic. I feel like they were the best years of my life – I had a sense of freedom, the like of which only Africa gives you. I am the kind of guy who has a problem accepting constraints and rules and I felt in my element over there.

'I often used to hear the word nonchalance from my coaches in the early days. Some Europeans take our apparent calmness as something provocative, but it's not that at all. An African guy will simply feel strong and untouchable; it's something you have in your genes, nothing to do with being pretentious. It's just a character trait you are born with.

'Mentally speaking, an African is solid. He knows how to be jovial even when things are going badly. It's a way to show you're relaxed and can deal with the situation.'

Throughout his astonishing life Didier has been able to 'deal with the situation': from the heartache of leaving his parents when barely a toddler, through the mean streets of Parisian suburbs as a teenager, the football failures of his early years and the enmity of fans before they were won over by his skill and bravery. Throughout it all he showed the world courage, determination and integrity – all the qualities necessary to paint a true portrait of a hero.

## CHAPTER 30

# Exit Mourinho ... and Didier?

It wasn't to be long into the new 2007/08 season before the inevitable 'tears before bedtime' were literally being shed at Stamford Bridge as the relationship between Jose Mourinho and Roman Abramovich, stormy at best, grew to positively typhoon-strength in a matter of weeks.

Didier's remarks about Mourinho that summer made it pretty clear where he stood on the matter of the differences between coach and owner: 'If Jose left, it would hurt me, that's for sure,' he said, before adding ominously for his admirers, 'I am still at Chelsea, I have signed a new contract, but I was very successful in France and now I am successful in England. I love challenges and maybe I will look for a new challenge somewhere else in another country.

'Personally, it has been a great season for me. I had more than a month off after the World Cup and I was finally able to rest properly. I needed it. I've reached my personal objectives such as finishing as top goal-scorer and winning the respect of the

Premiership. But it has been a frustrating season, full of disappointments: the Premiership, the Champions League – losing in those competitions hurt us a lot.'

And another remark expanded further on his closeness with Mourinho, while indicating to some that he might not have the same instant rapport with any new man at the helm, when he said, 'If I disagree with my manager, I know how to tell him.'

In two separate interviews, he continued to put the message across to any who might not yet have received it, stating, 'I'm at the last big turning point of my career. It's time for one final big choice – should I stay or should I go? I am tempted to discover another world and to see what footballing life is like outside England. It would be a big disappointment if I never manage to play for teams that I dream of playing for. That would be terribly frustrating. Spain and Italy attract me a lot and, although I am a long way from saying farewell to Chelsea, you never know what can happen.

'If I think the club lacks ambition, then it is sure I will not stay too long. I'm 29 and I don't have much time to lose. I believed in being loyal to a stable club. But it is clear that, in such matters, players don't control anything.'

Weeks later, he added, 'For now things are still fuzzy, not clear. Yet any good offer could tip the scale in another team's favour. I have heard there are offers from Porto, Barca and the rest. But I've not made up my mind. There is no season I don't have many offers. Yet as a disciplined player I look at my career, which is uppermost, and my family. I would love to stay in England. I want to improve on my last season's performance and to win more titles in England. But any strong economic pull can make me change my mind.'

At least when the new season arrived there was some football to concentrate on rather than the verbal games being played off the pitch.

The traditional curtain-raiser Community Shield Game against

# EXIT MOURINHO ... AND DIDIER?

Manchester United was lost on penalties, but Chelsea continued their astonishing home record with a 3–2 victory over Birmingham City in a game that saw Didier come on as substitute.

He was on the field from the start of the next league game at Reading and, even though a rare Petr Cech error gave the home side the lead, Didier dominated the second half and laid on an equaliser for Frank Lampard before exchanging passes with Salomon Kalou on the edge of the area and then bending the ball home in his trademark style for what turned out to be the winner. The season seemed to be continuing in an almost predictable manner, on the field at least, with a Frank Lampard penalty earning a point at Anfield against Liverpool and then a solitary goal from the England midfielder proving enough to claim all the points at Portsmouth.

But trouble was just around the corner and matters came to a head at a remarkable pace. First came a 2–0 loss at Aston Villa – Chelsea's first defeat in 19 Premiership matches – and a knee injury to Didier. The next day's headlines were all on Abramovich's rapid exit from the Villa directors' box as soon as the home side scored their second goal.

Mourinho simply said, 'The owner leaves the stadium when he wants to leave. I went to see England versus Germany and I left early because of the traffic.'

Just as bad was a disappointing goalless match with Blackburn Rovers at Stamford Bridge, which caused Mourinho – who threw his TV monitor away in disgust during the match over a disallowed Chelsea goal – to bemoan the absence of stars such as Didier in one of his more colourful similes: 'To make omelettes, you need eggs. No eggs, no omelette. It depends on the quality of the eggs. In supermarkets, you have class one, two or three eggs. Some are more expensive than others and give you a better omelette,' he philosophised. 'When the class one eggs are in Waitrose and you can't go there, you have a problem. Do we have the squad to cope with our injuries? It depends on the injuries.

## DIDIER DROGBA

For me, the problem is not to have three or four players out, but which three or four are injured.

'When you have Drogba, Lampard, Michael Ballack and Ricardo Carvalho out, you are speaking about 40 per cent of the team, the spine of the team through defence, midfield and attack. After that, you go for Claudio Pizarro because he's the second target man and a direct replacement for Drogba, but he's out. Then you have Wayne Bridge out, which means Ashley Cole is the only left-back and plays every minute of every game. The problem is the importance of the players for the team. When you speak about Drogba and Lampard, you speak about maybe more than 50 per cent of the goals the team scores. They are important injuries. That's the reality. I'm speaking about it because you asked me. I don't want to cry about it. I have to work with the players I have.'

Eggs or no eggs, the inevitable was about to happen. After the defeat at Villa Park, Mourinho's odds on being the first Premiership manager of the season to split with his club had been slashed by one bookmaker from 66–1 to 20–1. They were to get even shorter after a night of European misery at Stamford Bridge in Chelsea's Champions League Group B match against Norwegian 'no-hopers' Rosenborg.

Although they dominated possession, Chelsea trailed at half-time and it took an equaliser from Andriy Shevchenko, playing instead of the injured Didier, to earn them even a point in front of an embarrassingly low crowd of under 25,000 fans, some of whom booed the team off the pitch.

No wonder Mourinho complained, 'I'm very disappointed. We had about 20 chances and scored one goal. So, to score two, maybe we need 40 chances; to score three, maybe 60. From the 20 chances, maybe 15 of them were not even on target. One in the net and some others the goalkeeper saved. We can speak and speak but the history of the game is we couldn't score more than one goal in 20 shots. I'm alarmed, I'm not happy.' The end was in sight.

## EXIT MOURINHO ... AND DIDIER?

The day after the match, the word was out – Jose Mourinho and Chelsea were no longer together. Some reports said he'd quit, others that he'd been sacked. The official statement from the club was that he'd left by 'mutual consent' and a brief statement to that effect, also thanking him for his efforts, was placed on the club website.

Only months before, he had said, 'There are only two ways for me to leave Chelsea. One way is in June 2010 when I finish my contract and if the club doesn't give me a new one. It is the end of my contract and I am out. The second way is for Chelsea to sack me. The way of the manager leaving the club by deciding to walk away, no chance! I will never do this to Chelsea supporters.'

Yet, by 6 p.m. on the night after the Champions League game, Mourinho had sent text messages to five members of the first-team squad telling them the news; by midnight, the entire squad knew.

The atmosphere at the club's training ground shortly after 10 o'clock the next morning, Thursday, 20 September, was practically funereal as Mourinho arrived to say his farewells. He spoke to the players in turn, as he moved around the large changing room thanking them for what they had done and passing on his good wishes for their wives and children.

Eventually, he came to Didier. Placing his hands on the player's arms, he spoke in a voice slightly louder than he had used with the other men so that all in the room could hear. 'You are one of the best strikers in the world and you have made yourself into one of the best players. I am very proud of you, Didi – and you should be proud of yourself,' he told him. 'You have worked hard and you are a winner. Always remember you are a winner.'

Then he embraced him, giving the giant striker a massive, irresistible hug. Didier broke down in tears, so great was the emotion and the heartache he felt.

There were more kind words, this time for Frank Lampard, while Florent Malouda comforted countryman Didier, as emotion welled up in the giant striker's body.

Didier later said, 'I learned that the manager was going when he told me personally – before the club made it official. It was a shock because I literally did not believe it could happen to a guy like him. When Mourinho went to say goodbye for the last time in the dressing room, it only lasted five minutes but it was an immensely strong moment and very moving. To watch him empty his locker so quickly and with such little fuss was terrible. Some around me were crying. It's a shame if you are sensitive. He kissed us, one by one – except a few!

'Then he said, "I wish you good luck to you and to your families and I thank you all. Even those who betrayed me." Mourinho didn't stay a second longer after that because I think he would have burst into tears.

'Then it was like fireworks in the dressing room. I really feared that everything was going to explode. Finally, a sense of resignation sank over us, and my initial feeling – just like a lot of players I think – was to feel alone. It was almost like being an orphan after the departure of a father.'

He added, 'My opinion is that results were only an excuse for getting rid of him. Perhaps his honesty and his way of saying what he thinks were not appreciated by everyone at the club... Sacking Mourinho has done a lot of harm to the squad. I still don't know why we changed manager after just a month of competition.'

He also spelled out what the entire world knew: 'I took the whole thing badly and perhaps I put too much sentiment in my relationship with the coach. When the manager left, he quickly said that he would like to work with me again but in such deals nothing is simple. He knows that I dream of the Spanish and the Italian league. I must win either La Liga or Serie A and there are, perhaps, only five clubs in the world that make me dream. They are Barcelona, Real Madrid, Inter, AC Milan and Marseille. There are not 50 clubs which can inspire my passion and my hunger to win, but these ones do.'

## EXIT MOURINHO ... AND DIDIER?

He described his years at Chelsea as 'the most beautiful of my career' but made it clear that he wanted to leave once the summer of 2008 arrived.

Amid the turmoil, the club issued a formal statement saying, 'It is only right that we explain the reasons behind Jose Mourinho leaving Chelsea and also recognise the immense contribution he has made to the club and to English football. We announced that Chelsea and Jose Mourinho had agreed to part company by mutual consent. The key phrase here is that there was mutual agreement. Jose did not resign and he was not sacked. What is clear, though, is we had all reached a point where the relationship between the club and Jose had broken down. This was despite genuine attempts over several months by all parties to resolve certain differences. The reason the decision has been taken is that we believed the breakdown started to impact on the performance of the team and recent results supported this view.'

Publicly Mourinho replied by saying on the club website he was 'proud' of his work at Chelsea and described his time at the club as 'a beautiful and rich period' of his career.

'I want to thank all Chelsea FC supporters for what I believe is a never-ending love story. I wish great success to the club, a club that will be forever connected to me for some historical moments. I wish the players happiness in football and in their family life.'

The news of Mourinho's departure sped around the world, and not just to British and European nations; his sudden exit merited column inches in publications as far removed from the beautiful game as it was possible to be, such as the *Washington Post* and the *New York Times*.

The man chosen to replace the charismatic Mourinho was hardly from the same mould. The little-known Israeli director of football at the club, Avram Grant, took over the helm and, although new men in charge often bring immediate improved results, it wasn't to be the case with Grant. Unfortunately for him, Chelsea's first match under him was at Old Trafford and the 2–0 result can hardly have come as a great surprise, given that United were awarded a disputed penalty and the Blues had to play a large chunk of the match with just 10 men after John Obi Mikel was sent off.

A 4–0 Carling Cup win at Hull hardly signified a return to form and to follow it with a goalless draw at home to near-neighbours Fulham meant Chelsea were in the middle of one of their poorest runs in recent years.

So a Champions League match at Valencia in early October seemed fraught with danger, especially when the Spaniards took an early lead. Yet again, as he had done so often on foreign fields in the Champions League, Didier made his mark. First he played a role in setting up Joe Cole's equaliser and then Cole returned the compliment to provide the pass that enabled Didier to score the spectacular second-half winner.

Victories over Bolton and Middlesbrough – with Didier scoring – meant that Chelsea's 'mini collapse' seemed to be over and the later stages of Europe beckoned with a 2–0 win over Schalke at Stamford Bridge courtesy of a goalkeeping error that let in a Malouda shot and a fine header from Didier.

Didier's public denouncement of the manner of Mourinho's departure and especially his own intention of leaving the club when appropriate could hardly be seen as attempts to endear himself to the supporters. Yet his value to the side was plain for all to see. Frank Lampard put it into words: 'It is important he stays because you want players like Didier playing alongside you, that's for sure. He makes his decisions and, even with all the controversy surrounding his decisions in the last week or two, he's put in two performances which show what he's all about. He's the best, it's as simple as that. There are different types of player. There's Wayne Rooney, who is a fantastic, absolute world-class player who likes to come off his defender and score. But in terms of an out-and-out striker there's no one as good as Didier, with his all-round game, his pace, his power. He's a team player. He scores goals with his head or his feet. He's the best. He's a great lad in the dressing room as well. He'll always fight to the end. The way he's played over the last two years – there's no one better in world football.'

Manchester City were soon to find out that Lampard was a pretty shrewd judge when they turned up at Stamford Bridge. An impressive start to the season saw them riding high under Sven-Goran Eriksson, but Didier scored twice in the 6–0 rout, Chelsea's first home win by that margin in the Premiership.

The Chelsea goal feast continued when they won a thrilling Carling Cup match with Leicester, 4–3 despite trailing with just four minutes of normal time left, and Didier returned to the line-up for a 2–0 win at Wigan.

He was on the goal trail again when he headed Chelsea into the lead at home to Everton, but a brilliant overhead kick by Tim Cahill in the 89th minute meant two dropped points at home brought an end to Chelsea's winning streak. Importantly, conceding a late equaliser was to be a recurring theme during the coming season, and it was to be one that would cost Chelsea dear.

Derby were beaten 2–0 away before Didier chose a bitterly cold night in Norway to give a masterclass in the art of leading a forward line. The victims were poor Rosenborg whose draw at Stamford Bridge had precipitated Mourinho's departure.

It was as if Didier bore a grudge. He terrorised their defence for over an hour; his sheer power, movement off the ball and aerial strength left them floundering. He scored twice, injuring his back while blasting the first, but could have had more, as could his team-mates. Grant showed mercy on the Norwegians and brought Didier off – no doubt to spare him too – with Chelsea three goals up and on their way to a 4–0 triumph. But in the hour he was on the pitch Didier gave an awesome display of attacking power, one that would have destroyed any side in Europe that night. It also served to emphasise that, with Didier at his best, the side were a far more potent attacking force than they were without him, no matter who replaced him.

One of the more unusual ways of trying to stop Didier came in the 1–0 home victory over West Ham United when a 'fan' shone a green 'laser' beam into his face during the match, leading to a police investigation of the incident. But it didn't prevent Didier setting up Joe Cole for the only goal of the match. It was to be one of his last acts centre stage for a while as the worrying knee injury he was battling with meant he was ruled out of the victory over Sunderland and the goalless draw at home to Valencia and it left a question mark over his appearing in the massive match away to Arsenal.

Avram Grant said, 'The decision will depend on his health. If he can play, then that is OK. If he cannot and he needs surgery, we will do it. We hope that he will be fit whether it is for Arsenal or other games. We don't want him to miss so many games and have to have surgery, but we have to wait and see. The only thing that I think about is if it is good for him or not. I have spoken with him, and it is not easy because he always pushes to play, even if he does not feel so good. But there is no striker in the world like him. He is a striker with power, technique, an intelligent player, the best in the world.'

Matters came to a head when Chelsea club doctor Bryan English said on 8 December, 'Didier's knee locked yesterday afternoon and the decision was taken to have the operation immediately in the medical interests of the player. The procedure went well and he will begin his rehabilitation as soon as possible.'

There were fears that the knee op might mean Didier would be sidelined for two months, but by the first week in January he was coming on as substitute in the Cup victory over Queens Park Rangers.

Unfortunately for Chelsea supporters, it didn't mean that Didier would soon be helping them in the Premiership title chase, as he was off to the African Nations Cup in Ghana, along with

## EXIT MOURINHO ... AND DIDIER?

Mikel John Obi (Nigeria), Salomon Kalou (Ivory Coast) and Michael Essien (Ghana).

'I don't think my absence should really affect our chances, although I would have loved to be a part of the team now,' he confessed before leaving for Africa. 'Chelsea are definitely good enough for the title – even when I'm not there. I think Shevchenko, Ballack, Wright-Phillips and others are doing really well and scoring good goals. There are others who can step in and score too. Don't forget it's not only Drogba that's out, other good players are not playing now as well and yet Chelsea still win. It shows that Chelsea do not rely on a particular player. All players are important.'

Though not fully match-fit, he played against much-fancied Nigeria in the opening 1–0 victory of the African tournament and said afterwards, 'It is an important victory because we won against our main rivals for top spot in the group. Nigeria were the most dangerous team and I feel the most important job has been done.'

Didier scored the opening goal in the much easier 4–1 victory over Benin that followed and again got the opener – his 32nd goal in 50 internationals – in the comfortable 3–0 win over Mali, his wife's home side. The quarter-final against Guinea, who were without injured Celtic stopper Bobo Balde, was a 5–0 romp with Solomon Kalou scoring twice and Didier netting again.

A Ghana v Ivory Coast final beckoned, but both these fancied sides were defeated in the semi-finals; Ghana to a solitary goal from Cameroon and Didier's 'Elephants' to the eventual winners Egypt 4–1 in a bad-tempered game.

During the tournament, Didier had plenty of time to ponder on his new team-mate at Stamford Bridge, Nicolas Anelka, the £15 million striker the club had signed from Bolton, a player called 'Le Sulk' by some for his apparent moods on the field. If Didier was worried about the competition for the striking role, he certainly didn't show it when he said, 'Anelka is a good forward

– but he will only complement me rather than fighting for the position with me. You know I speak French too, so we'll be buddies. Perhaps we can use the language to our advantage during a match.

'I don't think it will affect my position in the team when I return. Do people expect me to start fighting Anelka? No, we're friends. We all welcome him into the club. I am not bothered at all; I'll keep scoring no matter who joins us.'

When Didier returned from international duty, it was to find Arsenal at the top of the Premiership and Chelsea trailing Manchester United in the hunt to catch the Gunners. Champions League prospects were brighter, though, and a goalless draw at Olympiakos in Greece boosted their chances of progressing to the next round.

But Chelsea came down to earth not so much with a bump as a deafening crash when they took on London rivals Tottenham at Wembley in the Carling Cup Final. Despite Chelsea opening the scoring with a Didier 'special' from a free-kick, Spurs won 2–1, the eventual winner coming from the unlikely figure of their centre-half Jonathan Woodgate. The loss in itself would have been bad enough, but there was instant criticism of Grant's team selection and the omission of Joe Cole, as well as reports of training-ground arguments before the match.

If anything, this setback seemed to inspire the Blues, temporarily at least. West Ham were flattened 4–0, despite Frank Lampard harshly being sent off, and Olympiakos went the same way, trounced 3–0 in the second leg of their European tie, before another bizarre defeat brought havoc again. This time it was in the unlikely setting of Barnsley where a 1–0 defeat in the FA Cup was considered by most observers to be the worst result since Abramovich bought the club. At least Didier was spared criticism, as he and Frank Lampard missed the game – believed to be a key factor in the defeat by many fans.

However, victories over lowly Derby and Sunderland

maintained the late chase for the title, although two vital points along with a two-goal lead were thrown away in a pulsating 4–4 draw at Spurs, when the home side's ultra-late equaliser was to prove crucial as the season's climax approached.

Didier had scored in the eight-goal thriller and also hit both goals that saw off faltering Arsenal in a 2–1 victory at the Bridge. The Gunners' early season flow had dried up, and now it was Manchester United who Chelsea – boosted by the win at The Emirates – were chasing. Didier was confident: 'We can overturn the gap at the top of the Premier League. People thought we were dead and buried when Jose Mourinho left, but we are through our most difficult period.'

Turkish side Fenerbahce were outplayed in the Champions League first leg yet somehow managed to win 2–1, but the Blues eliminated them with a 2–0 response in the home second leg, while Middlesbrough and Manchester City were beaten in the domestic competition. Chelsea were in with a fighting chance of catching United, but Didier's recurring knee problem meant he missed the home game against Wigan, which was to add another nail in their title hopes when Emile Heskey's injury-time equaliser yet again turned three points into just one in a game that Chelsea should have considered a home banker.

There was no clear favourite, though, when Chelsea took on Liverpool yet again in the Champions League. The teams seemed destined to be drawn together in the competition with the 'Pool coming out narrow – and usually controversial – victors in games that were inevitably tight and where goals were scarce.

So it was that a Dirk Kuyt goal seemed to be enough to give Liverpool victory in another pulsating match at Anfield until Salomon Kalou swung in a hopeful cross from the left in the dying seconds of the game. Norwegian defender John Arne Riise dived to head clear, but only succeeded in powerfully diverting the ball into his own net. Anfield fell silent as Liverpool were left to wonder if they would rue those missed chances.

## DIDIER DROGBA

By this stage of the season, the 'must-win' games seemed to be taking place almost daily. Next was the crunch match at home to Manchester United, which, with hardly any games remaining, the Blues had to win to stay in with a chance of the title. For once, the goal-scoring hero wasn't Didier but Michael Ballack. First he gave Chelsea the lead and, after Wayne Rooney's equaliser, the German calmly converted a late, and inevitably disputed, penalty to clinch the 2–1 victory. However, it wasn't a case of Didier avoiding the limelight. In one bizarre incident, he and Ballack argued openly and furiously over who would take a free-kick on the edge of the United area, and early on in the game Didier accidentally caught Nemanja Vidic in the face with his knee and the United defender was carried off as a result. Even after the game, the fun and games continued when a party of United players 'warming down' clashed with Chelsea stewards. The victory meant Chelsea were still in with a fighting chance of winning the title, but it was dependent on United slipping up in their few remaining games.

The dust had hardly settled on the Stamford Bridge pitch when, four days later, Liverpool arrived for the second leg of the Champions League semi-final. It was to be a night where Didier again showed why he was so highly praised by those who admired the way he lead a forward line. If he needed any inspiration, Didier even kept a picture of Liverpool boss Rafa Benitez – who had taunted him with remarks about 'diving' – above his dressing-room peg. It seemed inevitable, therefore, that it would be Didier who gave Chelsea a first-half lead with a low shot. Fernando Torres, Liverpool's on-fire striker, equalised in the second half, but Frank Lampard, in his first game since his mother's tragic death from pneumonia, restored the Chelsea lead with a penalty before Didier wrapped up victory with another executioner's goal near the end. A Ryan Babel reply for Liverpool was too little, too late – Chelsea were in the final of the Champions League for the first time. Didier, ecstatic with the result, said, 'To get to the final is amazing. We played very well. We have waited for so long to get there. It is fantastic for the club.'

And so it was. The greatest prize in club football was within their grasp as the attention of the soccer world turned to Moscow on the night of 21 May.

Manchester United had secured the title in the Premiership and thus made Chelsea pay dearly for those squandered points against lesser sides, meaning the Moscow match was the Blues' only hope of winning a trophy that season.

The Luzhniki Stadium game was to have all the classic elements that make up the 'Didier Drogba Story': controversy in the run-up to the match, insults flung around with abandon, remarkable football, physical clashes that made grown men wince – and recriminations and heartache to end it all after 120 nerve-jangling minutes.

First came the verbal battles, with Wayne Rooney saying of Didier, 'When he's at his best, he's an unbelievable player. He's big, strong, he scores goals – left foot, right foot, headers – and at times he's unplayable. But sometimes he seems as if his head's not quite there.'

And, prophetically, Serb defender Vidic added to the mix when he said, 'Sometimes he goes in very strong and sometimes he pretends he is very weak. He can pretend he fell down to win a penalty but the referee knows that. The Champions League Final is a big game and I'm sure the ref will know his job.' There were those who were very shortly to disagree with that verdict.

But the biggest storm before the game was caused by Didier himself. In France to promote his biography, he revealed that, when he signed for Chelsea in 2004, 'It just wasn't the team I wanted to join.' To make matters worse, he even admitted to clandestine Italian meetings with AC Milan in August 2006, pretending to Jose Mourinho he was travelling to see a dentist in Paris. For once the bond between the two men was broken, albeit temporarily, and Mourinho was furious when he discovered the deception. The manner of Mourinho's departure had even prompted angry Didier to threaten not to play for the club until he was talked out of such a drastic course of action by friends.

It was hardly ideal preparation for Chelsea's first Champions League Final, which started badly when Cristiano Ronaldo's header past the orange-clad Petr Cech gave United a 26th-minute lead in front of 67,310 fans on a late Moscow night. But to the Chelsea fans' relief Frank Lampard nimbly equalised on the stroke of half-time.

In the 78th minute came the moment that turned the match – and, almost inevitably, it involved Didier. There seemed to be no danger to United as he tried to control the ball a few strides outside the penalty area with a clutch of red shirts around him. Yet somehow, even though he seemed to be off balance, Didier managed to wrap his right foot around the ball with enough force to send it past the helpless Van der Sar in goal – and against the left-hand post. Given the strength and determination that Chelsea had shown in the second half, it would have been a foolish man who would have bet against them to hold out for the 12 minutes remaining if that shot had gone in.

As it was, the game went into overtime and, from being a possible match-winning hero, Didier was about to experience a Russian nightmare. In the 26th minute of an increasingly bitter extra-time, a fairly minor battle broke out over a disputed throw-in. Soon players from both sides were shoving and jostling each other as grudges from the game – and previous encounters – surfaced.

Vidic joined the throng and, in a moment's petulance, Didier gave his face an innocuous slap. It didn't even have the force to make the Serb flinch, but it was hard enough to end Didier's night. The referee was just yards away and clearly saw it, so, no matter how ineffectual the blow was, he had raised his fists and struck an opponent. It was a red card.

## EXIT MOURINHO ... AND DIDIER?

As a storm raged overhead, he exited the battle, not to be seen again that night.

The inevitable penalty shoot-out followed. Denied Didier's services, skipper John Terry, an embodiment of all that Chelsea stood for, stepped up to take the spot kick that could have won the trophy for them, Ronaldo, of all people, having missed his earlier. Poor Terry's 'standing' left leg gave slightly as he hit his shot which beat Van der Sar but thumped against the post and bounced clear. Terry looked as though the miseries of the world were all piled on his broad shoulders.

The game that could have been won was on the point of being lost. Anderson and Giggs subsequently scored for United as did Kalou for Chelsea, but Nicolas Anelka's attempt was easily blocked by the tall Dutchman in the United goal and, at 1.34 a.m. local time, the game was United's 6–5.

The rain hadn't even stopped before many were speculating that Didier's moment of anger might have been his last as a Chelsea player. Within days, both Avram Grant and first-team coach Henk ten Cate had their contracts terminated and a host of candidates were named, and then discounted, as their replacements.

But, in the middle of the European Championships, the man who was to take over at the helm was officially announced. The Portuguese national coach, 59-year-old Luiz Felipe Scolari, known throughout football as 'Big Phil', had been tempted to take the job for a salary reported to be a staggering £6 million a year. A new era at Stamford Bridge loomed large yet again.

And Didier Drogba? For years, he had constantly been linked with top clubs in Spain and Italy and had made no secret of his willingness to move if the right chance came along, but only one thing appeared certain. Wherever he would be kicking a football for a living next, controversy, excitement and, of course, goals, would no doubt be there too.